Women's Participation in
Mexican Political Life

Women's Participation in Mexican Political Life

edited by
Victoria E. Rodríguez

UNIVERSITY OF TEXAS AT AUSTIN

Westview Press
A Member of the Perseus Books Group

Copyright © 1998 by Westview Press, A Member of the Perseus Books Group

Published in 1998 in the United States of America by Westview Press, 5500 Central Avenue, Boulder, Colorado 80301-2877, and in the United Kingdom by Westview Press, 12 Hid's Copse Road, Cumnor Hill, Oxford OX2 9JJ

Library of Congress Cataloging-in-Publication Data
Women's participation in Mexican political life / edited by Victoria
E. Rodríguez.
    p.   cm.
    Papers originally presented during meetings held at the University
of Texas at Austin in April 1995 and April 1996.
    Includes bibliographical references and index.
    ISBN 0-8133-3529-9 (hardcover). — ISBN 0-8133-3530-2 (pbk.)
    1. Women in politics—Mexico—Congresses.   I. Rodríguez, Victoria
Elizabeth, 1954– .   II. University of Texas at Austin.
HQ1236.5.M6W65   1998
320'.082'0972—dc21   98-20771
                                                                                CIP

The paper used in this publication meets the requirements of the American National Standard for Permanence of Paper for Printed Library Materials Z39.48-1984.

10   9   8   7   6   5   4   3   2   1

Somos Mujeres Muy Listas

Esto no puede ser nomás que una canción
Quisiera fuera una declaración de unión
Política, de formas tales
Que olvidemos las broncas que tenemos a raudales.
Si me criticas no voy a morirme
Si he de morir quiero que sea por México
Por México, por México
Eternamente por México.
Si alguna vez me siento relegada
Voy a pensar en esta unión lograda
Mujeres, mujeres
La fuerza está en las mujeres.
Tenemos que ponernos muy listas
Para quedar incluidas en las listas
Mujeres, las listas
Somos mujeres muy listas.

—A song composed by and for the women attending
the Women in Contemporary Mexican Politics II
conference held in Austin, Texas, April 1996

Contents

List of Tables and Figures   ix
List of Acronyms   xi
Preface and Acknowledgments   xv

1 The Emerging Role of Women in Mexican
Political Life, *Victoria E. Rodríguez*   1

Part 1
The Context: Women in Political Life Worldwide

2 Women in Politics: Mexico in Global Perspective,
Kathleen Staudt   23

3 Mexican Women's Inclusion into Political Life:
A Latin American Perspective, *Nikki Craske*   41

4 Ten Theses on Women in the Political Life
of Latin America, *Joe Foweraker*   63

5 *Supermadre* Revisited, *Elsa M. Chaney*   78

Part 2
Women in the Mexican Political Arena

6 Women and Power in Mexico:
The Forgotten Heritage, 1880–1954,
Carmen Ramos Escandón   87

7 De la A a la Z: A Feminist Alliance Experience
in Mexico, *Marta Lamas*   103

8 Everyday Struggles: Women in Urban
   Popular Movements and Territorially Based
   Protests in Mexico, *Vivienne Bennett*   116

9 The Role of Women's Nongovernmental
   Organizations in Mexican Public Life, *María Luisa Tarrés*   131

10 Gender and Grassroots Organizing:
   Lessons from Chiapas, *Lynn Stephen*   146

Part 3
Women in Politics: Government and Political Parties

11 Women and Men, Men and Women: Gender Patterns
   in Mexican Politics, *Roderic Ai Camp*   167

12 Feminist Policies in Contemporary Mexico:
   Strategies and Viability, *Alicia Martínez*
   and Teresa Incháustegui   179

13 Women in the Local Arena and Municipal Power,
   Alejandra Massolo   193

14 Women in the Border: The *Panista* Militants
   of Tijuana and Ciudad Juárez, *Lilia Venegas*   204

15 Conclusion: *Haciendo Política*—The Mexican Case
   in Perspective, *Jane S. Jaquette*   219

References   229
About the Editor and Contributors   248
Index   252

Tables and Figures

Tables

1.1	Women's representation in the last sixteen Mexican congresses	12
1.2	The July 1997 congressional election, by party: How did the women fare?	13
3.1	Women's representation in Latin American chambers of deputies	46
3.2	Women's representation in Latin American senates	48
9.1	Areas of activity of women's NGOs	137
9.2	Level of specialization in the areas of activity in women's NGOs	138
11.1	Distribution of women graduates representing the Salinas-Zedillo political generation in higher education	172
11.2	Teaching experiences of female politicians	173
11.3	Prominent female figures in the executive branch, 1994–1998	175
13.1	Female mayors in Latin America	197
13.2	Municipal governments, by party and state, governed by women, 1998	201
13.3	*Regidor* positions by gender in five large *panista* cities, 1995	202

Figures

2.1	Engendering politics in democratic regimes	25
2.2	Women's and men's participation pyramids	27
2.3	Women's representation in government, 1994	28

Acronyms

ANFER	Asociación Nacional Femenina Revolucionaria (National Revolutionary Feminine Association)
ARIC	Asociación Rural de Interés Colectivo (Rural Collective Interest Association)
CCRI	Consejo Clandestino Revolucionario Indígena (Clandestine Revolutionary Indigenous Council)
CDP	Comité de Defensa Popular (Popular Defense Committee)
CEDAW	Convention on the Elimination of All Forms of Discrimination Against Women
CEDEMUN	Centro de Desarrollo Municipal (Center for Municipal Development)
CEN	Comité Ejecutivo Nacional (National Executive Committee)
CFM	Consejo Feminista Mexicano (Mexican Feminist Council)
CIM	Consejo para la Integración de la Mujer (Council for the Inclusion of Women)
CIOAC	Central Independiente de Obreros Agrícolas y Campesinos (Independent Central of Agricultural Workers and Peasants)
CMC	Congreso de Mujeres por el Cambio (Congress of Women for Change)
CNC	Confederación Nacional Campesina (National Peasant Confederation)
CND	Convención Nacional Democrática (National Democratic Convention)
CNI	Convención Nacional Indígena (National Indigenous Convention)
CNM	Convención Nacional de Mujeres (National Women's Convention)
CNOP	Confederación Nacional de Organizaciones Populares (National Confederation of Popular Organizations)
CNPA	Coordinadora Nacional Plan de Ayala (National Coordinator Plan de Ayala)

CNTE	Coordinadora Nacional de Trabajadores de la Educación (National Coordinating Committee of Education Workers)
COFIPE	Código Federal de Instituciones y Procedimientos Electorales (Federal Code for Electoral Procedures and Institutions)
CONAMUP	Coordinadora Nacional del Movimiento Urbano Popular (National Cooordinator of the Urban Popular Movement)
CONAPO	Consejo Nacional de Población (National Population Council)
CONPAZ	Coordinación de Organismos No-gubernamentales por la Paz de Chiapas (Coordinating Committee of NGOs for Peace in Chiapas)
CTM	Confederación de Trabajadores Mexicanos (Confederation of Mexican Workers)
DIF	Desarrollo Integral de la Familia (Integrated Family Development)
EMILY	Early Money Is Like Yeast
ENP	Escuela Nacional Preparatoria (National Preparatory School)
ERA	Equal Rights Amendment
EZLN	Ejército Zapatista de Liberación Nacional (Zapatista National Liberation Army)
FDN	Frente Democrático Nacional (National Democratic Front)
FEMAP	Federación Mexicana de Asociaciones Privadas de Salud y Desarrollo Comunitario (Mexican Federation of Private Associations for Health and Community Development)
FLACSO	Facultad Latinoamericana de Ciencias Sociales (Latin American Faculty for the Social Sciences)
FMLN	Frente Farabundo Martí de Liberación Nacional (Farabundo Martí National Liberation Front)
FNALIDM	Frente Nacional por la Liberación y los Derechos de las Mujeres (National Front for Women's Rights and Liberation)
FNOC	Frente Nacional de Organizaciones y Ciudadanos (National Front of Organizations and Citizens)
FPTyL	Frente Popular Tierra y Libertad (Tierra y Libertad Popular Front)
FSLN	Frente Sandinista de Liberación Nacional (Sandinista National Liberation Front)

FUPDM	Frente Unico Pro Derechos de la Mujer (Sole Front for Women's Rights)
FZLN	Frente Zapatista de Liberación Nacional (Zapatista Front of National Liberation)
GEM	Grupo de Educación Popular con Mujeres (Group for Women's Popular Education)
HDI	Human Development Index
ILAS	Institute of Latin American Studies
IPN	Instituto Politécnico Nacional (National Polytechnic Institute)
IPU	Inter-Parliamentary Union
ITAM	Instituto Tecnológico Autónomo de México (Autonomous Technological Institute of Mexico)
ITESM	Instituto Tecnológico y de Estudios Superiores de Monterrey (Monterrey Institute of Technology and Higher Studies)
LASA	Latin American Studies Association
LSE	London School of Economics
MAS	Mujeres en Acción Sindical (Women in Action in Unions)
MEMCH-83	Movimiento para la Emancipación de las Mujeres Chilenas (Movement for Women's Emancipation)
MNM	Movimiento Nacional de Mujeres (National Women's Movement)
MT	Movimiento Popular Urbano Territorial (Urban Territorial Popular Movement)
NAFTA	North American Free Trade Agreement
NGOs	Nongovernmental Organizations
PAN	Partido Acción Nacional (National Action Party)
PCM	Partido Comunista Mexicano (Mexican Communist Party)
PIEM	Programa Interdisciplinario de Estudios de la Mujer (Interdisciplinary Program for Women's Studies)
PMT	Partido Mexicano de los Trabajadores (Mexican Workers' Party)
PNR	Partido Nacional Revolucionario (National Revolutionary Party
PR	proportional representation
PRD	Partido de la Revolución Democrática (Party of the Democratic Revolution)
PRI	Partido Revolucionario Institucional (Party of the Institutionalized Revolution)
PRM	Partido de la Revolución Mexicana (Party of the Mexican Revolution)

PRONASOL	Programa Nacional de Solidaridad (National Solidarity Program)
PRT	Partido Revolucionario de los Trabajadores (Workers' Revolutionary Party)
PSUM	Partido Socialista Unificado de México (Unified Socialist Party)
PT	Partido del Trabajo (Labor Party)
PUEG	Programa Universitario de Estudios de Género
PVEM	Partido Verde Ecologista Mexicano (Green Party)
SERNAM	Servicio Nacional de la Mujer, Chile (Women's Ministry)
SM	single-member (systems)
SNTE	Sindicato Nacional de Trabajadores de la Educación (National Union of Education Workers)
UN	United Nations
UNAM	Universidad Nacional Autónoma de México (National Autonomous University of Mexico)
UNDP	United Nations Development Programme
UNE	Ciudadanos en Movimiento (Citizens on the Move)
UNICEF	United Nations International Culture and Education Fund
UP	Unión del Pueblo (The People's Union)
UU	Unión de Uniones (Union of Ejido Unions and Solidarity Peasant Organizations of Chiapas)

Preface and Acknowledgments

The chapters that make up this volume were originally presented at either one of two consecutive meetings held at the University of Texas at Austin in April 1995 and April 1996. The meetings brought together, for the first time ever in an international academic setting, a distinguished group of scholars from Mexico, the United States, and Europe with a key group of over fifty women who have exercised leadership positions in various arenas of Mexican political life during the last fifteen years. In a remarkably friendly and mutually supportive environment, created by the openness of the political participants and the intellectual stimulation of the academic presentations, women from all walks of political life in Mexico candidly talked about their entrance into the political scenario, the obstacles they have encountered at every turn of the way, and their expectations for the future.

The "neutral" setting provided by the University of Texas at Austin, away from journalists, conflicting schedules, telephone calls, and other interruptions, allowed in each of the two meetings a vigorous and candid exchange of ideas among academics, politicians, and activists. It was particularly thrilling to observe and listen to the exchange among the political women, as they agreed on common-ground gender issues yet continued to disagree on others more directly related to party alliances or ideological positions. Indeed, many of the participants in both conferences pointed out that the neutral forum provided by meeting in Austin was the *only* opportunity for them to meet at all, given that they would not be likely to do so in their own home country. For three days at least, in each of these two meetings, Mexican women could put aside their institutional rivalries and ideological disagreements and concentrate upon the ways in which they could exercise their leadership to meet the challenges and advance the position of women in Mexico's political life.

The first meeting, "Women in Contemporary Mexican Politics" in April 1995, served as an open forum to discuss a wide range of issues affecting Mexican women's political participation in a global perspective. After an inspiring opening address by former Texas governor Ann Richards—a formidable example herself of the political presence women can have—the participants and attending public concentrated for two days on analyzing gender and politics in Mexico (see Rodríguez et al. 1995 for a complete transcript of Governor Richards's address and for a synopsis of the presentations and discussion sessions). Among the key political women present were Amalia García, Rosario Robles, and Leticia Calzada from the PRD; Cecilia Soto, who had just run for the presidency the year before as a candidate adopted by the PT; and a large group of key *panista* women, led by Consuelo Botello, María Elena Alvarez, María Teresa Gómez Mont, and Ana Rosa Payán. Also attending were some of the more prominent political women in other areas, such as Marta Lamas, Patricia Mercado, and Cecilia Loría, all of them key figures in Mexico's feminist movement. In order to cover the breadth of women's political participation, the sessions analyzed their role in formal politics (parties, government) and informal politics (social movements, NGOs). Among the academic presentations at that meeting were the chapters in this volume by Vivienne Bennett, Roderic Ai Camp, Elsa M. Chaney, Joe Foweraker, Marta Lamas, Carmen Ramos Escandón, Kathleen Staudt, and María Luisa Tarrés, all of which have been completely revised and updated for this book. Each of the academic sessions was followed by a roundtable discussion that integrated women from different political persuasions and areas of activity. The final roundtable ended with the consensus that a second meeting was imperative, preferably in Mexico but if not then again in Austin, in order to continue the unfinished discussions, particularly those surrounding the issue of affirmative action for women in politics.

In the event it was to be Austin, this second meeting, "Women in Contemporary Mexican Politics II: Participation and Affirmative Action" in April 1996, picked up these themes and focused the discussion on women's increasing political participation, especially in local and regional politics, and the debate surrounding the issue of quotas for affirmative action initiatives. The format was similar to that of the first meeting: formal presentations by the academics, followed by extended commentary from the women politicians. The presentations at the 1996 meeting by Nikki Craske, Alicia Martínez and Teresa Incháustegui, Alejandra Massolo, Lynn Stephen, and Lilia Venegas are included in this volume, revised and updated. We also had new presentations from some of the academics attending the 1995 meeting—Vivienne Bennett, Elsa M. Chaney, Marta Lamas, Carmen Ramos Escandón, María Luisa Tarrés, and several others. Among them, special mention must be made of the presentation by Judith Gentleman on women in the national security arena, which stirred considerable discussion. The most telling insights, once again, came from the roundtable discussions in which the political women openly and constructively agreed and disagreed on a number of issues. On this occasion, the keynote opening address was given by María de los Angeles Moreno and the closing remarks by Beatriz Paredes, two Mexican leaders who have risen to occupy positions of great prominence in Mexico's political landscape (see Rodríguez et al. 1996 for a complete transcript of their remarks). In addition to many of the political women who had attended the meeting the year before and returned to Austin for this second occasion, other prominent women joined the group, including Cecilia Romero from the PAN, Laura Itzel Castillo from the PRD, and María Elena Chapa from the PRI. Other leading women, such as Laura Carrera and Clara Jusidman, were also present. Once again, the meeting ended with the proposition to meet the following year.

That third meeting took place in Guadalajara, Mexico, in April 1997, in the broader context of the Twentieth International Congress of the Latin American Studies Association (LASA). For the first time since 1983 a LASA congress was held outside the United States; in addition, as I was serving as program cochair for that congress, the opportunity to hold a third meeting, this time in Mexico, presented itself. In the prelude to the 1997 midterm elections such an opportunity could hardly be resisted. Once again, the meeting brought together an impressive array of women in Mexican political life and of academics from Mexico, the United States, and Europe, many of whom had attended the Austin meetings. Jane Jaquette, then president of LASA, joined the group and participated actively in the Guadalajara meeting. Several of the politicians present were also at the time candidates for office. Although the electoral competition among the three main political parties was heating up, the women who participated in the roundtable discussion (Amalia García, PRD; Cecilia Loría, independent; María de los Angeles Moreno, PRI; Luisa María Calderón, PAN), speaking for their parties' position, were refreshingly measured and respectful, even though they continued to make strong ideological pronouncements. Although no consensus was reached on gender issues, it was clear from this meeting that women in Mexican politics have come of age and reached a high level of healthy political rivalry. Their male counterparts could learn much from the poise and political maturity exuded by these women in their political personae.

The pressure and temptation to continue these yearly meetings persist, but there has also been a strong feeling that some of the principal issues discussed at the meetings be made available to a larger public. This book not only encapsulates those particular issues but presents an insightful and comprehensive overview of the position of women in the political tapestry of contemporary Mexico.

In selecting the chapters to be included in this book, special care was taken to ensure that, as a whole, the book was representative of various academic disciplines and, more important, covered the range of activities in which women have become politically active. Thus, the chapters in this book analyze the various ways and the various arenas in which women participate in the political life of Mexico: in elected and appointed government positions, as feminists and grassroots leaders, as members of rebel groups and nongovernmental organizations, and so on. The range of discussion also extends to various political parties, different regions of the country, and different levels of government. Thus, the collective analysis is balanced along ideological positions, party affiliations, and areas of activity. Care was also taken to have a strong section on women's involvement in politics worldwide and in Latin America in order to provide a comparative context for the Mexican women. And finally, an effort was made to cross national boundaries and pull together the expertise of Mexicanist, Latin Americanist, and gender scholars from Mexico, the United States, and Europe.

In mounting the conferences and meetings that eventually led to the publication of this book, I have incurred a large number of debts. First and foremost, I wish to thank my husband and (favorite) colleague, Peter Ward, for his unwavering support. His encouragement and interest in my work have been a constant source of strength and inspiration. His advice has always been reassuring, and our discussions have helped me in many ways to clarify my views; in the course of many conversations, indeed, we have concluded that he is the more feminist of the two! His support as director of the Mexican Center at the University of Texas at Austin was instrumental in providing the academic setting to bring together such a stellar group of academics and politicians for the 1995 and 1996 conferences. As an academic couple, we have been fortunate to welcome into our home many of our academic and political friends. In fact, the social events organized at our home during the conferences have strengthened friendships and enriched those meetings in numerous ways. For example, the song that is presented as this book's epigraph was composed after a garden dinner led to an evening of music and camaraderie—quite literally, an evening of wine, women, and song. Close to one hundred academics and women from all parties, levels, and areas of activity sat around singing old and new Mexican melodies to the tune of three guitars. After the majority of the guests left, a small group stayed behind and worked on the composition of the song, which was sung the following day at the closing session of the 1996 meeting. With all conference participants singing in unison with the public at the auditorium, the session closed with a renewed solidarity among the women that was also a nationalist inspiration.

I wish to gratefully acknowledge the financial support that made the meetings possible, in particular support from the Ford Foundation Mexico City office and from both the Mexican Center of the Institute of Latin American Studies (ILAS) and the Lyndon B. Johnson School of Public Affairs at the University of Texas at Austin. I especially wish to acknowledge the continued support throughout of Peter Cleaves (ILAS) and Judy Caskey (Lyndon B. Johnson School). My gratitude also goes to the staff of the Mexican Center and of ILAS, who were inundated with a flurry of activity trying to orchestrate the logistics of these conferences. Working on the travel and lodging arrangements relating to more than fifty women coming to Austin was a mammoth task alone, and for this my heartfelt thanks go to Xóchitl Medina and Betty Padilla. Thanks also to my students, for the work they put into the conferences and for acting, as one of the conference participants put it, as the "guardian angels" of the Mexican women while they were visiting Austin. I hope the excitement of those meetings was a memorable experience of their graduate education.

The editorial tasks of putting together this volume were ameliorated immensely by Debbie Warden, who at various times in the preparation of this manuscript operated as computer expert, editor, and research assistant—not to mention as therapist and always as a friend. Her assistance and meticulous care in compiling and formatting the manuscript were priceless, and all of us who contributed to this book are in her debt.

The essential task of translating some of the chapters from Spanish into English was performed by Santiago J. Rodríguez. To his talents we owe the fluent translation of the chapters by Marta Lamas, Alicia Martínez and Teresa Incháustegui, Alejandra Massolo, María Luisa Tarrés, and Lilia Venegas. A special note of appreciation goes to Sharon Hogan Mastracci for her collaboration in diligently preparing the book's index as well as Figures 2.1, 2.2, and 2.3.

I am deeply grateful to all the contributors for their patience and commitment to this project and this research. Even though at times it seemed as though the book would never see the light because of foreseen and unforeseen delays, their continued support and willingness to revise, update, write, and rewrite in response to my queries and requests have made this anthology one of such high quality. The quality of the production process was also greatly enhanced by the efficiency and thoroughness of Karl Yambert, Jennifer Chen, and Elizabeth Lawrence at Westview Press.

And finally, a special note of thanks to the women in my family. To my mother, who has always taken pride in me personally, and in particular to my sister, Laura, for her friendship, for caring about my work, and for teaching me—from her own insights and in her capacity as spouse of a Mexican politician—a different perspective about women in the political life of Mexico.

Victoria E. Rodríguez
Austin, Texas

❀ 1 ❀

The Emerging Role of Women in Mexican Political Life

Victoria E. Rodríguez

> *I cannot understand democracy without the participation of women. The struggle that began many years ago has not finished. The year 2005 is the goal for parity.*
>
> —Senator María Elena Chapa (PRI), August 1997

The July 1997 midterm election in Mexico has been widely hailed as historic. For the first time in over seventy years of one-party rule, the governing elite has become genuinely plural. The Congress is now led by the combined opposition forces of the Partido Acción Nacional (National Action Party, PAN), to the right of the political spectrum, and the Partido de la Revolución Democrática (Party of the Democratic Revolution, PRD), to the left. Although the Partido Revolucionario Institucional (Party of the Institutionalized Revolution, PRI) remains the dominant party and governs nationally, there have been important opposition gains at the city and regional levels. Specifically, over 50 percent of the country's population is now governed by the opposition at the state and local levels, and more significantly, the three largest and most important metropolitan areas are in the hands of parties other than the PRI: Guadalajara and Monterrey have gone to the PAN, and the Federal District (Mexico City proper) went to the PRD on July 6, 1997. In the context of what was relatively recently called "a perfect dictatorship," a dramatic political opening is underway in Mexico.

If the 1997 election was historic, then how did the women fare? On the face of it, and compared with the situation that reigned before, the numbers look promising: Seventeen percent of the 1997–2000 Congress now consists of women (i.e., they occupy 85 seats out of 500). By way of contrast, in the United States women occupy 51 of the 435 seats in the House of Representatives, or 11.5 percent. And according to the Inter-Parliamentary Union, women now hold 10 percent of legislative seats in Latin America and the Caribbean, trailing behind the world average of 11.5 percent. The six countries in the world with the highest representation of women in their legislatures are Denmark, Finland, the Netherlands, New Zealand, Norway, and Sweden (the percentages in these countries range from 22 to 39 percent). The seventh is another Latin American nation—Argentina—which boosted its female representation with the passage of a quota law in 1993, from 5 percent in 1991 to 28 percent in 1995. Thus Mexico's 17 percent, although a step forward, still lags far behind that of many other countries. But if in Mexico the numbers themselves are significant, more significant yet is the trajectory Mexican women have followed to arrive at this level of formal representation and to position themselves as key actors in the country's transition to democracy.

This book explores the emergent role of women in Mexican politics and their increasingly important presence in the country's political life. To date, the mainstream literature on politics in Mexico—abundant as it is—has said little about women, even though their participation as formal political actors has increased dramatically in the last fifteen years. The political participation of women, although well documented in other Latin American countries, has been seriously neglected in the Mexican case, and only until recently has it began to grow as a field of study (see, for example, Fernández Poncela 1995; Hierro, Parada, and Careaga 1995; Martínez 1993; Massolo 1994d; Tarrés 1992). If this lack of scholarly attention can be explained, to a certain extent, by the fact that men continue to dramatically outnumber women in the Mexican political elite, it remains puzzling that their gains have been relatively ignored. The number of women in formal political office has increased steadily since the early 1980s, and as indicated above, the percentage of women in the legislature is comparatively and relatively high.

Roderic Camp points out in Chapter 11 that only one out of every fourteen members of the so-called political elite in Mexico is a woman. But again one must look beyond the numbers. Despite the dramatic underrepresentation of women in high-level appointed and elected positions, the quickening political participation and increased visibility of women in other arenas is now beginning to place them in a position to play a critical role as political actors. Women have become increasingly influential in the policymaking process through their activism in nongovernmental organizations (NGOs) and urban popular movements at both the local and the national levels. They have also become key actors in the electoral process, and not only because they make up more than 50 percent of the electorate. Women monitor elections, orchestrate campaign events, run campaigns, join marches and demonstrations in record numbers, and of course increasingly run for office and contend for the top positions within the political parties' internal structures. As elsewhere in the world, Mexican women have come of political age. As Jane Jaquette writes, "The growing participation and representation of women in politics is one of the most remarkable developments of the late twentieth century. For the first time, women in all countries and social classes are becoming politically active, achieving dramatic gains in the number and kind of offices they hold" (1997a:23).

This book analyzes the different forms of women's political participation and activism in Mexico in a systematic way and anticipates what the future holds for women in Mexican political life, thereby seeking to open a new path of scholarly inquiry in both the United States and Mexico. Because an important part of the analysis presented here documents the rise of women as political actors, the chapters in this book also seek to contribute to the growing literature on Mexico's democratization process. As elsewhere in Latin America, Mexican women are in a key position to steer their country's incipient political transformation.

Struggling for Political Rights and Equality

The dramatic opening that has occurred in the political and electoral processes of the last years in the Mexican system has brought to the fore a number of actors who previously had little or no say in the political and policy decisionmaking processes, which were overwhelmingly dominated at all levels by the PRI. In addition to the major gains of the opposition parties, led by the PAN and the PRD, the birth and growth of a new civic culture in Mexico have triggered new forms of activism and political participation. Previously repressed or ignored actors, such as women, independent agrarian organizations, and indigenous groups, have begun to organize and mobilize in order to press their demands. In so doing, they have attracted national and international attention. The Chiapas uprising of 1994, which counted among its ranks numerous women, was perhaps the most vivid illustration of this emergent political presence. Mexican women are organizationally and politically astute and well set to take advantage of this opening. In pursuit of their political rights and in their struggle for equality, they have devised a variety of strategies, as will be discussed below.

As elsewhere in Latin America, Mexican women are becoming a political force to be reckoned with. As Lourdes Arizpe puts it, "everywhere, women are mobilizing themselves. This phenomenon, which though not new, is only just becoming visible" (1990:xvi). Indeed, the political mobilization of women in Mexico is not new at all, dating as it does to the early part of this century. In the early 1900s women began to campaign vigorously for recognition as citizens, focusing their struggles on suffrage and equality. As Carmen Ramos Escandón describes in her chapter in this book, women built coalitions wherever they could, continued those fights through the mid 1900s, and were finally successful in winning the right to vote in 1953 (see also Miller 1991). Nevertheless, by the late 1950s, only a handful of women occupied prominent political positions. The first woman elected to Congress was Aurora Jiménez Palacios, from Baja California, in 1954, and the first woman elected as governor was Griselda Alvarez, from Colima, in 1979. Altogether, between 1954 and 1989, a derisory 229 women held high-level positions in the three branches of government (Silva 1989), and to date only three women have been state governors. Into the 1990s, in spite of women's constitutionally recognized equality and being the electoral majority, the playing field has remained unequal. Today, however, their presence is increasingly noticeable.

According to the last national census (INEGI 1990), women constitute 51 percent of Mexico's population. The majority live in urban areas and are under thirty years old. Of the female population, 37 percent are under the age of fifteen. Birth rates have fallen dramatically, with the average number of children being 3.8, or half that of the early 1970s. Education levels have increased steadily, though women still tend to have higher illiteracy rates than men (25.5 percent compared to 16.7 percent male) (Inter-American Development Bank 1995:201). Although higher education rates have also increased, with women representing 40 percent of university graduates, access to university remains a privilege of the elites. And as is the case in other parts of the world, women tend to concentrate in what are traditionally considered to be "female" career areas, such as education, nursing, and social work.

In the economic sphere, women have also become increasingly noticeable and active, mostly as a result of the economic crises of the 1980s and 1990s, which placed unprecedented burdens on women to become providers as well as caretakers for the family and the home. Women now constitute almost one-fourth of the economically active population in Mexico; in urban areas, where most women reside, this percentage is significantly higher (see INEGI 1993; García and de Oliveira 1997). These figures apply only to the formal labor sector and ignore the thousands of women who work as domestic servants or in other areas of the informal economy that are often not included in national statistics. Even though the stereotypical image of Mexican women is that they take on paid work while they are young and single, the composition of the female workforce has changed drastically and now includes large numbers of middle-aged wives and mothers, a growing percentage of whom are also heads of households (see Chant 1991; González de la Rocha and Escobar Latapí 1991; Roberts 1993; Staudt 1998).

This increased presence of women in the economic sector has also helped to trigger their political activism. At the formal level, women have gradually gained access to elected office, appointed positions within the bureaucracy, and top party structures at the federal, state, and municipal levels (see Fernández Poncela 1995; Hierro et al. 1995; Martínez 1993; and the chapters by Roderic Camp, Alejandra Massolo, Lilia Venegas, and Alicia Martínez and Teresa Incháustegui in this book). At the informal level (i.e., outside of government and political parties), women have invariably been the backbone of urban social movements and other organized forms of protest that demand basic services for their neighborhoods, pay equity and better working conditions through labor unions, and in many cases simple equality and fairness from the state in the delivery of goods and services (Bennett 1995a; Carrillo 1990; Foweraker 1995a; Jelin 1990a; Massolo 1994d; Stephen 1997). This political activism, both formal and informal, has transformed the role of women in the political process.

Becoming Politically Active

Just as the range of political activities in which women are engaged varies widely, so do the reasons for their becoming politically active. A series of in-depth interviews conducted in 1995–1997 with over eighty women who are politically active in Mexico (Rodríguez forthcoming) as well as other data (Camp this volume; Martínez 1993; Silva 1989) make it apparent that in the formal sphere of politics women overwhelmingly tend to come from the middle and upper classes, are highly educated, and in many cases belong to prominent political families. For example, Griselda Alvarez, Mexico's first female governor, comes from a long line of politicians: Her great grandfather was the first governor of Colima, and her father, also governor of the state between 1919 and 1923, was active in the Revolution and a friend of Venustiano Carranza. For politically active Mexican women, more often than not, political activism began at an early age, either by being exposed to politics through family life or by their joining some politically organized group while at university. Indeed, many of them were student leaders, who very early in their careers joined a political party and gained a position in government. Such is the case, for example, of Beatriz Paredes, who became a state *diputada* (congresswoman) at the age of nineteen—and later, among other things, federal congresswoman, governor, undersecretary, ambassador, party secretary, leader of the peasant sector, and senator (she is now in her late forties). Although some of these women are avowed feminists and have used their political office to advance women's causes, a large number of them are there, quite simply, for the thrill of politics and the exercise of power. One wonders how surprising it may be to some people that, as Camp describes in Chapter 11, these women are virtually indistinguishable from their male counterparts in their background, performance, and career tracks. Their policy agendas are also very similar.

Women who engage in other aspects of political life through social movements, NGOs, and other grassroots organizations become politically active often for very different reasons than those of their female counterparts in government. During the interviews alluded to earlier it became apparent that in numerous cases their involvement was originally triggered by a traumatic event: the 1968 student massacre in which friends were killed or arrested, the 1985 earthquakes in Mexico City, or the disappearance of a loved one. The interviews conducted also showed that although the women who lead the organized groups in these areas of activity tend to come from the middle and upper classes and are relatively highly educated, an overwhelming number of the groups' members are working-class women (Rodríguez forthcoming; see also Tarrés 1996). And although the leaders and organizers may join a group in pursuit of a cause for ideological reasons or in pursuit of the common good (e.g., human rights, environmental issues), a decided majority of activists in popular movements—both leaders and followers—have concrete demands for goods and services around which they organize. As is demonstrated in the respective chapters by Vivienne Bennett, Joe Foweraker, María Luisa Tarrés, and Lynn Stephen in this book, the mobilization of women at the informal level and their ability to impact policy decisions have turned women into a formidable political force. Measured in terms of political efficacy, therefore, Mexican women appear to have gone considerably farther in the informal than in the formal sphere of politics—at least to date.

Strategizing Women's Issues

The wide variation in the reasons why women become politically active and involved is reflected in the goals and objectives they pursue as well as in the strategies they adopt. As is true for women elsewhere, the assumption is that in Mexico women in politics, especially those in government, will automatically support and promote women's causes. Although this may be accurate in some cases, the majority of women in Mexican politics tend to concentrate their struggles on other matters. With the exception of feminist groups and those NGOs that are devoted exclusively to promoting women's issues (e.g., reproductive rights, violence against women), the bulk of women's political activism tends to concentrate on fighting for public goods and services (at the informal level) and on supporting specific pieces of legislation and government programs in social policy (at the formal level). There are some notable exceptions, however, especially for those women who are able to bridge the informal and the formal spheres of politics and sustain their struggle for women's rights. In the new Congress, feminists are preparing strategies to convince legisla-tors that the budget needs to be revised in order to provide better for women's health care, job training, and access to credit for businesses. And Patria Jiménez, who became the first openly gay woman to be elected to Congress in July 1997, also has a firm gender agenda. As leader of a les-bian group, El Closet de Sor Juana, she has devoted her political activities to fighting for women's rights and gay liberation in Mexico. Her policy agenda as she entered Congress firmly centered on better health care for women, reproductive rights, and tighter laws to ban discrimination against women seeking credit and protection of their property rights.

Gender concerns come in second within the majority of women's policy agendas, trailing behind whatever their principal policy priority area may be (fiscal policy, human rights, transportation, education, social welfare, health, and so on). Yet, in any way possible, most of the women who are po-litically active seek to support and promote women's issues. Women in government have been a critical force in passing legislation targeted at women, ranging from rape laws to education programs to child care facili-ties. Outside of government, organized groups have benefited women in a variety of ways, from providing training programs and health care facilities to unionizing domestic servants. Not one of the politically active women I have interviewed formally or conversed with informally in the course of my research has indicated that she does not care for women's concerns. In-deed, some of them categorically stated that while such concerns are criti-cally important to them, their agendas are so full that gender issues some-times have to come in a poor second—if at all. This situation was clearly confronted by María de los Angeles Moreno when she was head of her party, the PRI. Having received the party in its worst shape (up until then) after the 1988 election, she was faced with the impossible task of putting the party together and regaining some legitimacy for it. But being the highest-ranking woman in the political system overall, all women's eyes turned to her. Her hands tied with party affairs, she had little time for women's causes and was criticized rather harshly for this. Ironically, she is an avowed feminist, and since leaving the party presidency has become in-creasingly involved with women's groups in and outside government.

Only a handful of women interviewed appeared to be rather dismissive of explicit gender-related issues, but even they felt that if to support a par-ticular program benefited women, so much the better. Altogether, only a very small proportion of women in politics concentrate single-mindedly on women. As most others pointed out to me, the social and economic needs in Mexico are so many and so pressing that gender inevitably still takes a back seat.

Because there are still relatively few women who are politically visible and even fewer yet who carry real political weight, women appear to be

developing a sense of solidarity that cuts across party lines, political ideologies, and areas of activity. For example, this gender solidarity emerged
when women of all parties and ideological positions united in support of
the passage of the rape law in the early 1990s under the leadership of
Amalia García, then a congresswoman for the PRD. Now that very senior
political women have been elected to the Senate, it will be of great interest to observe the positions that they take. In July 1997 some of the most
prominent women from all three political parties became senators: from
the PRI, Beatriz Paredes, Elba Esther Gordillo, and Rosario Green; from
the PAN, Ana Rosa Payán and María Elena Alvarez; and from the PRD,
Amalia García and Rosalbina Garavito. Moreover, two leading feminists
have been appointed to the incoming Cárdenas administration in the Federal District: Rosario Robles as secretary of government (the highest appointed position in the administration) and Clara Jusidman as secretary
of social development. All these women represent, indeed, *"las planas
mayores"* (the heavy-hitters).

However, both in my conversations with and my observations of political women in Mexico, it has become clear that women's political loyalties,
first and foremost, rest with the political party or organization to which
they belong. Gender loyalty, for all practical purposes, comes in (a distant)
second. Even among women of the same party, it is noticeable that their solidarity and loyalty rest with policies and programs, political patrons and
mentors, career plans and ambitions—not with the other women in the
party. Here, too, women were quick to point out that if some (additional)
gender solidarity could be developed, then so much the better. Indeed,
when the pressure is really on (as is the case, for example, during elections),
women tend to show greater unity. As an illustration, on June 23, 1997, two
weeks before the election, a coalition of women from all political parties put
aside their ideological differences and signed an accord to seek certain reforms to protect women. Among their priorities is the need for better laws
to make fathers responsible for their children and to ban discrimination in
employment and salaries. Through this nonpartisan agreement, the coalition of women is also seeking to outlaw a controversial practice to which
women of all ideological persuasions are united in opposition: forced preg-
nancy testing of women applying for jobs. There are, however, some issues
where a compromise is out of the question, abortion being a case in point:
The PAN follows an immovable antiabortion philosophy, whereas the PRD
advocates abortion rights and a national referendum on decriminalizing
abortion. The PRI is split down the middle.

Yet almost without exception, all of the political women I have studied
in Mexico have shown a willingness to put aside personal and ideological
differences with other women and come together in the one political goal
that unites all women: their recognition as political actors. Building al-

liances is probably the most widely recognized strategy for women to fulfill their aspirations and responsibilities as emerging political actors in Mexico's democratization process. As Kathleen Staudt, Nikki Craske, Marta Lamas, Jane Jaquette, and Alicia Martínez and Teresa Incháustegui argue in their respective chapters in this book, there is strength in numbers (see also Jaquette 1997a). The goal for Mexican women is to reach the "critical mass" that will allow them to advance their position and that of all women in Mexican society. Building alliances with other women across party lines and areas of activity, irrespective of being feminists or not, is the one opportunity for women to improve their political position and gain influence in the policymaking process. But alliances are not necessarily exclusively gender based; many of the strongest alliances of women have been built with men. In government in general, and in the Congress in particular, this strategy of forging alliances with male actors has resulted in positive outcomes. As Consuelo Botello, a former congresswoman from the PAN put it at the 1996 meeting in Austin, "our strength is with our *compañerOs* [male colleagues] in the Congress as much as it is with our *compañerAs* [female colleagues]." The alliances with men of women active in informal politics have also been critical for their success in securing goods and services.

Building Strength in Numbers: Are Quotas the Answer?

In an attempt to foster the building of alliances to promote women's causes and to fulfill their principal objective—political representation—politically active women in Mexico have pursued other strategies. Among these the most noteworthy is the effort to institutionalize a quota system within government and in the organizational structures and candidate lists of political parties. As is well documented in the literature, the quota system has been enormously successful in Scandinavian countries (see Jaquette 1997a and the chapter by Kathleen Staudt in this book), it recently led to a doubling in the representation of women in Britain's House of Commons with the sweeping Labour Party victory, and it is being avidly contemplated and adopted throughout Latin America. This move to establish quotas for women in politics has been fostered by the networking among women's groups, from the Beijing conference in 1995, as well as from the growing focus on women's issues in international development organizations. But more to the point, as Jaquette puts it,

> the surest way to achieve an increased number of women in national legislatures is to adopt a quota system that requires a certain percentage of women to be nominated or elected. . . . If the trend continues, quotas will soon pro-

duce a quantum leap in women's political power. For the first time, women will form a "critical mass" of legislators in many countries, able to set new agendas and perhaps create new styles of leadership (1997a:32, 34)

Following the lead of the Scandinavian countries, in 1991 Argentina was the first country to institute a formal quota system in Latin America. The Ley de Cupos (Quota Law) required all political parties to have at least 30 percent women in their electoral slates and showed impressive results in the first election following this legislation, held in 1993: Women's representation in Congress soared overnight from 5 percent in 1991 to 21 percent, and then to 28 percent in 1995 (Jones 1996:76). Impressed by these results, Latin American women discussing the issue of quotas at Beijing were determined to establish quotas in their own countries. The second country to follow suit was Brazil, which in 1995 adopted a law requiring all parties to have at least 20 percent women in all their slates for the 1996 municipal elections and is now formally considering extending the law to include national office. Under the quota system followed in the 1997 congressional elections, women legislators increased by nearly 40 percent. In 1997, Ecuador passed a quota law in February, Bolivia in March, and Peru in June, all of them requiring a minimum 20 percent women in every electoral slate. Venezuela is now considering a 30 percent quota law, which is most likely to pass.

Other Latin American nations also encourage political parties to nominate more women in their candidate lists but provide little enforcement. Mexico, like Panama, has passed legislation encouraging parties to promote more women to public office but has provided no effective enforcement mechanisms. For example, article 41 of the PRI's statutes says "*se promoverá*" ("will be promoted"), and article 1 of the Código Federal de Instituciones y Procedimientos Electorales (Federal Code for Electoral Procedures and Institutions, COFIPE) only says "*se considerarán*" ("will be considered"). In addition to the vague language, there is no mention of enforcement. In other Latin American countries where no quotas exist, individual parties are making the effort on their own. The Sandinista Front in Nicaragua and the National Liberation Front in El Salvador both have internal quotas for their parties' leadership.

The efforts at affirmative action through a quota system, always a contentious and controversial issue, have divided Mexican women. On the one hand are those who argue for quotas as the only effective mechanism for reaching the critical mass that women need in order to gain political strength. This argument follows the line that a minimum 30 percent of women in government and political parties will guarantee that women begin to be given their rightful political place and be more likely to have their demands met. Quotas are the only way to guarantee women access to power. On the other hand are those who oppose the institutionalization of a quota on the grounds that it is discriminatory, devaluates the political abilities of women, promotes underqualified women, and is unnecessary because the women who are qualified will rise on their own merit anyway. Moreover, in the view of those who oppose quotas, a set number of women in government and political parties is no assurance that they will promote and support women's causes. The number of women in government is not important; what matters is their commitment to gender issues and to advancing the position of women in society.

In broad terms, the institutionalization of quotas is favored by the PRD and the PRI and opposed by the PAN (see Rodríguez et al. 1996). Of the three major political parties, the only one to formally and explicitly institute a quota system both within its internal party structure and its candidate lists is the PRD. Only recently did the PRI follow suit, after a rather hushed debate during the party's annual assembly in 1996. The PAN continues to be opposed.

Although the results of the quota system for the number of women in the PRD are far from glowing—indeed, it has never really reached its 30 percent quota—the numbers of women in government and parties continue to grow. After the 1997 election, in addition to the scores of women who won a seat in Congress, women won 26 percent of the seats in Mexico City's Legislative Assembly. This number, which includes women from all political parties, is the highest ever in that body. And there is further hope. Senator María Elena Chapa (PRI) hopes to achieve parity by the year 2005, and Senator Amalia García (PRD) hopes that a 50/50 goal will materialize both in parties and government for the election of the year 2000. In fact, as becomes apparent in looking at Table 1.1, the data consistently show that women fare better in presidential elections than in midterm elections. For example, the number of women legislators increased from 42 to 59 in the 1988 election (a presidential one), dropped to 44 in 1991 (a midterm election), then rose to 70 in 1994 (a presidential election). The exception that may prove this rule is that the total number of women in Congress actually increased to 87 in the 1997 midterm election. Indeed, taking congresswomen from the PRI as an example, in the 1991 midterm election they obtained 23 seats; in 1994, a presidential election, that number almost doubled to 41; in the 1997 midterm election it dropped to 35 (see Table 1.2). This raises the expectations for the election of the year 2000, which will be a presidential one.

Yet women are far from satisfied and remain critical of the way the quota system operates. The biggest complaints center around women's placement on the candidate lists and the districts for which they are nominated to run. The female proportional representation candidates are placed so low on the list that it is impossible for them to get in through

TABLE 1.1   Women's Representation in the Last Sixteen Mexican Congresses

Presidential Period	Legislature	Chamber of Deputies			Senate		
		Men	Women	Total	Men	Women	Total
1952–1958 Adolfo Ruiz Cortines	XLII (1952–1955)	161	1	162	56	0	56
	XLIII (1955–1958)	156	4	160			
1958–1964 Adolfo López Mateos	XLIV (1958–1961)	154	8	162	58	0	58
	XLV (1961–1964)	176	9	185			
1964–1970 Gustavo Díaz Ordaz	XLVI (1964–1967)	197	13	210	56	2	58
	XLVII (1967–1970)	198	12	210			
1970–1976 Luis Echeverría Alvarez	XLVIII (1970–1973)	184	13	197	58	2	60
	XLIX (1973–1976)	212	19	231			
1976–1982 José López Portillo	L (1976–1979)	215	21	236	59	5	64
	LI (1979–1982)	368	32	400			
1982–1988 Miguel de la Madrid Hurtado	LII (1982–1985)	358	42	400	58	6	64
	LIII (1985–1988)	358	42	400			
1988–1994 Carlos Salinas de Gortari	LIV (1988–1991)	441	59	500	54	10	64
	LV (1991–1994)	455	44	499	60	4	64
1994–2000 Ernesto Zedillo Ponce de León	LVI (1994–1997)	426	70	496	112	16	128
	LVII (1997–2000)	413	87	500	109	19	128
Total		4,472	476	4,948	566	64	630

Source: Programa Nacional de la Mujer, *Más Mujeres al Congreso* (Mexico: PRONAM, 1997), pp. 231–232.

TABLE 1.2 The July 1997 Congressional Election, by Party: How Did the Women Fare?

Party	Total Number of Seats Won	Total Number of Women	Total Number of Female Candidates Nominated by Direct Election	Total Number of Women Who Won by	
				Direct Election	Proportional Representation
PAN	122	16	38	3	13
PRD	125	29	41	11	18
PRI	239	35	43	22	13
PVEM	8	4	95	0	4
PT	6	1	64	0	1
Total	500	85	281	36	49

Note: The data in this table are not compatible with the data in Table 1.1 because the electoral results were preliminary. Some congressional seats were up for contestation. The definitive data are presented in Table 1.1

Source: Data compiled by author from Enfoque, Sunday Supplement to Reforma, August 10, 1997.

this route. And the candidates for direct election are nominated for districts where the party knows it has no possibility of winning. Even worse, some parties (notably the PRI) nominate many of the required 30 percent women as *suplentes* (alternates)! As Patricia Espinosa from the PAN puts it, referring to the 1997 election and to her party, "one has to see the places occupied by women: the large majority, the fat list, was in unwinnable districts" (*Enfoque,* August 10, 1997; my translation). And María Elena Chapa's assessment from the PRI: "Yes, I will open the door to you, but only to municipalities that don't mean much to my party. . . . I'm testing you. Go, woman" (*Enfoque,* August 10, 1997; my translation). However, as Table 1.2 shows, there appears to have been a positive effect at least for the female candidates of the PRI, since they had the highest proportion of women candidates winning in the seats contested. The issue, as Amalia García from the PRD states, is deeper: "The challenge of the minimum percentage is not its application as obligatory, but rather to transform the collective conscience, the culture of both men and women" (*Enfoque,* August 10, 1997; my translation).

There is little doubt that the figures discussed above, in addition to the scores of women elected to state congresses and other offices at the local level, have placed women in a position to become much more important as political actors in the new millennium. Just within the PRI's national ranks, it is very telling that two of the party's three sectors are headed by women, with Beatriz Paredes leading the peasant sector (Confederación Nacional Campesina [National Peasant Confederation, CNC]) and Elba Esther Gordillo the newly reconstituted popular sector (Confederación Nacional de Organizaciones Populares [National Confederation of Popular Organizations, CNOP]). Gordillo, in addition, only recently left the leading position of the teachers' union, the Sindicato Nacional de Trabajadores de la Educación (National Union of Education Workers, SNTE), which is the largest and one of the most powerful unions in Latin America. And the recently established Women's Bureau in the Ministry of the Interior is headed by Dulce María Sauri, a senior member of the PRI; her seniority and her support for women and gender issues throughout her career bodes well for the bureau. More significant yet is the appointment in January 1998 of Rosario Green as secretary of foreign relations (she had just won a seat in the Senate in the 1997 election). For the first time in history, a woman is at the helm of one of the highest-ranking ministries. Until her appointment, women had only been head of ministries considered to be "second tier": Fisheries, Environment, Tourism. The accomplishments of this stellar group are indeed stellar. But for the majority of Mexican political women, the playing field is far from level, and there is still a considerable societal and cultural negative baggage attached to being a woman in politics and to promoting women's causes.

The ongoing struggle of women to be recognized as political actors (in a gender-free sense) has effectively led Mexican women to "nest" their struggles within a larger concern for social justice and equality. Particularly in this era of transformation in the political system and as a new civic and political culture develops, women have begun to articulate their concerns as part of the larger discourse that demands democratic opening and a wider space to incorporate previously neglected actors. Opposition parties, women, and indigenous groups are among the principal players in Mexico's process of democratic transition, as is evident in the attention they have received both nationally and internationally. The repeated claims for democracy, equality, and social justice are readily evident in the platforms of these three key new actors. Just how these demands will be transformed into specific policies and programs is the task that lies ahead. A task, perhaps, that may come to be performed by the daughters of the women who are currently struggling to establish their political representation in Mexico's emerging democracy. The daughters, as Elsa Chaney would put it, of the *supermadres* of the 1990s.

Organization of the Book

The book consists of fifteen chapters, divided into three parts. The first part, The Context: Women in Political Life Worldwide, provides an overview of the status of women in the political life of Latin America and other parts of the world. The chapters in this first section serve as a contextual setting for the discussion of women in Mexican political life that follows in the remainder of the book. How do Mexican political women fare when compared with women in other countries?

In Chapter 2, Kathleen Staudt argues that women's political participation is crucial for promoting democracy throughout the world but that undisputably men continue to monopolize political space. Based on an extensive study she conducted for the United Nations Development Programme (UNDP), Staudt puts Mexico in global perspective, focusing on patterns of women's representation and on explanations for variation in representation. Effective practices and lessons from her study are highlighted, as is their applicability to the Mexican case. Additionally, she offers a conceptual model that posits relationships for engendering politics. In the concluding section of the chapter, Staudt outlines what she considers the most promising practices and lessons for engendering democracy. These include "critical mass" numbers in executive and legislative bodies, increased participation at the local level, effective voter turnout, monitoring government accountability to women, and building coalitions with men who support engendering democracy.

Building upon Staudt's global perspective, her assessment of UN initiatives, and the strategies she proposes for engendering democracy worldwide, in Chapter 3 Nikki Craske focuses on women's political participation in Latin America. In this chapter Craske examines the opportunities and constraints confronting women who seek a political role, especially in the electoral arena, and compares Mexico with other countries in the region, particularly Argentina and Chile. The comparison is based on different policies adopted by Latin American governments, such as quota laws, women's ministries, and UN conventions. Based on her assessment of the background and outcomes of Argentina's Ley de Cupos and Chile's Servicio Nacional de la Mujer (Women's Ministry, SERNAM), Craske argues that it is difficult to discern a policy that could be used as a model for the rest of the region. Mexico, to date, has tended to be less interventionist on the "women question," evading a formal use of quotas and women's ministries. In terms of women representatives, however, Mexico is in a better position than most of its Latin American neighbors.

Chapter 4, by Joe Foweraker, is both thoughtful and thought provoking and provides a comprehensive review and discussion of the theoretical and comparative literature on women's mobilization in Latin America. From this literature he draws ten theses about the role of women in political life in Latin America generally and Mexico specifically. The ten theses around which Foweraker builds his argument are the following: (1) Women's mobilization is new in form and degree; (2) women's mobilization is different from feminist movements; (3) women's mobilization is rooted in traditional female roles; (4) feminism is successful in extending women's political agenda; (5) women's mobilization is mainly led by men; (6) women's mobilization creates new political identities; (7) women's mobilization changes the division between public and private; (8) women's mobilization targets the agencies and apparatuses of the state; (9) women's mobilization expands citizenship rights; and (10) women's mobilization extends political representation.

In Chapter 5, Elsa Chaney outlines the main points from her 1979 classic work *Supermadre: Women in Politics in Latin America* and examines some of the flaws in her own earlier arguments. She argues, nonetheless, that the many aspects of her original thesis endure today and are reiterated by more recent scholars who have done work on the subject (e.g., Sonia Alvarez and Jane Jaquette). She concludes that women's entry into the formal political arena, after some gains, is waning. The full changes will become apparent after studying the political daughters of the women she interviewed in her original work.

Part Two, Women in the Mexican Political Arena, analyzes the different arenas of political activity outside of formal political institutions in which women have played a critical role. The chapters in this section focus specifically on Mexico and provide a thorough discussion of women in urban popular movements, NGOs, and other organized groups of collective action through which women have attempted, with varying degrees of success, to influence public policy and governmental decisionmaking procedures.

In Chapter 6, Carmen Ramos Escandón provides a historical overview of women's participation in Mexico, focusing specifically on three "historical moments": (1) the relationship between women and the state's power structures of the Porfiriato, from 1880 to 1917; (2) the spontaneous political participation of women and the breakdown of barriers between their public and private spaces during the Revolution; and (3) the coalition of women's organizations that united under the Frente Unico Pro Derechos de la Mujer (Sole Front for Women's Rights, FUPDM) during the 1930s. In Ramos's view, these three "moments" illustrate the different ways in which women have related to political power structures in Mexico and serve as strong reminders that the current women's movement has a rich heritage that must not be forgotten.

Chapter 7 takes us into the 1990s. Marta Lamas provides an "insider's view" of Mexico's feminist movement, reflecting on her personal experiences within the movement and focusing specifically on the creation and activities of De la A a la Z. This group, put together under Lamas's leadership, was composed of seven leading Mexican feminists of differing political ideologies and persuasions who sought to put the Italian principle of *affidamento*—women trusting other women—into practice. De la A a la Z also sought to demonstrate that the group (and the feminist movement) could have political efficacy. The group's experiences and its political impact were mixed. As Lamas questions, can Mexican feminists overcome their personal and political differences and establish an alliance that will allow them to introduce their proposals into the public policy agenda and obtain more representation for women in politics? This same question is taken up later in the book by Alicia Martínez and Teresa Incháustegui. Lamas concludes that De la A a la Z was, above all, a political exercise of Mexican feminists who dared to be different.

Vivienne Bennett, in Chapter 8, focuses on two types of grassroots activity of urban poor women in Mexico: urban popular movements and territorially based organizations. The first part presents an overview of the evolution of urban popular movements in Mexico in which Bennett emphasizes how, from the 1970s to 1985, women were major participants in these movements but never leaders. From 1985 onward, however, women not only created new movements but also became leaders. The second half of the chapter analyzes territorially based organizations of urban poor women. Bennett concludes that as the Mexican government cuts social spending, urban militance by poor women is likely to increase.

As she persuasively argues, social activism has become a part of their everyday life and everyday struggles.

María Luisa Tarrés based Chapter 9 on a research project on women's NGOs in Mexico. She notes that NGOs have grown considerably since the mid-1980s, at the precise time when a crisis of legitimacy within the political system was beginning to develop. Women's NGOs grew in a context characterized by the breaking of old attitudes that for many years dominated Mexican culture and popular mobilization. Tarrés examines the characteristics of women who join and build women's NGOs, their bases of support, their areas of activity, the public they serve, the obstacles they more frequently encounter, and their commitment to participating in Mexico's democratic transition. She concludes that women's NGOs work on diverse subjects and activities, which makes them heterogeneous, but are united by a common cause: combating the subordination of women in the different arenas of private and public life.

Chapter 10, the last chapter of this section, closes the circle of women's political activity outside of formal political institutions: from the women's movement pioneers of the turn of the century, to feminists, to women in popular movements and NGOs, to the female soldiers of the Chiapas uprising. Drawing upon her fieldwork in Chiapas and incorporating some of her insightful interviews with Zapatista women, Lynn Stephen examines arenas in which women have organized in Chiapas and how these women's organizations have both built upon and challenged past limitations of local women's organizing. She emphasizes how the integration of women into the democratization process currently under way in Mexico was in many ways inspired by the Zapatista women and their revolutionary laws. In the groups organized by Zapatista women, as well as in their documents and manifestos, democratization is proposed as a critical ingredient for improving the lives of women, both in the public and the private spheres.

The third and final part, Women in Politics: Government and Political Parties, is devoted to analyzing the role of women in formal political arenas. The chapters in this section provide a profile of these women and discuss how they are recruited and drawn into formal political institutions at the national and local levels, the obstacles and challenges they face, and the alternative strategies they pursue in their efforts to enhance their political presence within the system. The concluding chapter provides a final overview of the book and suggests future directions for women in the political life of Latin America in general and of Mexico specifically.

Using his extensive archival database, in Chapter 11 Roderic Ai Camp examines the career tracks of Mexican female politicians. He provides a comprehensive analysis of women's and men's access to political careers, identifying similarities and differences between men and women in the process of recruitment and career advancement. Emphasizing women's educational, family, and career backgrounds, Camp identifies the paths women pursue to reach the apex of the political system—compared to men—and offers some thoughts on what this means for the future of women in Mexican national politics.

Alicia Martínez and Teresa Incháustegui, in Chapter 12, reflect on the accomplishments of the Mexican feminist movement in terms of the inclusion of women into formal political structures and institutions (government, political parties) and the movement's political efficacy. Building upon the chapters by Kathleen Staudt and Nikki Craske, Martínez and Incháustegui analyze the quota system in Mexico's political parties as a strategy to increase the number of women in politics and conclude that quotas not only have been ineffectively adopted and implemented but also have failed to produce a "critical mass" of women in Mexican political institutions. Even though the number of women in elected and appointed positions as well as within the parties' leadership has increased, the entry of women into Mexican politics has been rather fortuitous, that is, not the result of organized tactics such as affirmative action. Quotas are not the solution for Mexican women. Martínez and Incháustegui argue that the problem is deeper and calls for alternative strategies that are compatible with the workings of the Mexican political system. In their view, which resonates with that of Lamas, the feminist movement in Mexico needs to reconsider its strategies for increasing the presence of women in politics and its political efficacy by building alliances. The starting point, they argue, is to establish solid relationships among the movement's various groups, the political parties, governmental institutions, and all other decisionmaking arenas where the role of women in politics—and their future—is determined.

Moving from national to local politics, in Chapter 13 Alejandra Massolo argues that the localities have been the principal place where women have fought the longest and where they are more effective. Following Vivienne Bennett's argument, Massolo also contends that the neighborhood and local social settings are where women have protected their roles and interests and fought their battles. She analyzes the activities of women in localities and their presence in local government. She discusses the fluctuating numbers of women in municipal governments headed by different political parties and in different regions of the country, the positions they hold in municipal governments, and the successes and obstacles they have encountered.

Lilia Venegas continues the analysis at the local level in Chapter 14. She details why two northern cities—Tijuana, Baja California, and Ciudad Juárez, Chihuahua—were chosen for her study and what makes them more prone to militancy within the PAN, the opposition party to the right of the political spectrum that has won consistently in state and local elections throughout the country since the electoral opening of the early 1990s. Venegas explores various social aspects that influence women's decisions to join the conservative PAN and the role they play within the party's activities. She argues that for the past decade the main role of women within the PAN has been almost limited to cleaning up every electoral mess in those two cities. As electoral processes have become cleaner and more effective, however, *panista* women are left with two alternative choices: One is to return to the private sphere; the other is to continue their political activism by running for public office, holding an appointed position in government, or occupying a leading position within the party. Venegas offers some insights on those women who have chosen the second alternative.

Chapter 15 draws overall conclusions from the separate contributions and addresses the major issues raised in the book. In an insightful and provocative chapter and building upon her expertise on women and political participation, democratization, and feminism, Jane Jaquette looks back on previous feminist research practices and outlines her perspectives for the participation of women in the political life of Latin America as both Mexico and the region turn to democracy.

PART ONE

The Context: Women in Political Life Worldwide

❀ 2 ❀

Women in Politics:
Mexico in Global Perspective

Kathleen Staudt

Political Space Belongs to All Citizens
—**Inter-Parliamentary Union**

With the eloquent statement that opens this chapter, an Inter-Parliamentary Symposium synthesized its 1989 conference. Democracies ought to draw on the voices and participation of both women and men, in balanced, shared, and partnered ways. Yet the historical legacies and figures from most countries point to a stark reality: *Men monopolize political space.* Political monopolies are likely to produce policy results that are neither gender fair nor accountable to women.

Women's participation has been crucial in the transitions to democracy in Latin America (Jaquette 1994). But that risky participation has not necessarily borne fruit for women in the form of greater representation or more responsive policies. Continued women's participation is crucial for consolidating democracies and, in so doing, transforming their process. With Julieta Kirkwood's famous quotes about *"una nueva manera de hacer política"* ("a new way of doing politics"), Jane Jaquette goes on to discuss a political process that needs change:

> In its usual and even democratic forms, politics is an alien and alienating world to most women, not because (as some researchers have argued) it is too abstract or too complicated, but because it is often perceived as destructively competitive, morally compromising and hostile to those women who do try to enter it through the conventional channels. Part of the desire that women's groups have to remain autonomous is to distance themselves from the corrupting pressures and the competitive power plays that they believe will divert them from their goals. (1993:6)[1]

23

With the 1995 Fourth World Congress on Women, the United Nations Development Programme (UNDP) made women's representation a central feature of its annual *Human Development Report*. Using data from a background study prepared for UNDP (Staudt 1994),[2] in this chapter I put Mexico in global context, focusing on patterns of women's representation and on explanations for variation in representation. In the course of analyzing institutional variations, promising practices and lessons from the more successful country cases are highlighted. A conceptual model is offered that posits relationships for en*gender*ing politics.[3]

My argument on Mexico follows, in highly condensed form. Viewed in global and hemispheric contexts, the Mexico experience through the early 1990s has not been promising, either in terms of representations or of democracy responsive to women. In institutional terms, Mexico might *seem* to have conditions favorable for women's democracy; its framework offers regular, multiparty elections with several leftist parties that address women's participation; parties compete for legislative seats allocated through both single-member and proportional representation. Mexico has vigorous and vibrant feminist organizations, along with extensive women's participation in grassroots neighborhood organizations. Together, these two kinds of groups offer the promise of an expanded policy agenda, a "new way of doing politics," and a "new political culture" (Arizpe and Velázquez 1994; Tarrés 1989). Women dialogue across party lines over their representation and issues (selections in Rodríguez et al. 1995, 1996). But those who "man" top decisionmaking positions in the major parties have rarely accorded these matters high priority. With this old political culture in place—both at national and local levels—organizations that represent women's issues have been reluctant to taint their involvement through engagement with mainstream politics or to settle for the meager payoffs awarded them. Nevertheless, women are "building bridges" to the establishment and "translating" feminist discourse (Lamas et al. 1995a) into language that allows them to press the crumbling male monopoly from inside and outside the system.

Engendering Politics: A Conceptual Model

Will gender-balanced participation make a difference for a democracy that responds to women? The question can be answered by focusing on women's movements and groups and on official representation. Movement activists attempt, sometimes successfully, to broaden and transform the policy agenda; they also create a climate of expectations that men and women political officials be accountable to their needs.

Women's representatives behave in less predictable ways, depending on their career pathways into politics, their gender ideologies, and their

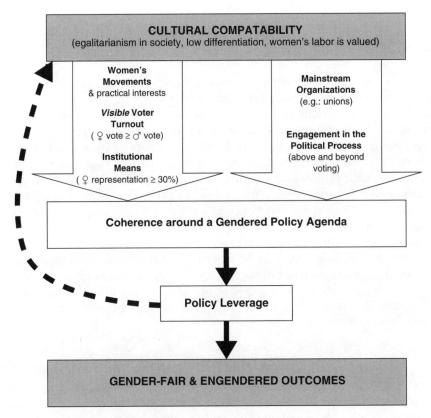

CULTURAL COMPATABILITY
(egalitarianism in society, low differentiation, women's labor is valued)

Women's
Movements
& practical interests

Visible Voter
Turnout
(♀ vote ≥ ♂ vote)

Institutional
Means
(♀ representation ≥ 30%)

Mainstream
Organizations
(e.g.: unions)

Engagement in the
Political Process
(above and beyond
voting)

Coherence around a Gendered Policy Agenda

Policy Leverage

GENDER-FAIR & ENGENDERED OUTCOMES

FIGURE 2.1   Engendering Politics in Democratic Regimes

sources of support. In the best case scenario, women representatives are connected to interests and ideas supportive of gender fairness. When working under the condition of "critical mass" numbers, beginning with 15 percent "skewed representation" and moving toward "balanced representation" of 35 percent or more (Kanter 1993), women are able to build coalitions with other women and men to accomplish those goals. In the worst case scenario, women representatives are beholden to men who seek to perpetuate a status quo that privileges men.

Figure 2.1 posits pathways toward engendered political outcomes, drawing on socioeconomic factors that feed conventional politics and are in turn affected by political outcomes. Moving from the top down, cultural compatibility establishes the ease by which women organize for change both in women's movements and in mainstream organizations, such as unions. Compatibility emerges in societies that stress egalitarianism and value public female labor or reduce the construction of gender "difference" (see the section "Explanations for Low Representation"). Low fertility is assumed to link with less differentiation. Women's organizational activities that increase female value can foster greater compatibility.

Moving to conventional politics, women's voices and choices are connected to public decisionmaking. Female voter turnout is nearly equal to and/or surpasses male turnout, but this turnout must be *visible* to the electorate, to candidates, and to elected officials. Also, more than voting must occur. Women's groups must opt to *engage with* (Nelson and Chowdhury 1994) the political process rather than avoid it, as is quite common in many countries (Charlton, Everett, and Staudt 1989) and among radical women's factions. Both voting and organizational engagement are assumed to invoke a gendered policy agenda around which people—men and women alike—will cohere.

Finally, representatives and officials act on a coherent gendered policy agenda, especially when built upon critical mass numbers of women's voices. These actions will provide policy leverage, such as equality laws and women's machinery (the UN term for women's bureaus, equality ministries, and so on), that feeds back to strengthen voting and organizational engagement.

Low Representation Levels

In all but a handful of countries, women comprise an eligible electorate of half or more. Yet women's representation withers to 16 percent in local councils, 10 percent in national legislatures (parliaments and congresses), 7 percent in national cabinets, and 4 percent of chief executives (presidents and prime ministers). These mid-1994 figures come from the Inter-Parliamentary Union (IPU) and the UN Division for the Advancement of Women (Staudt 1994). The women's pyramid portrayed in Figure 2.2 is a striking contrast to men's inverted pyramid. Although figures on women chief executives and national representatives are commonly cited, women's participation at other levels is less visible. Only since 1989 has the UN kept track of women cabinet members.[4] Yet cabinet and local representation merit strong consideration.

Local participation provides an experienced pool of women available to serve at other levels. As decentralization becomes more meaningful (see Rodríguez and Ward 1992, 1994 on Mexico), the significant decisions that are made about taxing and spending have different effects on men, women, and female household heads. Recent constitutional changes in India reserve a third of Panchayat (local council) seats for women. At least 800,000 women will consequently be in a local political pool. In Germany, more than 1,200 equal rights offices operate at local levels.

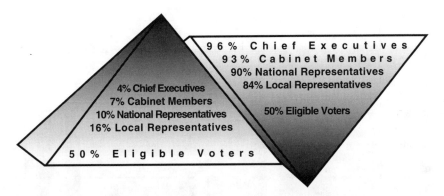

FIGURE 2.2   Women's and Men's Participation Pyramids

Cabinet work, which spans both legislative and executive/bureaucratic branches of government in parliamentary systems, is a special strategic location from which to exercise decisionmaking power. In presidential forms of government, appointed cabinet members work primarily in the executive branch departments. They represent their agencies to the legislature and thus engage in sustained contact with those representatives.

Few countries have a critical mass of women on cabinets. Whatever their proportions, the portfolios to which women are assigned fall generally in the areas of social welfare, women's affairs, education, and culture—all of which are seldom considered to be the more powerful ministries, such as foreign affairs, defense, and finance (Staudt 1989). Finland is the current world exception, with a woman central bank director and minister of defense.

Mexican men generally appoint several women to cabinet-level positions but not in positions considered powerful or close to the president (in this executive-dominant presidential system).[5] For example, the fisheries post is a cabinet slot allocated more than once to women in Mexico. When cabinet posts were announced after the 1994 elections, one large newspaper headlined the story with the words "Los Hombres del Presidente" ("the president's men") and pictured three women. One might interpret this as editorial simplification, which reduces "people" to "men." Another interpretation might view these women as people seeking upward mobility in a man's political world, wherein connections to women's groups and women's issues have no place.

Women heads of state are more rare than those on cabinets. Although the symbolism of a woman president/prime minister is to be applauded, in no case has a single woman transformed political process and outcome. Nor do all women executives put gender fairness at the top of their pol-

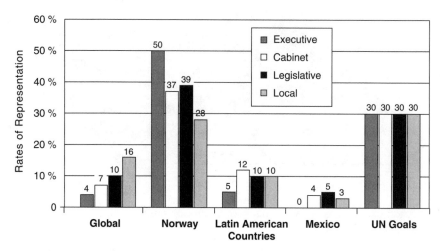

FIGURE 2.3   Women's Representation in Government, 1994

icy priorities. Margaret Thatcher, dubbed the Iron Lady, cut milk subsidies to children (thus the refrain, "Maggie Thatcher, milk snatcher").

Political work toward gender-fair policy outcomes is threatening to the status quo. Can mid-1990s woman executives in Turkey (Tansu Ciller) and Pakistan (Benazir Bhutto) spend political capital in such ways? Former Philippines president Corazon Aquino's record was mixed on poverty alleviation (in a feminized-poverty context), but she signed the executive order to create and implement a Development Plan for Women, under the direction of the women's commission, with sixty staff members, augmented by a "sisters sorority" of focal points in government agencies and accountable relationships with women's organizations (in Rao et al 1991).

Several women have run for president in Mexican multiparty elections, although they were based in small leftist parties. Many voters view elections with cynicism in Mexico, given past manipulations of the vote count, along with unfair media and patronage privileges for the dominant party.

How does Mexico compare with Latin America, global figures, Norway (the most successful, gender-balanced polity), and UN goals? Figure 2.3 shows that mid-1994 Mexico had the lowest rates of women's representation in comparison with the others.[6] In particular, Mexico lagged in female representation at the local level (see Chapter 13). In many countries, political experience at local levels becomes a stepping-stone toward more experience at state and national levels. Further, local political work is frequently more compatible with women's still-extensive responsibilities in home and family, a common issue worldwide. Still, Mexico's rates are minuscule compared to other countries.

Global figures show gross underrepresentation. These levels are well below UN goals as well as the achievements of Nordic countries (Norway, Sweden, Finland, Denmark). Although women's representation is on the rise in cabinets, global legislative patterns have held fairly steady over the last decade, even taking a dip after the so-called transitions to democracy in the former USSR and Eastern Europe led to dramatic reductions in the high state-imposed female representation levels.

Let us now turn to explanations for those figures in the areas of human development priority, broadly defined culture, and institutions.

Explanations for Low Representation

Explanations for low female representation fall into three categories, each associated with empirical challenges. The first, human development, is amenable to some quantification, although the numerical precision may be more fantasy than reality in some countries. The second, culture, is notably difficult to define in comparable ways. The third, institutional, offers observable and concrete categorical differentiation, with procedural leverage for change.

Human Development

Since 1990, the UNDP Human Development Index (HDI) has ranked countries according to achievements in longevity, knowledge, and income. HDI ranking is a measure preferable to those based on poverty/wealth (such as the World Bank's per capita income ranking). Achievements and spending in human development result from political and individual struggle rather than the marketplace.

The top ten countries in the Human Development Index rankings are likely to have higher-than-average global levels of female representation. This is true of Canada (first), Switzerland (second), Sweden (fourth), Norway (fifth), Australia (seventh), and the Netherlands (ninth). Yet there are notable exceptions: Japan (third), which has especially low female representation rates of 3 percent women legislators and no cabinet members; France (sixth); the United States (eighth); and the United Kingdom (tenth). Conversely, of the bottom ten countries, only two have higher-than-average female representation levels (Chad, 168th, and Guinea-Bissau, 164th), but they are authoritarian rather than democratic regimes.

Mexico ranks in the top half (fifty-second) on the human development ranking. Those who analyze human development spending and outcomes often assume that low priorities signify little by way of gender differentiation. Mainstream policy documents render invisible the probable gender differentiation that characterizes human development indicators.

However, useful statistical analyses demonstrate with cold numbers how men and women experience those low priorities in different ways. Martínez (1993) provided ample documentation of the ways in which in Mexico women benefit less from public spending than men, from higher education spending to equal wage enforcement. Moreover, although Mexico manages a vigorous family planning program, laws and policies that support voluntary motherhood are not in place, resulting in much unnecessary female death from unsafe abortion attempts.

Culture

Cultural explanations fall into three categories. The first concerns gender differentiation, including prejudice against women. The second focuses on egalitarianism in the sense of how Dutch theorist Geert Hofstede views culture, that is, as collective programming in enduring values and norms that guide behavior (1984). The third arises from women's movements, which frequently emerge from "women's culture" or everyday women's lives and experiences.

Gender differentiation is more or less marked in all societies. Generally, though, childhood learning and adult experiences tend to encourage among men more interest in and background preparation thought suitable for politics. For example, gendered educational gaps are commonly found in training linked to politics, such as law and the military. If politics is to be transformed, political recruitment would draw on wider ranges of backgrounds, including those in which women specialize.

Male-female wage inequalities are also commonplace, even in Nordic countries. Women's labor force participation has risen over the last few decades, but they are often stuck at or near minimum-wage levels, in such jobs as foreign export–assembly factories.

In Mexico, officials maintain minimum wages below market rates. The burden of attracting foreign investment and of keeping inflation rates low thus falls on working people's backs. Many working people live below a poverty level, a line that some informed observers estimate to be three minimum wages (that is, three times the minimum wage) or less (Suárez and Chávez 1996). *Maquilas* (export-processing factories) are mixed blessings for women, for their earnings are stuck at one to two minimum wages (although other social benefits are included).[7] Informal work, in which women participate at higher rates than men (STPS/USDA 1992), produces a range of earnings. Benería and Roldán (1987) have analyzed the grim circumstances of home-based subcontracting work. Yet some informals cannot "afford" to work in factories, for their earnings—however unstable, without linkage to social benefits—reap more reward (see Hellman 1994, as well as the northern border studies by Roberts 1993; Staudt

1996; Staudt 1998). Although government studies rarely differentiate gender differences in wage earnings—whether through formal or informal work—other studies document a 25 percent wage differential, with women earning approximately 75 percent of men's salaries (Selby et al. 1990:123; Roberts 1993; also see Martínez 1993:51, by sector).

In countries in which money is crucial to political success, such as the United States, gendered wage inequality can be a serious problem for women. The most famous of women's groups to raise funds for U.S. candidates is EMILY, an acronym for Early Money Is Like Yeast (that is, it makes the dough [slang for money] rise).

Cultural traditions often foster traits that translate into political leadership for men and dependency for women. Voters, male and female alike, acquiesce to this tradition, and prejudice forms. Governments perpetuate these values with policies that privilege men with opportunities, responsibilities, and resources. The media often feed on prejudices, mocking or exaggerating the importance of female dress and appearance. Also, media overemphases on female sexuality do not inspire voter confidence in women leaders. Readers might count how many more naked or near-naked women they see in newspapers and television, compared to men, ranging from intellectual journals to crude entertainment shows.

Studies of the female political elite in near-male monopoly conditions show their unique characteristics and impeccable credentials (Staudt 1989). Their accomplishments seem to validate the Latin American proverb, "whereas a man may be made of silver, a woman must be made of gold" (Chaney 1979:110).

Women's "difference" has become an asset in some national politics, if only temporarily. Voters, disgusted with political corruption and scandals, turn to women who (rightly or wrongly) are identified with honesty and morality. The *supermadre* political women in Peru and Chile shared such characteristics (Chaney 1979). Japanese women made temporary gains with sentiments like these in the late 1980s. Norwegian voters sought a wider policy agenda that political women could bring. Voters chose women because they were women (Skard 1981:87).

Hofstede's quantification of cultural *egalitarianism* is the best and largest comparative effort relevant to this study. He generated 116,000 interviews in forty countries in this methodologically challenging, one-of-a-kind study (1984). Hofstede plotted countries on scattergrams along four dimensions, two of which are relevant here: High Power Distance (acceptance of unequal power distribution) and Masculinity (high female-male differentiation, valuing male characteristics).[8]

Hofstede's two dimensions are related to female representation in legislatures and cabinets. High Masculinity is moderately associated with low women's representation. High Power Distance is strongly associated with low female representation. Low Power Distance, or egalitarian cultures, have more than double the rates of women than the nonegalitarian ones. Notably, these egalitarian cultures—mainly Nordic countries—have used taxing and spending to redistribute wealth and opportunity in more equitable ways. Hofstede ranks Mexico second highest in Power Distance and sixth highest in Masculinity (1984:77, 189). Feminist scholars corroborate Mexico's traditions of male dominance. Lamas et al. analyze "men's aggressive/defensive masculinity," a full-blown ideology that is reinforced with Catholicism (1995a:327, 328). Further corroborating this nonegalitarian tradition is Mexico's severely unequal distribution of wealth, always prominent in tables in the World Bank's annual *World Development Report*. To the extent Hofstede's measurement is valid, such characteristics do not bode well for women in Mexican politics.

Cultural programming of this magnitude does not change overnight. Government efforts to redistribute wealth can make some dent in these patterns, though the era of structural adjustment and privatization renders this action less likely. Yet many women's movements and groups have emerged, even blossomed since the first UN conference in Mexico City in 1975, with potentials to improve egalitarianism and female value.

Women's movements develop leadership, experience, and female constituency strength to the political establishment, whether in separate or integrated form. After achieving female suffrage, revolutionary triumph, or independence, women's contributions are sometimes recognized in symbolic or real ways with policy concessions and political appointments. Curiously, in India, higher percentages of women were jailed during nationalist struggles (10 percent) than percentages seated in the national parliament (Swarup et al. 1994:368)!

Female suffrage came late in Mexico (1953) compared to the rest of the hemisphere. Gender differentiation has rarely been reported in the media for candidates and for turnout. If Mexico resembles other countries, female voter turnout was likely less in the first decades after their franchise. Although officials bemoan "abstentionism," one wonders whether they took this seriously for women. Of course, several major parties have feminine sectors to mobilize women's votes. With greater attention to public opinion surveys and exit polls in Mexico, the popular media have begun to differentiate men's and women's opinions and behaviors. This gender visibility might make candidates and parties more attentive to women, to their expanded policy agenda, and consequently to a new political culture about which others have written, as noted earlier.

Women activists are a diverse and diffuse populace, with some suspicions of the state, political representatives (including women), and party/state subsidized women's programs. Other activists are reformers, willing to engage with the state.

Under Latin American authoritarian regimes, women's and mothers' groups (searching for disappeared family members) had good reason to be suspicious. Their willingness to use whatever political space existed, at great risk, helped create the mass base for mobilizing opposition and making transitions to more democratic regimes. Yet few were elected and appointed to office (selections in Jaquette 1994). Brazil's Commissions on the Status of Women went to great lengths to retain connections with women's organizations, though ultimately their dependence on state budgets during economic crisis led to their demise (Alvarez 1990b). In Mexico, Lamas and others have analyzed the move from feminist organizational autonomy to limited engagement with the state, as feminists build new bridges (1995a). Human rights activists have pricked the moral conscience of the state and concerns of the wider public through calling attention to political disappearance and assassination in Mexico. The presidential candidacies of Rosario Ibarra de Piedra can be viewed in this way.

Others worry about the sometimes paltry returns or overcompromised solutions that feminists' engagement with the Mexican state produces. Bartra (1994) analyzed major concerns about the state's still-limited attention to violence against women in the form of rape, harassment, and wifebeating. The general secretary of Mexico's Consejo Nacional de Población (National Population Council, CONAPO), also an official delegate to the 1995 World Conference on Women in Beijing, expressed his public outrage over violence against women. According to José Gómez de León, the reduction of violence against women should be a top government program priority; violence is "truly deplorable and disgusting.... [W]omen are literally living out their lives in constant fear" (in FEMAP 1995).

In many Mexican urban areas, women are the mainstay of grassroots neighborhood organizations. Women, as household managers, have perhaps the largest stakes in access to water, electricity, sewer, and other services. As Alejandra Massolo puts it, "urban politics are women's politics" (cited in Craske 1993a:134; also see Venegas 1995; Vélez-Ibáñez 1983; and Chapter 8). Using Maxine Molyneux's (1985) brilliant distinction between "practical" and "strategic" women's interests, with the latter addressed to female subordination, women's urban politics can be understood as an expression of practical interests. Yet women's very involvement creates a sense of citizenship, says Massolo (cited in Bennett 1995b:79; see also Massolo 1994d:16), with prospects to redistribute household power relations (Staudt and Aguilar 1992; Craske 1993a). Urban women activists ought to be moving into local representation positions, but men there appear to monopolize power more fervently than at other levels.

To what extent do women vote or turn out to vote at rates comparable to or larger than men? Few countries regularly report and tabulate turnout by gender. In the cases of Costa Rica and the Philippines, women's turnout rates equal and surpass men's in most elections. In Japan, women's turnout is visibly higher than men's, to little avail in increasing representation. As discussed earlier, in Mexico, differences in male-female registration, opinion, and turnout became far more visible in 1988 and especially with the 1994 elections and thereafter (Massolo 1994d:26). Perhaps a new sort of gender "abstentionism," historically a cause for official alarm, can stimulate a new sort of institutional reform to increase turnout and thus voters' stakes in the system.

Thus, high female turnout does not necessarily predict balanced political representation. Factors mediate the connection: awareness of the "gender gap" on the part of candidates and of voters and a gendered policy agenda, around which voters can cohere. Such a policy agenda was virtually absent in Mexico's 1994 presidential elections, except for parties of the left—most especially the candidacy of Cecilia Soto (Robles, Ruiz, and Ortega 1994).

Culture and gender differentiation, taken as factors explaining women's representation in politics, are dynamic but complex and can delay change. Viewed with a Mexico lens, they would not predict rapid change in gender-balanced representation. However, Mexico has no women's machinery inside government agencies. Such machinery, which exists in the majority of countries, often prompts government insiders to advocate change and coalesce with women's groups. Institutional factors offer promising alternatives and solutions. To this we now turn.

Institutional Factors

How do institutions of governance, including parties, legislative-executive decisionmaking, and electoral systems, affect women's representation? In countries with higher-than-average global norms, vigorous multiple parties provide policy choices to voters. In 34 countries, party quotas support women's candidacies and transform policy agendas with concrete goals, rather than promises. In 5 countries, laws reserve seats for women in national legislatures. In 44 countries, women obtain seats through appointment, generally to the upper house (senate). These institutional provisions work best when enforced at levels that promote critical masses of women (15–30 percent or more) in representative bodies (Staudt 1994).

Quotas, reserved seats, and appointments are adopted in conjunction with particular kinds of political systems. Proportional representation (PR) electoral systems are particularly amenable to party-driven progress in gender-balanced representation. Studies consistently show that women's representation is higher in proportional representation systems (Rule 1987, 1994; Norris 1985). Through internal party quotas (generally 30 percent or more), critical masses of women's names are placed on winnable seats of the list. In contrasting single-member (SM) systems, fewer parties compete for the ideological center, and a single winner takes the seat. Direct competition between a man and a woman candidate, in the context of anti–political woman prejudice, dooms gender-balanced representation.

Ideological parties blossom in PR systems. In the 1970s period and beyond, many centrist, left, and environmental parties installed healthy party quotas to seat more women. Nordic women now make up a third or more of the parliaments and nearly comparable numbers of cabinet seats. The Netherlands runs close behind. Green (environmental) parties frequently adopt the policy, "every other seat a woman" (i.e., 50 percent), although Greens win few seats. Even the German conservative party, the Christian Democratic Union, adopted 30 percent quotas in the 1994 election after realizing its support among women was dwindling. Small margins of victory make a big difference in these mostly European parliaments wherein the chief executive also directs the legislative process.

Even though many Latin American political systems offer proportional representation, rates are stuck below global levels. Noteworthy exceptions include Costa Rica, Cuba (a one-party system), several Caribbean countries, and Argentina, with its first-of-a-kind 30 percent quota law for all parties.

The 1991 Ley de Cupos in Argentina was passed in Congress with strong support from the president, the Consejo Nacional de la Mujer, and the President's Gabinete de Consejeras Presidenciales (Jones 1996). The law requires that all parties list 30 percent women on winnable seats. Some parties resisted, but the law was enforced with the threat and action of lawsuits. For the decade before the law, women's representation was stuck at 4 percent; after the law, it rose to 21 percent (1993) and then 28 percent (1995). The quota law fostered "contagion effects," according to Jones. First, seventeen of twenty-three provinces implemented quota laws, based on the national model. Second, 26 percent women were elected as delegates to the 1994 Constituent Assembly. Finally, the Chamber of Deputies proposed a gender quota law bill in 1994 for labor union officers.

In Mexico, just one party supports greater gender balance in its executive committees, rather than in its candidacies. The PRD seats no less than 30 percent women or men on its local, state, and national executive committees. Women seek increased candidacies and are discussing the quota strategy across party lines (Lamas et al. 1995a:344; selections in Rodríguez et al. 1995, 1996). With great wisdom, though, women worry that female quotas could produce more women representatives in "face" only, rather than in substantive terms. Similar concerns have been raised about affirmative action for women in government (Pérez Duarte 1994:89). Future studies should attend to whether women launched into positions via quotas come into politics from women's organizations, bringing a new public agenda and a new kind of politics that responds to women as well as men.

Global data on 1994 representation show striking differences between PR and SM systems. In the seventy-four SM systems, women's representation levels fall below global norms; in forty-six PR systems, rates surpass global norms. PR works no miracles, however. Several PR countries, such as Greece, Uruguay, and Turkey, have severe underrepresentation.

Nineteen countries mix PR and SM, either in each legislative body or within each house. Mexico offers a mixed system. Mixed systems do better than pure SM, but averaging female representation rates brings totals just above those of SM. When contrasts are made in single countries, however, PR's advantages shine. In Germany, women won 12 percent of seats from SM votes and 28 percent of seats from PR in the 1987–1991 period (Rule 1994:17). Germany's 1994 election produced an even more dramatic 39 percent gain for women in PR seats. France elected 4 percent women to its National Assembly with its SM system but 21 percent of the French delegation to the European Economic Community (now European Union) Parliament with a PR system (Norris 1985:99).

In frustration with exclusion or meaningless policy platforms, women have formed their own parties. Among the many countries where this happened historically are Canada, Chile, Egypt, Finland, Iceland, Norway, Philippines, Republic of Korea, Russia, Sweden, the United States, and the former Yugoslavia. Although women's parties win few seats, especially in SM systems, women's exit or threats to demobilize women supporters from established parties can pressure mainstream parties for change. Iceland's Women's Alliance (the women's party) did produce dramatic gains on municipal councils, gaining up to 18 percent of seats.

Sometimes parties are frustrated by an inability to recruit women to these (men's?) organizations. Successful recruitment strategies have used the following: family-friendly meeting times; family-friendly meeting space, with child care provided; and women's branches. Even though women's branches have the potential to empower women in parties, they can have quite the opposite effect when women are isolated, marginalized, and simply used as cheap labor to mobilize the vote. Research studies show very mixed pictures on their effectiveness.

Lacking quotas, successful parties use other voluntary means to increase women candidacies. They offer special campaign training workshops and subsidize campaigns for women.

Only five countries have established reserved seats for women in representative bodies. The percentage of seats for women is at token levels (e.g., Nepal, 3 percent; Pakistan, 10 percent, although women's 2 percent figure shows a lack of enforcement; Bangladesh, 10 percent). Only in Tanzania has the reserve seat "floor" not resulted in a "ceiling"; a total of 28 women serve, or 13 more elected than the 15 women appointed. Another unabashed success is Taiwan, where parties waste seats if women go unappointed. Parties have thereby been encouraged to recruit women at local, regional, and national levels (Chou and Clark 1994).

Of the numerous countries that appoint women, the record shows they add merely zero to fifteen in representative bodies that range from small to those that total in the hundreds. Such figures are paltry. Another problem with appointments is the uncertainty about females' accountability to women's policy interests.

Once in legislatures in sizable numbers, women form coalitions with other women and men to support gender-fair policies, laws, and public spending. In the Philippines, a Congressional Caucus for Women steers bills into laws. In Costa Rica, with support from former president Oscar Arias and Margarita Peñón (marital partners), a comprehensive Law for Real Equality was introduced in 1988. After two years of democratic debate in the legislature and larger society over matters such as stereotyped educational curricula and advertising that constructs women as sex objects, a compromise version passed (Saint-Germain and Morgan 1991). Besides a watchdog role for the National Center for Women's Development, the Ministry of Justice has enforcement and oversight authority, including an ombudsperson.

In both Costa Rica and the Philippines, a strong tradition of women's studies flourishes and links applied research findings to policymakers. In the United States, similar roles are played by the Rutgers University–based Center for the Study of Women in Politics and the Washington, D.C.–based independent Institute for Women's Policy Research. It is important that research go beyond the obvious or sometimes stereotyped policy issues, such as antifemale violence, wage inequality, and child care. Successful university- and government-based advocacy units focus on a "gendered policy analysis," that is, the ways that tax, economic, land, and health policies differently serve or burden men and women (along with female household heads who live in feminized poverty). They also break down statistical data by gender, to highlight inequities and the uneven distribution of government benefits (Martínez 1993). Groups can then use results as they engage with the political mainstream, including parties and representatives.

Conclusions and Implications for Practice

Men monopolize politics in all but a minority of countries. Data on chief executives, cabinet members, and representatives at national and local levels all show extremely imbalanced gender representation. Global representation rates have actually fallen slightly, a result of changes in Eastern Europe and the former USSR, where single-party authorities appointed women who did not necessarily represent diverse women in societies with weak civil organizations.

Yet the faces of those in politics are changing. In a sizable number of countries, women have dramatically increased their representation. Balanced representation has the potential both to make policies gender fair and to make a more democratic political process. In Mexico, female representation rates are below regional and global levels, especially at local levels.

In regard to low representation rates, three factors combine to explain these patterns. First, investments in human development (including women) are lacking, even in some rich countries. Second, cultural constructions of gender lead to exaggerated differentiation or the devaluation of women. However, women's groups now flourish in many places; their actions undermine devaluation and differentiation. Cultural patterns that sustain "power distance" and policy-driven inequality also aggravate female devaluation. Third, political institutions affect the ease of increasing female representation. PR multiparty systems appear most amenable to gender balance. Specific actions, such as party quotas and reserved seats, exist to provide mechanisms to quicken the pace of change. Argentina is a notable example, along with many European democracies.

This chapter has outlined the promises and disappointments associated with making democracy more real for women in Mexico. Women in Mexican feminist and grassroots organizations offer hopes for transforming an old male political monopoly into one with a new political culture and a new way of doing politics. Part of this newness is the long overdue responsiveness of government to key women's issues, among them violence, economic inequality, involuntary motherhood, and monetary policies that burden women and the poor in which women are overrepresented.

What are some promising practices and lessons to engender democracy? Although not all practices are transferable, some may be adaptable in various national settings.

First, "critical mass" numbers of women are fundamental to transforming policies and politics. One or two women do not represent a broad base for change, nor can they represent diverse women. In successful countries, 15 percent female representation in cabinets and in national and local councils has been a turning point. Thirty percent representation is a common goal, quota, and sociological turning point in studies of organization.

Second, goodwill and promises alone rarely foster change. Instead, concrete practices, such as party quotas or legally mandated quotas for all parties, have been successful techniques to improve gender balance. Such goals are useless unless enforced. Some countries reserve seats for women, but legitimate questions must always be raised about who appoints such seat holders and the groups to whom they respond.

Third, local and regional legislatures are important spaces for gender-balanced representation. In the impressive achievements of Nordic countries, albeit egalitarian and decentralized, women's local involvement was a stimulus for change. Quotas and reserved seats are also relevant at local and regional levels. India's new law will infuse massive numbers of new women into political recruitment pools who thereby can supply a more diverse pipeline into national politics.

Fourth, women's voter turnout is visible in most successful systems, as are gender gaps in turnout and abstentionism. Beyond that, though, parties in successful countries mobilize female constituencies with a gendered policy agenda that, if enacted, will promote gender fairness and responsiveness to women.

Fifth, citizens monitor existing laws and policies through mechanisms that introduce the idea of government accountability to women and then enforce it with authority. Many governments house women's machinery, such as women's bureaus, equality ministries, and ombudspeople; or they create commissions on which members of independent women's organizations share authority.

Sixth, independent women's movements and groups both engage with and criticize government shortcomings in successful countries. In those places where women's groups avoid the seemingly corrupt political establishment, policies and political practices continue to privilege men and burden women through massive taxing and spending authority. Self-help rarely generates resources that match those possible from government investment.

Seventh, women build coalitions with men who support engendering democracy. In such countries as Costa Rica, Tanzania, the Philippines, and Nordic countries, male support has been crucial to help engineer change and to deflect criticism from women.

Eighth, partnerships among women's groups, researchers, and policymakers bring attention to policy and representation inequity. Such research findings help to inform and improve public decisionmaking in a wide variety of countries.

Above all, success takes place in genuine democracies that prize good governance. Democratic processes would include transparent procedures, real choices, honesty, egalitarian policies, and strong civil organizations, including women's organizations. Without women's voices, can there be real democracy?

Notes

1. See also Arizpe and Velázquez 1994.
2. Parts of this chapter are highly condensed from that background monograph. Besides the quantitative analysis, I also analyzed five successful and five unsuccessful country cases in terms of female representation.

3. Sonia Alvarez was the first person to use the term *engendering*, but its use has increased in exponential ways by a variety of writers.

4. In 1989, finally, the UN put political representation on the intellectual and action agenda with its conference in Vienna (see Staudt 1989). Since then, the UN has collected cabinet data.

5. The appointment of Rosario Green as secretary of foreign relations in January 1998 is an outstanding exception.

6. The figure for local representation in Mexico represents mayors, not council members. Alejandra Massolo, expert on women's politics in Mexico, especially at local levels, verified the lack of alternative data ("Conference on Women in Local Government: Mexico and the U.S.," Universidad Autónoma de Cd. Juárez, December 2, 1994). Also see Massolo 1994a. I am also grateful to the Centro Nacional de Desarrollo Municipal, Secretaría de Gobernación, for their impressive computer disk, but it provides no way to extract data on women's *cabildo* representation.

7. The *maquila* literature is voluminous. See, for example, Fernández-Kelly 1983; Tiano 1993; Sklair 1993; Young and Fort 1994.

8. Masculinity is the weakest of Hofstede's dimensions, for social constructions of masculine-feminine occur diversely, at far less than global levels.

❀ 3 ❀

Mexican Women's Inclusion into Political Life: A Latin American Perspective

Nikki Craske

Latin America as a region has experienced a high degree of political activity over the past three decades, some of which has resulted in potent collective action. In many ways the experiences in the various countries can be compared, and one promising area of comparison is the political participation of women. It has been well documented that in many Latin American countries, women were particularly active in grassroots organizations that developed into anti-regime protests; however, variations are evident in the development of feminist organizations, women's party political participation, and, for instance, motherist groups. Although Mexico did not suffer the excesses of the military governments prevalent in the south, which had a massive impact on collective organization and which had a particular effect on gender relations (Jaquette 1989; Bourque 1989), nevertheless it has suffered its own authoritarian regime that has proved more resilient and that has its own discourse on gender relations.

The image of women as politically conservative has been a strong one in Mexico, resulting in the late awarding of franchise and the dismissal of "women's issues" by leftist parties in the past (not unique to Mexico); the negative interpretation of feminism has been a legacy of these attitudes. In this chapter I will be assessing the inroads women have made politically over the past decades and how Mexican women fare in comparison with others in the region. The failure to equalize gender representation, particularly in institutional politics, is widespread, but trends are emerging that indicate both the problems facing women and the choice of strategies to increase their representation. The issue of gender relations is part of the dynamism of contemporary Latin American politics; as relations are renegotiated, actors, both in formal and informal politics, absorb new discourses and resist others. The relationship between women as political, economic, and social actors and political parties is not static; neither is the way in which parties respond to the challenge of integrating women as political actors, which varies greatly. The similar lack of women in positions of power might suggest that gender relations throughout Latin America are uniform, but the way in which gender and gender relations have been constructed and, more important, challenged over the past decades demonstrates different patterns in the interaction between women and parties, governments, and political organizations as well as each other.

I will also examine the opportunities and constraints confronting women who seek a political role, particularly in the electoral arena, and compare Mexico with other countries in the region (the main countries for comparison will be Argentina and Chile). The comparison will be on the basis of different policies adopted by governments, such as quota laws, women's ministries, and UN Conventions. I argue that it is difficult to discern a policy or policies that could be used as a model for the whole of the region. It is important to make an analysis of the political conditions prevalent in a country before advocating policies, and there needs to be a consideration of what we are trying to achieve; for some countries the goal appears to be increasing the number of women representatives within electoral politics, whereas others concentrate their activities on developing women-friendly policies directed toward the female population (and voters!), with less attention paid to increasing the quantity of women in decisionmaking positions. Mexico, to date, has tended to be less interventionist on the "women question," employing neither quotas nor women's ministries, and there are only limited women-friendly policies. However, in terms of numbers of women representatives, Mexico is currently in a better position than most of its neighbors, despite the late extension of franchise.

Transitions

Widespread collective action in Latin America has shown ways in which actors can break out of roles set for them. The popular protest activities of the 1970s and 1980s gave visibility to a large group of people and issues generally ignored by political institutions. The military's attempt to quash politics led to its outbreak elsewhere; the closure of institutional avenues of expression politicized other activities. The new fluidity gave rise to the possibility of reconstructing politics in a way that was more inclusive (cf. Radcliffe and Westwood 1993); political identities emerged around race, class, ethnicity, and gender that could, and in some cases did, challenge political hierarchies both of authoritarian regimes and opposition organizations. The shift of political terrain away from institutional configurations allowed for alternative political spaces to emerge. When the most obvious form of politics, parties, and elections were removed from our vision, we could see more clearly organizations and political expressions that had previously been hidden. For some commentators these alternative expressions almost by definition had radical potential, since they challenged conceptions of politics, but others were more sober and indicated that personal development might not be affected by the politicization of some social identities; indeed, they could confirm a narrow arena for women's collective action (Perelli 1994). The decline of collective action and the reemergence of parties as the central focus of politics in most Latin American countries has illustrated quite clearly that any radical implications of collective action are not to be achieved in the short run (Escobar and Alvarez 1992; Foweraker 1995a). However, we still concentrate more on women's noninstitutional collective action (e.g., Jaquette 1994) and lack studies on the relationship between movements, parties, and the state, particularly with a gender perspective.

With the suspension of politics, the old discourses that served to give parameters to mass political activity mutated; the public and private divide was increasingly contested as both the military and collective organizations manipulated its meaning. Equally, the divisions between "social" and "political," "institutional" and "community" were also blurred as old divisions no longer helped us understand events, while political spaces opened and closed as they were first de- and then re-constructed. However, the left-right division and liberal and conservative interpretations of actors and issues were not challenged in the same way. It was not so much a case of manipulating or rewriting their perceived meaning as one of total denial and ignorance; if there was no politics, there could be no left and right. For a number of years opposition to authoritarian rule superseded other political identities as many movements coalesced around a single point: democratization. Perhaps because little attention was paid to the left-right division, it has emerged unscathed as a way of comprehending politics. This is not to say that there has not been a shift to the right or a decline of the left or that the left did not suffer disproportionately under authoritarian regimes, but that we still use the dichotomy to organize how we think of politics.

One of the great challenges of popular protest and the emergence of new political identities was that they do not fit into traditional ideologies, giving rise to such notions as the politicization of motherhood (Alvarez 1990a). But as parties have reemerged, so too have the discourses; consequently there is an attempt to label the many collective action groups as either left or right and for parties to coopt them and absorb their energy. Although there are many parties in Latin America that do not conform to a clear left-right model, not least the PRI, it is still widely used to discuss political attitudes. Along with the retrenchment of traditional political discourse there has been a redrawing of old dualisms—for example, public-private, social-political, and institutional-informal—in ways that generally prejudice women's collective action. The fate of female political activity is perhaps a good example of the fate of social movements generally, as the reality of exclusionary politics displaces hopes for inclusionary political systems. As parties have consolidated their role, women's political activity has become less visible.

Although a number of factors distinguish Mexico—the absence of military intervention, a hegemonic party system, a revolutionary history absorbed into popular culture, continuing problems of political legitimacy—it shares many similarities in the levels and types of female political involvement with its neighbors. There are also similarities in the ways in which women have been perceived as political actors: conservative, influenced by the Church, motherhood constructed as the predominant political identity, and apolitical. Although some of these perceptions may seem contradictory, it is of little consequence to those who adopt them. These characterizations constrained women's political activity, but during the period of enhanced popular protest they formed the basis of many women's collective action.

The degree to which women have maintained their political visibility into the 1990s depends on a number of factors that will be explored here: the relationship between political parties and grassroots organizations, the exchange between feminists and women's organizations, the role of female political elites, and the governments' concern for international appearance of "modernity." These relations have not just arisen over the past decades of widespread collective action but reflect a greater history of intervention and practices of political containment in all countries. With the narrowing of political spaces, women have to apply pressure from all sides to consolidate the gains made and to make future changes.

The Record to Date

Latin American women gained the vote between 1929 (Ecuador) and 1961 (Paraguay). However, the circumstances of attaining this basic citizen's right varied in different countries. In some cases (particularly Argentina, Cuba, Mexico, and Brazil), women militated to demand the vote, whereas in others the governments, quite often conservative ones (notably Ecuador), enfranchised women in the expectation that they would support the governments and bolster their position. The 1917 Mexican Constitution gave *citizens* the right to vote, yet despite the deployment of this ostensibly gender-neutral term, the vote was not extended to women on the grounds that they were subjects of the domestic arena and the family and thus would not develop a political consciousness (Fernández Poncela 1995:38). Miller (1991) asserted that one of the most "vociferous opponents of feminism" at the beginning of the century, when there were groups demanding women's emancipation, was the Confederation of Catholic Associations of Mexico. The first postrevolutionary governments were reluctant to extend the vote, and it was not until 1953 that this right was granted by President Adolfo Ruiz Cortines, a more conservative president than his predecessors, at which time only Colombia, Honduras, Peru, Nicaragua, and Paraguay had yet to introduce universal suffrage.

Mexico was similarly slow to appoint a woman cabinet minister, which it did in 1981 (Tourism); by then more than half the countries in the region had at least one female cabinet minister. In Chile there was a female minister for justice in 1952, but Argentina, with its share of prominent women in politics, waited until 1989 for a woman to be appointed as a minister, for foreign affairs (Valdes and Gomariz 1995). One area in which women appear to be advancing is the judiciary; in the case of Chile, Elsa Chaney explained it as the result of the limited financial rewards to members of the judiciary, whereas Roderic Camp attributed it to the need for fewer political skills (both in Camp 1995b:157).

Over the years, Mexico has been broadly typical of the region in terms of the proportion of female representatives it returned to Congress. With only three exceptions, average female representation in the lower house (Table 3.1) has not exceeded 10 percent in the region.[1] In a large number of countries women attained their highest levels of representation during the 1980s, although Argentina is a marked exception and partly reflects the legacy of Eva Perón and the Partido Femenino. More recently Argentina's Ley de Cupos (Quota Law), passed in 1991, has also dramatically increased women's presence in Congress from 5 percent in 1991 to 16.3 percent in 1993 to 26.9 percent in 1997. Chile, despite its well-developed women's movements, SERNAM (the women's ministry), and good relations between the two, had only nine women deputies (7.5 percent of the total) in 1993. Prior to the 1997 midterm elections (1994–1997 legislature), Mexico had its highest female representation, 14 percent; the previous high was in the 1988–1991 legislature, the first in which the PRI did not win an overwhelming majority. In the current legislature (1997–2000), women constitute 13.3 percent of federal deputies. The PRD had the highest proportion of women deputies (21.4 percent compared to 14.8 percent and 7.6 percent for the PRI and PAN respectively).[2] However, what is more worrying for the prospects of women's winning seats is that although in 1991 there was the highest number of women candidates to date, fewer were elected than in 1988, with the Partido del Trabajo (Labor Party, PT), Partido Revolucionario de los Trabajadores (Workers' Revolu-

TABLE 3.1   Women's Representation in Latin American Chambers of Deputies

Country	Years	Average (%)	Term (years)	Highest (%)	Representation (%)[a]	Comments
Argentina	1952–1997	7	3	21.6 (1955)	26.9 (1997)	1989 no women deputies
Belize[b]	1984–1993	2.34	4	10 (1991)	3.5 (1993)	
Bolivia	1979–1993	5	4	6 (1990)	6.9 (1993)	1945 no women deputies
Brazil	1945–1990	1.44	4	6 (1990)	6 (1990)	
Chile[c]	1945–1993	4.13	4	8 (1965)	7.5 (1993)	
Colombia	1994	11	4		11 (1994)	5.7% 1970 (only other year for which data available)
Costa Rica	1949–1994	5.8	5	14 (1994)	14 (1994)	1949 no women deputies
Cuba	1976–1993	24.5	5 (approx)	33.8 (1986)	22.8 (1993)	
Dominican Republic	1970–1990	7.8	4	7.6 (1982)	11.7 (1990)	no data 1974, 1978
Ecuador	1979–1994	2.7	4	5.2 (1994)	5.2 (1994)	
El Salvador	1982–1994	8.5	3	11.6 (1982)	10.7 (1994)	no data 1988
Guatemala	1954–1990	2.8	4	7.0 (1985)	5.2 (1990)	no data 1961
Honduras	1981–1993	7.1	4	11.7 (1989)	3.6 (1991)	
Mexico[d]	1955–1997	10	3	13.7 (1994)	13.3 (1997)	12.4% 1988–1991
Nicaragua	1979–1990	17.5	6	21.6 (1979)	16.3 (1990)	appointed at different times in 1979
Panama	1946–1994	4	4	8.1 (1978)	7.5 (1994)	
Paraguay	1968–1993	2.96	5	5.5 (1989)	2.5 (1993)	
Peru	1980–1992	5.5	5	5.5[e]	8.8 (1992)	Congress suspended 1992
Uruguay	1946–1989	5.7	5	8 (1954)	6.1 (1989)	including substitutes
Venezuela	1948–1993	5.24	5	9.9 (1988)	5.5 (1993)	1968 no women deputies
Mean		6.9		11.18	9.3	

[a]Percentage representation in most recent year for which data are available.
[b]Gained independence in 1984.
[c]No elections 1973–1990.
[d]Data for LVI (1994–1997) and LVII (1997–2000) legislatures from Mexican Embassy, London.
[e]Highest achieved before suspension of Congress in 1992.

Source: Table compiled by the author with data from the Interparliamentary Union.

tionary Party, PRT), and PRD being most open to female candidates. The failure of women candidates to be elected stemmed in part from the fact that they stand in seats where their party is weak and only 17.4 percent are in the first five names on candidate lists (Fernández Poncela 1995:55).

In the upper houses (Table 3.2) the picture is broadly the same. Women's average political representation barely reaches 6.5 percent, and in no country has it exceeded 10 (Belize, in which senators are appointed, is the exception). Indeed, throughout the region, women's representation is even lower in the Senate than in the Chamber of Deputies, although the current data in Table 3.2 show that things are looking more hopeful, with three countries exceeding 10 percent. As in the case of deputies, the Mexican Senate had its largest female representation between 1988–1991 (15.6 percent); it dropped to 4.7 percent in 1991–1994 and then increased to 12.7 percent in 1994–1997. After the 1997 election, this percentage decreased to 11.71.[3] Another notable breakthrough occurred in 1993, when women led both houses of Congress in Mexico.[4]

Mexico, in common with the majority of Latin American countries, has a highly centralized political system, which means that the focus of elections is at the national, and particularly presidential, level. As we have seen, women's representation is modest (although many northern, liberal democracies fare no better), and there have only been three occasions when women have been nominated as candidates for the presidency: Rosario Ibarra de Piedra in 1982 and 1988 for the PRT and Cecilia Soto for the PT in 1994.

So what is the record at other levels of government throughout the region, where most systems are federal? Mexico has only had three women governors,[5] the first elected in 1979, and none is currently sitting. Argentina still has none; Chile has five (9.8 percent of total). It may be surprising to note that Cuba has none, whereas five of Costa Rica's seven governors are women (71.4 percent of total). At the gubernatorial level there is no clear pattern to women's representation, although Costa Rica is the only country to exceed a 30 percent "ceiling." At the municipal level, women mayors are few; Uruguay has the most with 15.8 percent (1992), whereas, ironically, Costa Rica has none! In 1995 Mexico had 4.2 percent, a slight increase on 1994 (see Chapter 13). What appears to be a common pattern is that women are more strongly represented in smaller municipal governments, although as Pinto (1993) pointed out, many countries are undergoing municipal reform with an emphasis on decentralization, and therefore trends are difficult to detect. Others note that women engage in the same kind of commissions at the local level as they do at the national: health, social assistance, housing, human rights (Bruera and González 1993). However, over time this gender division of labor within political institutions is breaking down.[6]

TABLE 3.2 Women's Representation in Latin American Senates

Country	Years	Average (%)	Term (years)	Highest (%)	Representation (%)[a]	Comments
Argentina	1952–1997	5.7	6	17.6 (1952)	2.2 (1992)	no representatives 1958–1962
Belize	1984–1993	22.2	5	22.2	22.2 (1993)	senators appointed
Bolivia	1980–1993	5.6	4	7.4 (1991)	3.7 (1993)	no women before 1980
Brazil	1945–1990	n.a.	4	1.4 (1978)	2.5 (1990)	senators only 1978, 1990
Chile[b]	1945–1993	3.05	4	6.5 (1993)	6.5 (1993)	
Colombia	1994	6.9	4		6.9 (1994)	3.3% 1970 (only other year for which data available)
Dominican Republic	1970–1990	9.8	4	14.5 (1970)	no data	no data 1974, 1978, and 1990
Mexico[c]	1964–1997	8.5	6	15.6 (1988)	11.71 (1997)	
Paraguay	1968–1993	5	5	11.1 (1993)	11.1 (1993)	
Peru	1980–1990	5	5	6.7 (1990)	suspended	
Uruguay	1946–1989	4.1	4	10 (1950)	0 (1989)	no data 1971 and 1984
Venezuela	1948–1993	2.7	5	8.9 (1993)	8.2 (1993)	no women 1953, 1958, 1963, 1974, 1983
Mean		6.5		10.8	9.3	

[a]Percentage representation in most recent year for which data are available.
[b]No elections 1973–1990.
[c]Data for 1994–1997 and 1997–2000 from Mexican Embassy, London.

Source: Table compiled by the author with data from Interparliamentary Union.

Thus, although Mexico is currently no worse than the majority of its neighbors in terms of formal representation for women in the decision-making arenas, it clearly has room for improvement for women's political representation. Although Mexico has had more female governors and ministers than Argentina, the latter has been swifter to implement measures to improve congressional representation.

A common feature of countries in the region is that few of the women active in popular protest have secured entry to institutional politics. Even in Argentina, which has seen a massive increase in the number of congresswomen due to the quota law,[7] only one deputy, Graciela Fernández Meijide, was involved in collective action (as a human rights campaigner) prior to her election. In Mexico, political parties, notably the PRD and the PRI, have attempted to establish links between themselves and grassroots organizations, but since women are generally the backbone rather than the head of these movements, it is often the men who reap the rewards of earlier participation.[8] In Brazil the link between grassroots organization and parties is aided by the activities of the PT, which grew out of social movements in the late 1970s.

What we can deduce from these data is that women are increasingly active in institutional politics at all levels but that there are certain pessimistic conclusions to be drawn. First, it is the status of the position that is gendered, with women in greater numbers in the least influential positions (Camp 1995b). Second, although women were very active in community politics, it has been difficult for them to break through into electoral politics, even at the local level. This reflects the return of parties as the major political actor at this level and with them a particular political agenda. Thirdly, the reemergence of parties has brought with it the traditional political discourses of left-right, social-political, and public-private. Although women continue to be active in community politics, the issues do not fit neatly into the divides presented to them and often undermine their strength. Contrary to traditional notions of apolitical women who are uninterested in politics, in many cases women outnumber men as party members. However, they are still not being selected as candidates nor are they being elected to office.

Governments: Help or Hindrance?

In response to both the increased political participation at the grassroots level and changing international discourses, some governments have engaged in measures to promote, and to contain, women's political participation. These measures have included women's ministries, affirmative action programs (specifically quota laws), and the signing of the United Nations Convention on the Elimination of All Forms of Discrimination

Against Women (CEDAW). Mexico has a mixed record on such initiatives, and indeed it is not clear that the measures are beneficial.

There has long been a debate within feminism regarding engagement with the state or the pursuit of autonomy—that is, whether the state should be colonized as a strategy to further the position of women or shunned as a male construct with nothing to offer women. The different strategies can be seen in different parts of Latin America. In Chile there has plainly been considerable interaction between state bodies and feminists, the latter perceiving the state as an important tool to improve the quality of women's lives. Conversely, in Argentina, there is considerable suspicion on the part of feminists toward the state, although there have been episodes of interaction resulting in many changes of law. One of the problems with regarding the state as being either good or bad for women is that of ascribing to it a false homogeneity.

Although any engagement in politics requires compromises at certain points (the skill is to know which issues are negotiable and which are not), some areas of the state will act to exclude any kind of popular influence, whereas others will benefit from a more supportive attitude toward women. If women are to be equal citizens with constitutionally enshrined rights, the state has to be a prime site of struggle—a terrain rather than a unitary actor. As Alvarez points out, the ability to influence the gender impact of government policies depends on gender-conscious political action (1989a:213). In Mexico, a number of key feminists have chosen to work within the state to further the position of women (Bourque 1989). However, the state had different characteristics: on one hand, the paternal protector sanctifying women and particularly motherhood; on the other, the state as rapist using sexual torture against women defined as subversive (Charlton, Everett, and Staudt 1989).

CEDAW

The three strategies mentioned above—CEDAW, women's ministries, and affirmative action—are not equal in impact with regard to increasing women's political representation. The signing of the UN convention appears to have limited impact both on a global and regional level. CEDAW was adopted by the UN in 1979; the first Latin American government, Cuba, signed and ratified it in 1980 and the last, Bolivia, in 1990; Mexico ratified the convention in 1981.[9] Signing or ratifying the convention has had limited impact on increasing the number of women representatives despite articles that emphasize the need for women to be more politically visible.[10] In 1987, in those countries that ratified without reservation, women constituted 8.4 percent of parliamentarians and 5.6 percent of those in decisionmaking positions, whereas in those that signed with reservation or had neither signed nor ratified, women made up 5.8 percent and 6 percent of parliamentarians respectively. However, women's representation in decisionmaking was substantially lower in these countries, at 2.3 and 2.4 percent respectively (United Nations 1992:104).

Given that the convention seeks to be sensitive to the cultural differences across the globe, it is not a radical document, even though it does lay down some basic rights for women and has the potential for radical interpretation. The article on reproductive health, for example, could be used to support the legalization of abortion, illegal in all countries except in the most extreme circumstances.[11] However, it appears that, in general, signing of the convention has had little impact on legislation (government action on contraception and abortion, for example, has been very limited in all Latin American countries; Argentina relegalized the use of contraceptives but has done little to provide a public health contraceptive service) or on the levels of women's political representation. The impact is more symbolic than material.

The reasons for a government's signing such a convention may have less to do with ideas of promoting the advancement of women and more to do with the relationship with the international community (particularly if a country is seeking external legitimacy) or with the containment of women's political activity. We must consider, then, that the Mexican government signed the convention to demonstrate its "modern" character and as a way of preempting the convention from becoming the center of a protest campaign on behalf of the opposition.[12] Equally, international considerations are important, and Mexico is keen to prove itself a member of the "First World Club."[13]

Women's Ministries

Eighteen countries in Latin America have women's ministries of one kind or another.[14] The first such department was set up in 1960 in Cuba, but it was over twenty years before another such organization was established, on this occasion in Guatemala. The ministerial affiliation of women's departments is worth noting as a reflection of whether the government considers the issue central to government policy, related to other considerations, or whether women are a "minority" interest. The Federación de Mujeres Cubanas answers to the Ministry of Culture, Youth, and Sports! In many Latin American countries, women's ministries are part of the Office of the President, as was the case of Mexico's National Coordinating Committee for the 1995 Beijing Conference. The newly created (1996) Programa Nacional de la Mujer is part of the Ministry of the Interior (Gobernación). In four countries, women's advancement is overtly linked to their reproductive role by combining a ministry for women with that for children or the family (Costa Rica, El Salvador, Peru, and Uruguay). Only one, Bolivia, has a subsecretariat for gender (within the Ministry of Human Development), whereas in other countries there have been heated discussions regarding the meaning of the concept "gender," particularly prior to the UN Beijing conference. In Argentina, for instance, the term was banned in the Ministry of Education, leading to resignations. Argentina is unusual in having a *gabinete femenino* (a "shadow cabinet" made of women) to advise the president, although the cabinet has no binding role. Similarly, the country's Women's Council does not have ministerial status, unlike its predecessor that was disbanded in 1989.

The advantages of such a ministry are that it can coordinate activities aimed at improving the status of women in a given country and can act as a bridge between women's groups and the government. It has been seen in the case of Chile, in particular, that there is often room within such organizations for women who have previously been active in the women's movement. The Women's Ministry in Chile (SERNAM) commissions reports, coordinates activities between the government and the voluntary sector, and brings the issue of gender to the attention of other ministries. Although most governments have laws against domestic violence, the ministries can add legitimacy and pressure in the allocation of resources. However, it must be remembered that they are state bodies and that the ministers and other top positions are appointed by the incumbent party or parties. The top two appointees at SERNAM are women with little previous experience with women's issues and for whom the appointment was not necessarily seen as a promotion.[15] The presence of a "women's" minister can be designed to demonstrate a commitment to women's issues but may not help to advance the cause of women. In May 1995 the director of Argentina's Consejo Nacional de la Mujer resigned after a strong disagreement with the government policy on abortion, and months later there was still no new appointment. The impact of a women's ministry will depend on who is appointed as the head, and it is clear that it will not necessarily be a woman (or man) with an interest in gender issues. Moreover, the existence of a women's ministry might serve to marginalize women's interests and institutionalize traditional gender roles. Given the current economic constraints that weigh heavily on all Latin America governments, any activities that need high levels of state resources will be difficult to promote.

Mexico did have a National Commission for Women between 1983 and 1992, although the main thrust of the commission was to encourage women's participation in the development process. Similarly, in other countries women's political representation, even when targeted, only represents one area among many; issues of domestic violence, women in the workplace, the informal market, and indigenous women's rights are just some of the competing areas demanding resources from a women's department. Consequently, the existence of a women's department might have little impact on political representation even when it is staffed by people with a commitment to gender issues.

Affirmative Action

Most affirmative action in Latin America has resulted when parties passed statutes requiring a certain percentage of women on electoral lists. Argentina is a notable exception in that it changed the electoral law to require, specifically, that 30 percent of party list members for congressional candidates should be women. This accounts for the rapid increase in the number of women deputies since 1991. The law was proposed by an opposition senator, but without the backing of the president, Carlos Menem, it is doubtful that it would have succeeded. However, there have been problems in enforcing the quota, and some parties have been taken to court to ensure compliance with the law. The law was strengthened by allowing the Consejo Nacional de la Mujer to offer legal support to women who had been excluded by their parties. Furthermore, the quota only applies to the national congress, not the regional and local tiers of representation, although increasingly regional governments are passing similar laws. The previous Mexican president, Carlos Salinas de Gortari, stated that women were a priority for his government (Ramos Escandón 1994), but there was little material evidence of this commitment. Any kind of quota for women was ruled out,[16] although there are increasing demands for a quota and there may be changes under President Ernesto Zedillo. Despite Salinas's dislike of such legislation, the PRD has an internal quota system, and the ruling PRI also encourages women's representation through its women's sections. Furthermore, without the help of quota systems, Mexico currently has higher numbers of women ministers than Argentina.

One of the major arguments in favor of a quota law is that there would be a change in the political culture, since women would bring with them alternative methods of "doing politics." As Kathleen Staudt points out in Chapter 2, the notion of a "critical mass" needed to make the changes is popular, although there is less agreement about what the quota might be. Most suggest 20 or 30 percent as the minimum; in Argentina it is 30 percent, but since this is the quota for candidate lists it is probable that the number of deputies is not likely to rise above 25 percent. Riet Delsing discovered that attitudes toward quotas among party leaders in Chile are very mixed; some are opposed while others think it has to be 40 percent to have an impact and that 20–30 percent leaves women in a token position.[17] Reaching a critical mass might be important, but given the cooptive style of politics, it would seem sensible to consider timing as well. If the quota is gradually raised, the impact will be less than an overnight change, for example, from 5 to 40 percent female representation. In Argentina, the law is described as a transitory measure to instill a new culture, and therefore we must wait to see how long such a transitory measure will be necessary.

Notwithstanding the potential benefits, there have been many criticisms of quotas: first, that they will act as a "ceiling" instead of a "floor"; second, that quotas might guarantee quantity but not quality;[18] and finally, and most important from a Latin American perspective, that the measure is corporatist and therefore antidemocratic, creating sectors for different groups in society.

A major problem for women in many countries is the high degree of centralism that makes increased numbers of women deputies less significant. Thus, the political system itself is frequently the problem rather than the introduction of quotas and women's ministries, as demonstrated by the former USSR and its satellites. The Argentine experience has highlighted the debate about quality versus quantity and whether women's position has been improved at all by larger numbers of women deputies, but it is too early to make a clear assessment. Furthermore, in many countries in the region, government ministers are not drawn from these ranks, and therefore, even when they are women, they are not accountable to the electorate. There is also a problem with the selection procedure. It may be that a list should have 30 percent female candidates, but the selection appears to be undertaken by the same party elites as before, and these tend not to choose women active on women's issues. Women representatives should be as broad a cross section as the men, but there is a lack of interest on the part of many women deputies to espouse women's causes or offer a gender perspective, which is worrying. The women appear to be choosing party loyalty over gender, and many want to be seen to distance themselves from women's issues, not a dilemma that faces men. This would have particular implications in the Mexican case, where the PRI has long used divide-and-rule tactics. In most countries there appears to be a core group of women from diverse parties who are prepared to promote common themes, but it is not an easy alliance. Even with only nine women deputies, Chilean *diputadas* rarely agree on policies.

With this in mind, the likelihood of the Mexican government's establishing a formal women's ministry or a quota system depends more on the perceived benefits for government than it does on the arguments for democracy or pressure coming from women themselves. There is still an emphasis on national-level politics despite the greater potential for change at the local level (Saa 1993). Across the region it is grassroots organizations that have attracted the greatest female support, and therefore one way of promoting women's political involvement would be to establish closer ties between institutions and movements at the local level. Since the municipal level enjoys the lowest status within government, it could make a virtue out of necessity by putting women's marginalization from the major decisionmaking arenas to good use. The PAN's strategy over the past few years indicates that closer attention to the local and regional level may be more fruitful for women as well as opposition parties. Centralism is a problem for the majority of Latin American countries. However, in the Chilean case, parties so tightly control the candidacies for local and regional seats that there is no room for women who have become political actors through other forms of activity, and the parties are resistant to putting forward women as candidates.[19] Argentina displays many of the centralist characteristics familiar in Mexico, although it appears that the quota law is permeating the regional level and may, in time, become a generalized practice.

Parties and Women's Political Representation

Parties in Latin America tend to be weak structures, with rather underdeveloped ideologies and policies; furthermore, many do not survive very long, finding it difficult to establish themselves (see Mainwaring and Scully 1995). Relationships between parties and women have not always been smooth, and as Camp (1995b: 158–159) noted, it has often been initial access to executive positions that has limited women politically rather than their promotion once they are inside. The relationship between parties and women is governed by at least two factors: first, whether the parties encourage women as political actors, particularly regarding power positions within the parties and as electoral candidates; second, the gender impact of policies the parties are advocating.

The use of quotas may help increase women's representation in electoral politics, but policies still have a gendered impact that is not acknowledged, and "women's interests" often remain marginal to the political process. Traditionally within Latin America, so-called leftist parties have been more open to "women's issues," although lately there has been an offensive on the part of the right to generate support. The emergence of a politicized Catholic movement may be in response to what it perceives to be a moral decline or to the success of more liberal wings of the Church. The Church has long been an important actor in Latin American politics and has been a defender of democracy in some countries, but developments within the rightist group Opus Dei illustrate the ways traditionalists are absorbing modern discourses, including feminism (using the language of women's rights, for instance, or establishing women's studies departments at Opus Dei universities); unfortunately, little academic attention has been paid to these developments.

The links between parties and women's groups depend on attitudes of women's organizations toward the institutional arena, the needs of parties, and the strength of women's collective action. However, parties require loyalty, and the pervasiveness of a left-right divide can weaken the potential strength of women as political actors. Women's issues often involve policy issues that highlight tensions between women politicians and their party colleagues and also between women activists. There is an added dimension that as the women's movements and feminist movements grow more complex and the "easy" issues are dealt with, fault lines appear among women themselves. Even though this heterogeneity should be celebrated, it does cause problems for agreeing on strategies for the advancement of women.[20]

Throughout the region we can observe different relationships between parties and women activists, in part owing to the development of women's organizations themselves. In Argentina, the feminist movement is closely linked to psychology theory and practice, and many of the first groups comprised professionals in the field, a situation that has reinforced the divide between activists and more personal expressions of feminism. Here there are problems in developing collective, multi-organization activities, in contrast to Chile, where interaction among women's movements, parties, and popular protest has been more vigorous. A number of NGOs carry out their own studies; their publications are well-known and are often influential on policymaking, particularly at SERNAM. There also appear to be good relations in Chile between different types of women activists and the few women politicians who have gained entry into the national legislature. However, in those countries that have experienced a transition from military rule, the worries of encouraging another bout of military intervention appear to have put new pressures on popular organizations (Waylen 1993).

Parties generally have narrowed the political debate, to the detriment of popular participation, and there is little difference on major policy areas; overall, they emphasize a neoliberal economic order with minimum social expenditure. The greater costs of this will be offset by a poverty eradication program (nearly all countries have some kind of poverty alleviation policy) that, in turn, depends on encouraging individuals to shoulder the burden of economic adjustment, with an important role for women. The role of women within this new consensus is rarely discussed by politicians themselves, but there is an emphasis on the importance of motherhood as women's primary identity, with a secondary interest in remunerated labor. This allows flexible responses to labor demand while at the same time not undermining family welfare strategies that take pressure off public provision. Parties must perform a careful balancing act between developing rhetoric that will win women's support without alienating men or incurring commitments that would contradict economic policies.

It is difficult to obtain statistics on party membership, thereby frustrating a gendered analysis. In Chile, electoral data are easily obtained and in the past have indicated that women have favored conservative parties; the female membership of Renovación Nacional reinforces this, but recently it is apparent that women are joining all parties in greater numbers. In Greater Buenos Aires, women outnumber men in all the major parties. In Mexico, former PRI deputy Lorena Martínez commented that 58 percent of the PRI's membership is female (Rodríguez et al. 1995:44), but none of the three major parties in Mexico has had more than 25 percent women on its national executive committee (Fernández Poncela 1995:44–45). Yet, in talking to party activists from Chile, Argentina, and Mexico, it would appear that it is women who are behind the scenes, organizing the meetings and providing support.

The relationship between activists, parties, and nonparty political women tends to be most vibrant around single issues, which would mirror the structure of popular protest organization. In Argentina, relationships among the three are fragile and inconsistent. There have been examples of coordinated action (for instance, the campaign around the signing of the Ley de Cupos), but generally speaking, feminists in Argentina have maintained their distance from the state, and the interaction between feminists and grassroots collective action has not been as extensive as in other countries. Indeed, grassroots activity has not been on the scale of that in Mexico, Chile, and Peru. In Mexico a number of women's organizations seek to influence party platforms (Ramos Escandón 1994). If women's issues and a gendered analysis are going to be at the forefront of procedural politics, then cross-party tactics will always be necessary; and in most countries, including Mexico, such tactics are already used but often have to be renegotiated for each issue.

Diversity and Solidarity: Strategies

Politics is about the exercise of power and influence, and it is perhaps inevitable that for women motherhood would be a central political identity, given the symbolic power it has in the eyes of many in Latin America. However, being a mother does not provide a uniform political agenda, although it may introduce certain political practices and issues. Kaplan (1982) gave centrality to motherhood in her analysis of women's political action based on female consciousness and offered many insights into understanding the challenges motherhood posed to more masculine forms of politics. But motherhood has many problems of essentialism and can be a self-limiting political identity (Feijoó 1994; Perelli 1994); indeed, in the mid-1990s, we can point to few groups in which a specifically motherist political involvement has led to other political activities, particularly in the institutional arena. With the new challenges posed by the ongoing economic austerity and civilian rule, maintaining a broad front with other women's groups and other collective organizations has not been easy in any country.

The changes in the attitudes and actions of governments and parties have indicated that women are more established as political actors and that "private" issues can still be seen as legitimately political. Many analysts examining women's political activity challenge the utility of a public-private divide, arguing that it "invisibilizes" women's participation in all areas of life and constrains them when they achieve power positions.[21] However, Perelli (1994) defended the concept, saying that if the personal is always political, the logic of the common good is opposed. An added criticism must be that if we completely destroy the distinction, we are denying ourselves a place free from state intervention. Given the experiences of Latin Americans over the past decades, encouraging greater intrusion into all areas of life can hardly be welcomed. Many in power already want to restrict decisions that affect the most intimate areas of our life, such as sexuality and reproduction, and thus arguing for the demise of the public-private would only lend greater legitimacy to such policies. However, rather than leaving it to governments and parties to quietly reinstate a division that serves their socioeconomic aims, it is incumbent upon women themselves to redraw the line to satisfy their needs.

The political discourses of parties and institutions in the region are largely exclusionary to maintain elite, gendered, as well as race- and class-bound, preservation of power. Latin American women will only succeed in demonstrating their political subjectivity by developing multiple strategies (including struggling on the terrain of the state), colonizing parties, advancing ongoing independent organizations both feminist and "womanist," and building alliances with other groups. Foweraker (1988) highlighted the Mexican state's weakness to such transformative practices. No single strategy will make a great impact on its own, and the current world economic situation does not make it easy for anyone to effect egalitarian political change.

A key difference between parties and protest groups is the art of the possible. Many popular protest groups in Latin America have demands that they see as nonnegotiable, and they emphasize their independence from the state; the debate over engagement and autonomy is an important one (Munck 1990). However, it is inevitable that should they choose to engage with the institutional sphere, they will have to compromise, women's groups as much as any other. The passing of legislation requires the development of consensus building, and women's issues can be divisive. Abortion remains one of the most problematic issues—the Church remains implacably opposed to it, and both women and men are divided on the issue. However, given the calculated number of abortions practiced each year in the region, there are many engaging in the practice, even if their support for a change in legislation is unclear.[22] We need both pragmatic short-term strategies and longer-term projects to secure a future that is politically inclusive of women. Waylen (1993) has noted that it is women's groups seen to be concentrating on "practical gender interests" that have suffered during political transition, whereas organizations focusing on "strategic gender interests" have weathered political changes more successfully. For a longer-term approach it would be helpful to consider issues as having both strategic and practical implications, as doing so would aid the development of a two-pronged strategy for improving both the material conditions in which women live and their political influence.

Conclusions

The political participation of women in Mexico has many similarities with the situation in other countries in the region and beyond. Women are still excluded from major power positions, they find it more difficult than men to become elected, and political parties are less than welcoming to women. However, it is clear that women's participation at most levels is increasing. Furthermore, there is growing evidence to indicate that the label "apolitical" is inappropriate, even if we narrow the definition of politics to parties and political institutions; women are joining parties in larger numbers and in many outnumber men. Although the impact of mass popular protest movements appears not to be as great as had once been hoped, Latin America can never return to the days of the 1960s any more than Europe could return to prewar gender relations in 1945. Indeed, in some countries it would appear that the feminist movement is healthier than many other collective action groups.

Another important development in contemporary Latin America is the growing diversity of the women's movement. It ranges from radical feminism to nonfeminist groups, and the very term *feminist* is becoming less demonized and multiple in its interpretation. But what is clear from examples across the region is that issues will only be addressed in the institutional political arena when there is a significant body of opinion pressuring for change or if it is in the interests of political elites: Setbacks are common, such as the removal of the term *gender* in Argentina's Ministry of Education. Equally, parties have to be worked on and male (and some female) colleagues within them convinced of the centrality of women to the political process. It is simplistic to assume that women will somehow be "better" political actors than their male predecessors, introducing improved moral standards and cleaning-up the political act. Numerous examples in the region, notably Argentina, clearly show that women will have a limited impact on the tone of politics when they identify more strongly with the party hierarchies and practices and come from the same political elite. Women are as much products of the political process as men, and although women will introduce new issues and possibly new practices, there is a need for a "critical mass" to be reached quickly and maintained before lasting changes to political norms are achieved.

The period of transition was one of flux that facilitated the renegotiation of boundaries. However, in the consolidation phase governments have settled in familiar power relations around gender. They are currently focusing on economic issues: Mexico is still grappling with the fallout of the peso crisis, Argentina is dealing with record unemployment, and Chile is consolidating the economic gains made at great cost under Augusto Pinochet. Similarly, other countries in the region are also laboring under structural adjustment policies and economic restructuring. Women have succeeded in being heard more and are increasingly deciding their own terms of representation, but although there are numerically more women representatives, the impact on policies is muted. A major remaining problem is that the changes that are effected are tagged on to existing structures, and a fundamental questioning of the practice of politics has not been achieved. Women have been added to the equation without an overhauling of candidate list procedures, the high degree of centralism, lack of accountability of ministers and government officials, and less than transparent legal systems in most countries. It is in this environment that women's collective action is taking place. Consequently, little will be achieved without women's becoming involved in independent and opposition groups and rendering issues political by making them visible. As women become more visible so do many issues, and the shifting institutional and technical terrains constantly introduce new issues with implications for both gender relations and political priorities—issues such as assisted fertility, workplace technology, and changing working practices.

There are also many conceptual issues that need constant challenge, since they contain and control women's political activity. One is the question of political discourses that "invisibilize" women's issues, such as the left-right dualism that ignores matters that fit less easily along this continuum. Another is the homogenization of women, who are expected to prioritize gender needs over other identities in a way that ignores diversity and marginalizes them as political actors. The tension between diversity and solidarity is a difficult one and will not be easily resolved. Indeed, many party political activists talk of their "double militancy" between women's activism and party identity, acknowledging that both are necessary if not always possible for all. We are in an era when notions of universal solidarity are under attack, and developments in women's political activity in Latin America clearly indicate the problems of such an approach, even though mass movements have also shown themselves to contain massive transformative potential. The prospect for Latin American women is to have diversity of political activity in order to maintain pressure, develop strategies, and concentrate on improving the access of the majority of women to the decisionmaking arena through informed choice and autonomy. The art of the possible has to be combined with idealism. Women need to embrace both approaches and not use the differences to divide them when linkages can be made.

Notes

I would like to thank the British Academy for funding fieldwork for the comparative study in July–September 1995. I would also like to thank Rick Wilford for his valuable comments on this chapter.

1. It should be noted that the period in question for each country is not uniform, since it takes into account only periods of electoral rule.

2. Data are from the Mexican Embassy, London.

3. Senators are elected for a six-year term; however, half the senate is elected every three years, which accounts for different figures for 1988–1991 and 1991–1994.

4. Laura Alicia Garza Galindo in the Chamber of Deputies and Silvia Hernández in the Senate (Ramos Escandón 1994).

5. There are thirty-one governors in Mexico; their tenure is six years.

6. Archenti and Gómez (1994) have shown that in the Argentinian case women are increasingly involved in ministry commissions not associated with "women's issues"; however, Dip Graciela Fernández Meijide told me in an interview that she had not succeeded in participating on the economic commission she requested.

7. The Argentine quota law requires that 30 percent of candidates for Congress should be female.

8. This was the case of the independent organization I studied in Guadalajara (Craske 1993a, 1993b); cf. Stephen (1989.)

9. Many countries, including Argentina, Brazil, Chile, and Venezuela, have ratified with declarations or reservations; Mexico signed without reservation.

10. Article 7 states: "State's Parties shall take all appropriate measures to eliminate discrimination against women in the political and public life of the country . . . " (United Nations 1995); this could be used to support affirmative action on the part of national governments to increase women's participation in the major decisionmaking bodies.

11. Cuba has completely legalized abortion, and Mexico allows it when the mother's life is at risk.

12. It must be remembered that in 1981 a great degree of protest activity was orchestrated by the newly formed Coordinadoras.

13. This was particularly evident during the North American Free Trade Agreement (NAFTA) negotiations. A similar argument was made to me in relation to Argentina.

14. Under this rubric I include ministries, secretariats, departments, federations, and institutes that are designed to improve the status of women. That having been said, these organizations have different levels of power depending on their legal status.

15. Interview with Paulina Veloso, subdirector of SERNAM, August 30, 1995.

16. He is quoted as saying, "Más que cuotas en las cuales dejar a las mujeres en un rincón" ("More than quotas that will leave women in a corner") (*La Jornada*, March 9, 1990:3).

17. September 1995 conversation with Delsing, who is conducting a study for SERNAM on party leaders' attitudes to quotas for increasing women's representation.

18. The complaint of quantity without quality is one frequently heard in Argentina. It is worth noting that Augusto Pinochet significantly increased the number of women representatives at the local level when he appointed large numbers of women in the municipalities, but they did little to further the position of women. Indeed Pinochet was keen to disempower the Poder Femenino, which had played a significant part in encouraging his coup.

19. Chilean political parties have high levels of female membership; indeed the rightist Renovación Nacional has 62 percent. However, women account for few of the candidates at any level and even fewer of the representatives.

20. The tensions between the women's movement and the feminist movement are well discussed in Sternbach et al. (1992).

21. See Cubitt and Greenslade (1997) for a comprehensive critique of the public-private debate.

22. Estimated figures on abortion suggest that more than one in three pregnancies ends in termination in many countries in the region. In Mexico it is estimated to be about one in six (Valdes and Gomariz 1995:132).

❀ 4 ❀

Ten Theses on Women in
the Political Life of Latin America

Joe Foweraker

The ten theses on women in the political life of Latin America set forth in
this chapter are designed to construct a theoretical and comparative
framework for subsequent discussions of the role of women in Mexican
political life in particular. The theses are drawn from the extensive literature on women in Latin America, and each thesis summarizes an empirical generalization about the political practices of these women. Rather
than seeking to generalize about women as individuals, the theses are intended to characterize the emergence of women as a social and political
force and therefore focus on women's struggle to achieve political participation through increasing *mobilization*. The premise of the theses, and of
the greater part of the literature, is that women cannot enhance their political importance without such mobilization. But the overall political impact of the mobilization remains in doubt (and this doubt is reflected in
the theses). Will women's mobilization bring a sea change to the politics
of the continent? Or will the ancient fortifications of "malestream" politics
prove impervious to women's protests?

Thesis No. 1: Women's Mobilization
Is New in Form and Degree

Two main initial claims are made for women's mobilization across Latin
America: More women mobilize than ever before, and the mobilization is
novel in its organizational forms and ideological expression. Women's
mobilization began to increase rapidly from the mid-1970s on, and within
ten years it had reached unprecedented levels in Argentina, Brazil, Chile,
Peru, and Bolivia. Over the same period women had swelled the cadres of
revolutionary organizations in Guatemala, El Salvador, and Nicaragua.

Although there was some mobilization of rural women in countries like Peru and Nicaragua, which had undergone agrarian reforms, most women became active in the urban setting. This reflected a major generational and life-world shift, from a mainly rural to predominantly urban and industrial society (Foweraker 1995a). In this new society it was women who were mainly responsible for "building a community" (Caldeira 1990:48) and ensuring material survival (see thesis no. 3).

In Mexico this mobilization is evident in the rapid growth of urban social movements and of union movements in unions that have a female majority, such as unions of teachers, telephone operators, nurses, and garment workers (Foweraker and Craig 1990). There is no doubt that this increasing mobilization occurred during a period of very rapid political and electoral reforms and may have hastened these reforms (Loaeza 1989; Logan 1990). But this is difficult to prove. What is certain is that most arguments about the changing role of women and the impact of women's mobilization tend to be of *longue durée* and to focus on questions of political identity and political culture (Arizpe 1990; Radcliffe and Westwood 1993) (see thesis no. 6).

Thesis No. 2: Women's Mobilization Is Different from Feminist Movements

It is argued that the majority experience of women's mobilization derives from "female consciousness" (Kaplan 1982) or "practical gender interests" (Molyneux 1985), which express a sexual division of labor that assigns the responsibility for preserving life to women. Women's mobilization is therefore driven by the struggle for economic survival and family integrity. Feminist movements, on the other hand, are the minority experience that express "strategic gender interests" (Molyneux 1985) and the political struggle for women's liberation from multiple forms of gendered oppression. Hence it is alleged that "the majority of women who participate in the popular social movements are not mobilized by a feminist consciousness," since "feminism has very little to do with the reality of their lives" (Corcoran-Nantes 1993:159), or, similarly, that "the label feminist was almost unanimously rejected by working-class women" (Fisher 1993:205).

Underlying the ideological differences between feminism and "motherism" (Schirmer 1993) is the question of class, or of the divisions between working-class women and "elite women" (Safa 1980). Feminism, it is suggested, is restricted to the "fortunate" women of the middle and upper classes (Corcoran-Nantes 1993). But if this was true of the early decades of the century (Lavrin 1993:521), there is some evidence that it is now changing. In Chile, the feminist movement managed to transcend its middle-class origins and reach out to the poor women of the urban periphery

(Valenzuela 1990). In Brazil, "the politicization of gender within Church-linked community women's groups provided nascent Brazilian feminism with an extensive mass base" (Alvarez 1989b:36), and "feminists embraced the survival struggles of poor and working-class women and joined forces with the militant opposition" (Alvarez 1990a:265). In these countries, therefore, feminism has proved important to the leadership of grassroots movements (see thesis no. 5), as feminist struggles began to intersect both with the survival struggles of the urban poor and with the democratic struggles of the political opposition to the military regimes.

Nonetheless, feminists themselves are aware of the enduring differences between the "historical" and mainly middle-class feminists and the women from the urban movements (Sternbach et al. 1992). But they argue that such differences should not be allowed to buttress the binary categories of "practical" and "strategic" interests (Radcliffe and Westwood 1993:20) or "female" and "feminist" consciousness (Schirmer 1993), because these static categories simply reinforce the restrictive division between "private" and "public" and so serve to prolong women's subjugation (see thesis no. 7). The lesson of "the personal is political" is that all women are equally capable of political insight.

Thesis No. 3: Women's Mobilization Is Rooted in Traditional Female Roles

As a corollary to thesis no. 2, it is asserted that women's traditional roles as wives and mothers stimulate and legitimate their social protests and political participation (Safa 1990; Jaquette 1989). These roles determine women's preoccupation with economic survival and community defense and shape their demands. These demands address the issues of work, wages, cost of living, services, and housing and may focus on public utilities, schools, nurseries, clinics, transport, land titles, and tax. Any of these demands may promote mobilization, as may police or local government interference in the community. In this way private nurturing leads to collective action, in social movements, unions, and even political parties. The struggle for social survival defines the political agenda of women's organizations and creates their mass base, and this is especially true of women in low-income urban neighborhoods (Corcoran-Nantes 1990:225; Caldeira 1990).

Yet there is some doubt in the literature whether the traditional "networking" and survival activities of women in fact constitute grassroots mobilization as such (Cardoso 1987:32). The networks and other "traditional" activities such as those of many Catholic base communities may or may not compose the "micromobilization contexts" (McAdam, McCarthy, and Zald 1988) or the "pre-movement" conditions for social mobilization, and informal economy may or may not lead to formal political organiza-

tion. But there are no general rules that can determine whether the consciousness rooted in "community" (Safa 1980) or the associationalism of
urban neighborhoods will evolve into grassroots organization. It depends
on political context. What is sure is that initiatives as different as female
unionization in the Bolivian countryside (Jelin 1987) and antimilitary mobilization in Chile (Kirkwood 1983) have evolved from experiences of
community networks and popular self-help organizations.

In analogous and allied fashion, it is also debated whether women's
mobilization deliberately eschews political goals. The presumption is that
this mobilization is not proactive but rather reactive to state and market
pressures. In other words, women press for greater (material) participation in the political system as it is, rather than seeking to change it. But
these debates may simply misunderstand the process of social mobilization and the tendency for such mobilization to translate material into political demands (Foweraker 1993, 1995a). Women's groups, in particular,
can evolve "from economic into political organizations" once they realize
"that services that government has failed to provide to its citizens can be
obtained through coordinated mobilization" (Lavrin 1993:531), and practical demands for immediate improvements in living conditions can
spawn political demands for women's equality and an end to discrimination (Fisher 1993:206). In this way, originally material and limited demands can and do have a broader institutional and political impact.

Thesis No. 4: Feminism Is Successful
in Extending Women's Political Agenda

Social movements theorists (e.g., Habermas 1973, 1987) suggest that feminism is the only modern social movement to make universal moral and
legal claims in the Enlightenment tradition. It is therefore the only such
movement to be unequivocally "on the offensive." There is no doubt that
this impetus has succeeded in placing new "strategic" gender issues on
the political agenda, including domestic violence, sexual aggression and
rape, lack of reproductive control, clandestine abortion, discrimination
and harassment in the workplace, and economic dependence (Jaquette
1989:172). In Chile the Movimiento para la Emancipación de las Mujeres
Chilenas (Movement for Women's Emancipation, MEMCH-83) brought
together twenty-four of the huge range of women's organizations, and
Women for Life emerged as the principal axis of female mobilization
overall (Valenzuela 1990). In Brazil the issues of "militant motherhood"
drove the Female Amnesty Movement, the Cost of Living Movement,
and the Day Care Movement throughout the 1970s into the 1980s, and by
1985 "tens of thousands of women had been politicized by the women's
movements, and core items of the feminist agenda had made their way

into the platforms and programs of all major political parties" (Alvarez 1989b:18).

However, the awareness of and struggle for such strategic interests are far from being the majority experience of women in Latin America (compare thesis no. 2). In this regard the mass-based women's movements in Brazil and Chile (and possibly Peru) were exceptional in their feminist content, and only in very few instances has women's mobilization succeeded in winning such strategic goals. Once again, it is alleged that the question of class restricts the political scope of the feminist agenda, since only middle-class women have the time and resources to pursue this agenda. Elsa Chaney, in particular, has repeatedly observed that the women of Latin America who are publicly active and personally free have been mainly "liberated" by the work of the domestic servants in their employ (Chaney 1973, 1979; Chaney and García Castro 1989). In my view, this is partly a generational question, with formerly "feminist" issues now an integral part of the women's agenda of the younger generation in many cities of the continent (cf. Bourque 1985).

Thesis No. 5: Women's Mobilization Is Mainly Led by Men

Even where women are the majority presence, as in many urban movements and in some unions, the majority of the leadership tends to be male. It has been suggested that as many as 80 percent of participants in some urban movements are women (Corcoran-Nantes 1990), but male rule is still the rule (Caldeira 1990). Women's organizations also tend to have a tense relationship with political parties, especially those on the left, and despite the crucial role played by women in recent political struggles in Chile, Peru, Argentina, and Brazil, women's issues are still relegated to a poor second place, behind "class struggle" or male-dominated party platforms. Indeed, according to leaders on the left, the women massed in hundreds of organizations in factories and poor urban districts across the continent were to form a "rearguard" in support of the revolutionary project (Sternbach et al. 1992). Unions have proved even more recalcitrant, with women confined to women's sections, and little headway has been achieved in securing equal rights for women workers. Moreover, the influence of parties and even unions on women's organizations is often divisive and ultimately demoralizing (Kirkwood 1983; Valenzuela 1990).

In the case of the unions it is clear that "despite their increasing numbers in the labor force since the beginning of the century, women have been unable to rise to positions of national leadership in the labor movement" (Lavrin 1993:500). Their "segregation" into special and subordinate sections (Chaney 1973)[1] has prevented the development of autonomous organizations—as in the case of the Housewives' Committee in Bolivia, which was instructed to act as an auxiliary to the miners' union (Ardaya Salinas 1986). In the realization that women's issues remain secondary, as much for unions as for political parties (Bourque 1985:45), many women have opted for the kind of "double militancy" (Safa 1990) that might pursue union/party and women's goals simultaneously. Even "double militancy," however, has tended to weaken the women's agenda (Valenzuela 1990; Alvarez 1989b:45).

These observations are largely true of urban social movements, union movements, and political parties (with the partial exception of the PRD) in Mexico (Ramírez Saiz 1987a). Since the 1950s the predominantly female unions of telephone operators, textile workers, and teachers have consistently been led by men (Lavrin 1993:502). In the case of the contemporary teachers' movement, which mobilized self-styled "democratic" teachers, women's leadership roles were largely confined to delegational committees (Foweraker 1993). There are some exceptions, such as the 19th of September Garment Workers' Union (Carrillo 1990), in which women are the leadership, but these exceptions are themselves a small minority experience within the union sector overall.

Since the organizational or "institutionalized" leaderships are male dominated, the role of "outside" leaders may be especially important to women's organizations. Social movement analysis in general refers to the important part played by outside leaders such as lawyers, teachers, doctors, social workers, students, NGO activists, and pastoral agents of the popular church, who advise on organization, law, the political context, and negotiation with political authorities (Cardoso 1983:231). Many of these leaders have an almost natural place "inside" the community. They share the common experience of misery and oppression; they understand local realities; they promote and participate in "basist" or directly democratic decisionmaking. Union and (left-wing) party leaders, on the other hand, are seen as exercising influence from the "outside" and are tainted by a general suspicion of political parties and bureaucratic agencies.

In Mexico the student movement of 1968 was crucial to the gestation of a new generation of such popular leaders (Pérez Arce 1990; Foweraker 1993). This generation included educated *lideresas* (female leaders), both left-wing *políticas* (female politicians) and feminist activists. The role of the feminists has been important but often ambiguous. They may give organizational, legal, and strategic advice, but they facilitate the insertion of incipient organizations into the clientelistic power relations of "informal welfarism" (Massolo and Díaz Ronner 1983). They may provide an extensive network of support and solidarity, but their factionalism may prove as divisive as party affiliation (Carrillo 1990; Alvarez 1989b). Hence the relationship between women's grassroots organizations and feminist leaders is likely to be at once productive and uneasy. At best, it may create a powerful combination of class- and gender-based demands (Chinchilla 1992:45).

Thesis No. 6: Women's Mobilization Creates New Political Identities

The process of social networking and a subsequent engagement in social movement struggles tend to transform individual female identities (Scherer-Warren and Krischke 1987:62). In effect, social mobilization is the school where women learn to know themselves as political *actors* rather than as political *objects* (Foweraker 1993). Through mobilization they achieve new sociabilities and solidarities (Jelin 1990a:3) that underpin their increasing resistance to the "microdespotisms" (O'Donnell 1984) of the family, the school, the factory, and the college. With this new identity comes a change from passivity to combativeness (Jelin 1990a:50) that can begin to change civil society (Caldeira 1990:72).

Furthermore, new identities also mean a new politics, since it is alleged that women's "talk" and women's networking are different from the male domain of political parties and unions (Foweraker 1995a:57). Hence women's new identities resemble neither the "domestic female" nor the "political man." On the other hand, these changes in identity are not usually very visible, and the new politics rarely has a high profile. The Madres of the Plaza de Mayo are atypical in this respect. But where women and men mobilize together they are likely to change gender relationships. As the women teachers in Mexico suggested (tongue in cheek), "where the woman advances, no man dare retreat."

However, the costs of achieving such new identities can be high. The traditional double burden of work and family (Ramírez Saiz 1987a) now becomes a "triple burden" of work, family, and social and community struggle (Moser 1987). In particular, the change from passivity to combativeness can imply a loss of job, loss of (male) partner, loss of extended family support, and social opprobrium. But the incentives are also clear: a sense of self-worth, a new dignity, and a feeling of movement and liberation, described variously as an "oxygenation," a "new voice," or an understanding of social struggle as "a natural thing."

Women's new individual identities can coalesce into new collective identities, which are located and mapped in relation to each other and to other agents and organizations within civil society and the political system. At the same time the formation of collective identity may promote an increasing focus on "strategic" as well as "practical" gender interests (Molyneux 1985:234). Thus, there is no doubt that the women teachers of the teachers' movement in Mexico came to see their collective relationship to the male directors and supervisors of the SNTE as a form of gendered oppression

(Foweraker 1993). But collective action is complicated by the continuing power of patrimonialism and clientelism, both of which are capable of exacerbating personal power struggles and jealousies (Blondet 1990), and women's organizations are consequently both highly heterogeneous and sometimes deeply divided. Therefore it cannot be assumed that the new collective identities express unified interests, still less that there is such a thing as (undifferentiated) "women's interests" (Alvarez 1990a:226).

The notion of "women's interests" is complicated by class and ethnicity, on the one hand, and the process of political struggle, on the other. It is often observed in the literature that the experience of black and native Indian women is different from that of white women (Radcliffe and Westwood 1993) and that the opportunities for middle- and upper-class women are far greater than for working-class and poor women (Jaquette 1980:241). It remains moot whether class is the primary determinant of political attitudes, with gender a "secondary variable" (Jaquette 1980), or whether class and ethnic identities are constructed and refracted through gender identities (Radcliffe and Westwood 1993). But the analytical point is inescapable, and this is that the struggles that shape women's identities engage with the two interconnecting but semiautonomous systems of oppression, which are capitalism and patriarchy (Benería and Roldán 1987). At the same time, women's interests are defined and their new identities shaped in some degree by the process of social mobilization and struggle itself and in particular by the processes of political organization and strategic calculation (compare thesis no. 8) (Foweraker 1989a). In sum, there is nothing "essential" or "immutable" about women's interests or women's identities.

Thesis No. 7: Women's Mobilization Changes the Division Between Public and Private

As a corollary to theses nos. 3 and 6, it is alleged that women's mobilization shifts the boundary lines between the private and public worlds and between the spheres of reproduction and production. As a first step, women come to insist on "their right to leave the household in order to participate in the neighborhood association and base community" (Mainwaring and Viola 1984:39), and conservative opinion would keep women's activity within such associations and communities, which are "regarded as being an extension of the home" (Kirkwood 1983:629). But not only does entry into the public sphere have implications for the women themselves (as noted under thesis no. 6)—"releasing them from lives that are 'naturally determined' to enter the 'socially determined' world, where they can be the subjects, not merely the objects of political action" (Jaquette 1989:189)—but women's private or domestic concerns may now take on radical implications. Since the division between what is private and what is public is often state chartered and state sanctioned, such concerns may also impinge on the political system.

Past analyses of women's political roles in Latin America tended to see women as projecting their domestic concerns and responsibilities into the public sphere in a modest, benign, and nonconflictual way. This was the image of the *supermadre* who took her "nurturant and affectional tasks" into "the large *casa* of the municipality and even the nation," where she practiced a "microsocial approach to social change" that mainly addressed issues such as health care and child care and threatened nobody (Chaney 1973:104–105). But for the recent generation, material deprivation and state repression have altered this equation because "the repressive state apparatus and the market encroach increasingly on private life, undermining traditional social organization" (Arizpe 1990:xvii). In the Southern Cone (and Central America), especially, the repressive state set out to suppress all conventional channels of political representation and so suffocate the public sphere, but in attempting to "privatize" political life it effectively politicized private life (Oszlak 1987) and impelled women to struggle to defend their "traditional" world.

Women mobilized to defend their (previously) private world against disappearances, torture-rape, child theft, and other practices that violated the sanctity of the family (Franco 1992; Safa 1990). In this way women's rights tended to fuse with human rights, and human rights organizations became especially salient (Valenzuela 1990; Feijoó 1989).[2] The literature on these topics suggests that the experience of military rule endowed the claim that "the personal is political" with a special meaning (Jaquette 1989:205).[3] Thus women mobilized against the aggression of military regimes, taking their struggle into the public sphere (the symbolism of the Plaza de Mayo) and often joining the civilian opposition. As a result, military-authoritarian rule, which had set out to depoliticize men and restrict citizens' rights, "had the unintended consequence of mobilizing marginal and normally apolitical women" (Jaquette 1989:5), and eventually "women's resistance to military rule had made them more conscious of discrimination against them as women, at work, in the world of politics, and inside the home" (Fisher 1993:13).

It may be thought, correctly, that these Southern Cone experiences are not directly applicable to Mexico. But it may be noted that the Mexican government's record on human rights (and, by implication, its respect for the individual person and the private world) is poor and, by many accounts, getting worse (Foweraker 1995b). It is legitimate also to contemplate the longer-term effects of government and military incursions into the countryside of states like Chiapas and Guerrero. Moreover, it can be argued that the massive mobilization of Mexican women (in response to economic crisis and austerity policies among other things) has an analo-

gous impact in the public sphere. In other words, the boundary lines between private and public in Mexico are being changed by the growing
number of women who are prepared to act publicly and politically and to
insist on their right to do so (compare thesis no. 9).

Thesis No. 8: Women's Mobilization Targets the Agencies and Apparatuses of the State

At first sight this thesis seems paradoxical. On the one hand it was suggested that women's politics is a new politics that is distinct from men's
politics (see thesis no. 6) (Jelin 1987:50). On the other, feminists argue that
the domain of male politics *par excellence* is the state, which is seen as patriarchal and alien (Bunster-Burotto 1986).[4] But these arguments cannot negate
the practical necessity of addressing the state. In the first place, a great part
of women's mobilization seeks the kind of material resources that secure
family survival, and the state is often the main guarantor of their provision
(see thesis no.3). Consequently women's demand-making is often concentrated in the state as the provider of public services and public utilities. In
the second place, women's material struggles will inevitably be bound by
legal and institutional constraints, which often catalyze the translation of
material into overtly political demands, and it is important to note that, in
most countries of the continent, mass mobilization by women arose "while
institution building took place in the political system as a whole" (Boschi
1987:201). Finally, the massive presence of the state in Latin American societies means that new political identities, including those of women (see thesis no.6), are "constituted at the political level" in large degree (Moisés 1982)
and therefore in recurrent and intimate interaction with the state. Consequently, women's mobilization cannot (and should not) be conceived as
merely concerned with and confined to the relationships of civil society.
There is ample evidence for these assertions in the urban movements,
which are often a direct response to state policies.

In Mexico, the "transformist" project of the revolutionary state and its
pervasive influence in civil society have tended to strengthen these tendencies (Foweraker 1993). The Salinas administration, for instance, originally identified the *colonias populares* (working-class neighborhoods),
women, and youth as its priority constituencies as it attempted to combat
middle-class and popular discontent in the cities and harness community
participation to its own purposes (González de la Rocha and Escobar Latapí 1991). In the subsequent process of "institution-building" the former
CNOP was the sector most deeply affected by the process of administrative reform, and the Programa Nacional de Solidaridad (National Solidarity Program, PRONASOL) became emblematic of the regime's social
policies (Cornelius, Craig, and Fox 1994).[5] In effect, PRONASOL was de-

ployed to assuage the impact of the administration's economic reforms as well as to (re)generate community and political support for the PRI and the government. It is said that women have played an important part in PRONASOL programs in both city and countryside (Mujeres en Solidaridad), but very little is known of the net impact of the administrative reforms on women's mobilization or, more particularly, of the ways that the institutional initiatives (and the tensions between them) have affected the emergence and coherence of local women's leadership on the urban periphery. Some groups may have been able to achieve greater institutional purchase and material improvement as a result of the reforms, whereas others will certainly have been split and marginalized by government policies. This appears to be an important area for future research.

Thesis No. 9: Women's Mobilization Expands Citizenship Rights

Women's mobilization is understood as an integral part of a more general struggle for citizenship rights, and women's demands are increasingly stated in terms of rights (Foweraker 1995a). In Latin America, and in Mexico in particular, the struggle for universal rights mounts an automatic challenge to the particularism of clientelist and patrimonial power relations (Foweraker 1993). Women's rights are universal in this respect, in the Enlightenment tradition, and are therefore integral to the rights of modern citizenship, and women's mobilization also reinforces the struggle for other universal rights such as labor rights and human rights. Moreover, women's mobilization automatically implies their right to act outside of the domestic sphere, and their entry into the public sphere is essential if they are to claim in practice the rights they may enjoy in principle (compare thesis no.7). In entering the public sphere for the first time, women are demanding recognition of their rights as citizens (and rejecting representation by men, whether as spouses, neighborhood leaders, or politicians) (Safa 1990:355).

But there are real doubts as to whether women's mobilization has succeeded in vindicating and securing women's rights as such. As implied by thesis no. 7, "countries remaining under military rule in the 1970s postponed the reconsideration of women's legal equality" (Lavrin 1993:530), with the significant exception of Peru, where a native version of the Equal Rights Amendment (ERA) of the United States became part of the Constitution of 1979 (Bourque 1985). But things changed with the achievement of democracy. In addition, mass-based women's movements in Brazil, Chile, and Nicaragua were at least temporarily successful in extending their rights as political parties began to take up women's issues and include them on their political platforms. Brazil set up a National Council on Women's

Rights after 1985, but women's demands only found a very faint reflection in the Constitution of 1985. Argentina signed the UN Convention on the Elimination of All Forms of Discrimination Against Women, ratified a law on nursery education, legalized divorce, and reformed the so-called *potestad marital* (marital power); even so the Madres of the Plaza de Mayo were frustrated by the failure to prosecute most of those responsible for the Dirty War, and debates on domestic violence and abortion soon subsided. Uruguay passed equal pay laws and extended child-care facilities, and the long battle for equality before the law was finally won in Paraguay in 1992. Last, and in some ways least (given the level of expectations), the mainstream political parties in Chile paid lip service to women's equality but soon switched their policy emphasis to "support for the family"—despite the continuing proliferation of women's organizations. Thus, although it is true that the plethora of councils and special ministerial offices in these and other countries, such as Costa Rica and Venezuela, "helped to highlight the new political role of women" (Lavrin 1993:540), doubts remained over the depth or durability of women's newly won rights.

In Mexico, women's mobilization plays a key part in the broad struggle for civil and political rights, inside and outside the electoral arena. Mexican women won complete civil equality before the law in 1927 and secured the vote in 1953. Hence women's mobilization, like much other mobilization in Mexico, often aims to fill legal forms with a real political content and serves to strengthen the claim for *sufragio efectivo* (full suffrage) in particular. It is argued in the literature that specific social movements at specific times can sometimes color the preoccupations and define the demands and goals of social mobilization writ large (Snow and Benford 1992; Tarrow 1989). This was true of the civil rights movement in the United States of the 1960s and true in some degree of the Coordinadora Nacional del Movimiento Urbano Popular (National Coordinator of the Urban Popular Movement, CONAMUP) and the Coordinadora Nacional de Trabajadores de la Educación (National Coordinating Committee of Education Workers, CNTE) in the Mexico of the 1970s and 1980s. It seems clear that women's majority participation in these movements gave a special impetus to renewed claims on land rights, labor rights, and electoral rights, and women's mobilization has clearly contributed to these struggles and to the vindication of civil rights more generally (Foweraker 1995b).

Thesis No. 10: Women's Mobilization Extends Political Representation

The historical evidence in support of this thesis is not strong. Women won the suffrage in Latin America between 1929 (Ecuador) and 1961 (Paraguay), with fourteen nations extending the vote to women between

1945 and 1961 (Lavrin 1993). But the timing of these extensions did not correspond to overall levels of economic development, still less to degrees of female literacy or the strength of women's mobilization (Jaquette 1980). In Mexico, women's suffrage was delayed until forty years after the Revolution because it was thought that a majority of women opposed the secularization of the state and other projects of the ruling party, and women were granted the vote in Peru in 1955 because it was thought that their "conservative" vote could guarantee a conservative successor to Manuel Odría (Chaney 1973). Even after the vote was won for women, significantly fewer women than men were registered to vote across the continent, and only a tiny number of women were ever elected to high office (Jaquette 1980). The democratic transitions of the 1980s did little or nothing to alter this picture, with very few women elected to congress at either state or federal level in Brazil, fewer yet elected in Chile,[6] and not a single woman elected to the national legislature of Uruguay in 1985. In Nicaragua, in 1990, Violeta Chamorro became the first woman to be elected president of any Latin American country.

It has been argued that the women's movements provide a litmus test for the fate of social movements following the democratic transitions of recent years (Safa 1990). The auguries were good. At the moment of the plebiscite in Chile, a Woman's Command coordinated the attempts of party activists to reach women voters, and despite the conservative pattern of female voting, 52 percent of women voted against the prolongation of the Pinochet dictatorship. But following the transition, the political parties simply set up "women's sections" that were mere appendages to the main party organizations, and politics returned to "normal." In Argentina the National Women's Agency of the Ministry of Social Security was correctly seen as a palliative measure, and women's political careers continued to be tied to welfare initiatives such as the National Food Program and the National Literacy Campaign (*supermadre* revisited). In Brazil, where the women's movements had shown most political promise, their mobilization declined, and women's demand-making was reduced to pressure group activity. In fact, "ironically, the immediate effect of the return to 'democratic' politics was a fall in women's political activity, as male-dominated political parties and trade unions took center stage and national and local governments moved into areas in which women had worked" (Fisher 1993: 2). The inescapable conclusion is that nowhere did women's mobilization secure broader representation or more institutionalized participation of an enduring kind.[7]

In Mexico there has been no democratic transition of the kind experienced in the Southern Cone countries, and for many years Mexico's record of female participation in political life remained one of the poorest in Latin America (Staudt this volume; cf. Craske this volume). The federal participation rate was seen to improve with the change of administration in December 1994, with women now holding 17 percent of the seats in the legislature and three cabinet posts, and there is some evidence that changing sites of elite recruitment, from public to private educational establishments, is favoring women in some degree (Camp this volume). But the present participation rate at the municipal level is still significantly below the Latin American average (4.2 percent for Mexico compared to 6.0 percent for Latin America), with only 82 women mayors out of a total of 2,412 across the country in early 1998 (Massolo this volume). Thus, there is little possibility of creating an upward flow of recruitment from the municipalities and regions to the federal level, and where women have succeeded in gaining access to the higher echelons of the executive, legislature, or judiciary, they have tended to occupy those posts with the least influence over key decisions (Camp this volume; Martínez and Incháustegui this volume). The PRD may have shown one way forward by imposing a 30 percent minimum female quota for party lists and so increasing the proportion of women PRD deputies.

Yet, the proportion of women elected or appointed to political posts may not provide a full measure of the political impact of women's mobilization in Mexico. Thus, it might be argued that women's mobilization achieves greater autonomy for women's organizations (and organizations with a female majority) and that such autonomy is a condition of effective representation in a corporatist and clientelist system like Mexico's. It might further be argued that the struggle for (universal) rights (see thesis no. 9) weakens the mechanisms of clientelist control that act to deny effective representation within the political system. This increasing resistance to "vertical" controls was evident after the 1985 earthquake in Mexico City, where urban movements and neighborhood associations developed their own reconstruction projects that the government was sometimes forced to recognize and implement (Ramírez Saiz 1987b). There is strong evidence that women not only mobilized around these projects but also assumed the leadership of the new movements, with some of the women leaders subsequently winning electoral posts (Bennett this volume; Tarrés this volume). However, there are clearly no guarantees that increased mobilization can achieve greater or more effective representation. The present renewed combination of economic crisis and austerity policies may well mean that the bulk of women's mobilization will again be oriented to material demands and the defense of basic living conditions on the urban periphery.

Notes

1. It has been observed that women are similarly segregated within academic analysis, with women's issues addressed in a separate section or chapter of many

academic publications (Corcoran-Nantes 1993). Thus, the question of gender is recognized but not integrated into much of mainstream social science.

2. Approximately one third of the 20,000 people murdered and "disappeared" in Argentina between 1976 and 1983 were women (Fisher 1993).

3. A more radical view suggests that it is the conservative view of the mother as the pillar of society and of the home as the core of social stability that first makes the private "political" (Boyle 1993). Indeed, Poder Femenino's invasion of the public by the private during the campaign of the *cacerolas* in Chile clearly preceded that of the Madres of the Plaza de Mayo (demonstrating, if such demonstration were needed, that women's mobilization is not necessarily progressive). Boyle goes on to observe that, by the mid-1980s, it was the women of the poor urban barrios of Santiago who were banging their pots in unison, so consciously subverting this symbol of right-wing mobilization.

4. It is further observed, recalling the argument of thesis no.7, that "military regimes exhibit the impulse of the state to secure and defend the patriarchal structure and the privileged status of 'masculinity' more blatantly than do other authoritarian states" (Bunster-Burotto 1986:300).

5. As a result of the reform process the CNOP was transformed first into the UNE (Citizens on the Move) and then into the Frente Nacional de Organizaciones y Ciudadanos (National Front of Organizations and Citizens, FNOC), and the new Movimiento Popular Urbano Territorial (Urban Territorial Popular Movement, MT) was designed to undermine the autonomous urban movements and absorb their "natural leaders." A primary objective of these institutional reforms was to separate the urban movements in the MT from the citizens, professionals, and "new social movements" in the FNOC. The MT was therefore intended to focus on the problems of the urban periphery, with the equally new Sociedad Urbana concentrating on popular organizations in the major cities (Craske 1994).

6. In 1992 there were seven women out of 120 deputies and three women out of forty-four senators in Chile.

7. One exception was Argentina's imposition of a 30 percent minimum of women candidates on party slates (the Ley de Cupos).

❁ 5 ❁

Supermadre Revisited

Elsa M. Chaney

Because my book, *Supermadre: Women in Politics in Latin America,* was one of the first works on political life and women in the region, I have been asked to take a critical backward look at my main theses—ideas that have had a certain resonance in the field—to see to what extent they might hold true today. I should add that as the author of the work, I do not entirely agree with some of these theses!

First published in 1979 by the University of Texas Press, the book is out of print in English, but a second printing in Spanish recently was issued by the Fondo de Cultura Económica in Mexico (Chaney 1993). The 167 interviews on which the study is based were carried out in the late 1960s in Peru and Chile among the first generation of women in elective office at the national and municipal levels and of women in high bureaucratic posts. The study included the entire universe of women in office at that time in Peru and a purposive sample of about one-sixth of the women in formal political and bureaucratic positions in Chile. Peru and Chile were chosen for their contrasting political cultures: the former still a traditional society where women were just emerging; the latter a society in which women already were highly visible in the universities and the professions.

The principal thesis of *Supermadre* is simple: Many women at that time thought that voting was a civic duty—an appropriate, even obligatory, activity for women. Far fewer women and men were convinced that women should run for office.[1] The majority of those who did so envisioned their role in electoral politics, and even their presence in the bureaucracy, as an extension of their motherhood role in the family to the larger family of the *municipio* or the nation.

The first generation of women who sought political and bureaucratic posts in any numbers were encouraged to become active in the atmosphere of hope generated by the figures of Presidents Fernando Belaúnde in Peru and Eduardo Frei in Chile. However, these women tended to legitimate their political activism in their own eyes, and in the eyes of the public, as doing what women had always done: mothering, now in a larger arena. This stance steered many of them into roles traditionally reserved to women in the private sphere: health, education, welfare, care of children and the elderly, the arts, and culture. Eva Perón, in charge of social welfare in her husband's government, perfectly articulated the *Supermadre* thesis:

> In this great house of the Motherland, I am just like any other woman in the innumerable houses of my people. Just like all of them I rise early thinking about my husband and about my children . . . and I go about all day thinking about them and a good part of the night. . . . [T]hen instead of dreams, marvelous projects occur to me. . . . It's that I so truly feel myself the mother of my people. (Perón 1951:313–314; my translation)

Some women in the bureaucracy did not occupy fields stereotyped as "feminine": Twenty percent of those in my study were running important departments (but below the ministerial or subministerial level) dealing with budget and taxes, planning, census, and statistics.[2] Bureaucratic women, however, also tended to justify their presence in terms of the *Supermadre* image: Women, they said, are more honest, more hardworking, less "political" than men.

Many women at that time—even those who had chosen a public career—viewed politics as a "dirty business." Some in the first generation of women in public life had worked in securing the vote for women, and they reiterated one of the main tenets of the woman suffrage movements: that women would "purify" the political process. A high official in Chile injected a humorous note into her comment:

> One advantage in being a woman in public service is that we really are left out of the *politiquería* that goes on. Whenever you telephone a man who holds a public post, he is sure to be away from his desk; of course, he's out in a corridor somewhere talking politics with the other men. A woman official feels out of place doing this. She prefers to go to her office, sit at her desk, and do her work. (Chaney 1979:135)

My reflections in this chapter center around two questions: First, what difference did it make that women defined their public roles in terms of stereotypical images of the feminine? And second, does the *Supermadre* image still prevail?

I believe that one consequence was the great number of women who found the *macho* rough and tumble of politics more than they had bargained for and who withdrew after one term in office. In times of crisis or in special periods (as when women received the vote), women moved into the public sphere. When the emergency was over, they and the men expected them to "go home." A *regidora* (councilwoman) who planned to withdraw told me:

> Let me be honest with you about my feelings. I go to meetings when the party needs numbers, but not often otherwise because meetings seem to me a waste of time. I stood as a candidate because the party wanted my name— but I don't have any ambitions. I find this one experience very entertaining, even though I was against becoming active for a long time. But this will be it. (Chaney 1979:137)

A former woman senator in Peru, where senate sessions were held in the evenings, told me that she had to endure constant gibes—a principal reason she decided not to run for reelection: "What does your Señor think about your being out at night?" "Does your Señor like sleeping alone?" (Chaney 1979:144). Still others were candidates in spite of themselves. In Peru, being elected *concejal* (councillor) depends on the percentage of the vote one's party commands in the district and one's place on the ticket. One reluctant candidate told me: "I wasn't expecting even to be a candidate. Then the party put me No. 6 on the list, which was rather risky as it turned out, because all up to and including No. 8 were elected" (Chaney 1979:103).

Because of this ambivalence and reluctance to stand for reelection, as each entry "wave" of elected officials receded, only a few stalwarts were left on the beach. As a consequence, not enough women remained to create a critical mass of women officials. In my study, only seven Chileans and Peruvians in elective offices (out of ninety-six) professed interest in a political future.[3]

Another consequence of the *Supermadre* bent of so many women: Such an approach was not necessarily positive (later, I will specify under what conditions it may be very positive). If women really believed or believe that running a country is like running a house, they're in trouble.

Defining a public career in terms of the *Supermadre* image also correlated with a strong tendency toward conservatism. Not many women in the survey talked about deep structural change in the economy and polity. Thirty-five percent of the sample who advocated no structural changes and only limited improvements in terms of their own mandates were classified as "housewives" in their approach to public service. Another 58 percent who mentioned at least one structural change and had a broader vision of their mandate were classified as "reformists." Only 7 percent of the total spoke in terms of deep political and economic change and saw their roles in those terms; these were classified as "revolutionaries." A job description such as the following put an interviewee in the revolutionary category: "My reason for joining the ——— Ministry was not only the possibility of applying a new method of social service but also of motivating a group of very influential people who, in turn, have the possibility of influencing the masses. This post, directly and indirectly, gives me the opportunity to influence many" (Chaney 1979:149).

What about the positives and negatives of the *Supermadre* vision in public service today? The idea—with a somewhat different focus—has endured: In recent times scholars who work on women's social movements, notably Alvarez (1990a), Churchryk (1989a), and Jaquette (1994), write about women who justify their activism in terms of "militant motherhood" and "subversive motherhood."

My own view now is that I was perhaps too negative in judging the *Supermadre* approach, influenced as I was by the idealism and radicalism of the 1960s in the United States. In the last chapter of my study, however, I did attempt to show that it might be unwise to try to change women's approach and that in the future politics itself might undergo changes that would bring so-called feminine issues, then considered quite marginal and unimportant, to the center of the political arena. I discussed the following questions:

1. Why try to change women's preference for the important "feminine" fields in which they were engaged? Even if it were possible to convince Latin American women that they should leave feminine-stereotyped fields, who then would carry out these important tasks? Were those who found my approach in *Supermadre* "anti-feminist" too much influenced by the almost exclusive concentration of women's liberation in the United States on gaining entrance for women into "masculine" fields? In my study there never was any question that women who wanted to go in other directions should be encouraged to do so. But what about the women who did *not* want to go in another direction?

2. Would it not be more logical to challenge women in public life and the professions to reform, rethink, revamp, and recreate "their" fields? In Latin America, women in the 1960s and 1970s were largely in charge of so-called female professions: They taught in the universities, the medical auxiliary fields, social work, psychology and allied professions, the arts, and literature. Often they were the heads of the university departments in these fields. When they moved into the bureaucracy, they could move up and also be in charge: Men generally had other agendas and viewed these professions and posts as female terrain; in contrast to the United States, men occupied only the very top positions.[4]

3. Finally, I asked whether these fields would always be marginal. Writing in 1970, I tried to show that the family and motherhood had a particular importance for Latin American women. As we moved from an industrializing to an information age, women's values (there was never any implication that men could not also hold such values) would move to the center of political discourse:

> A [new] view is beginning to be expressed today within the feminist movement: that without the values for which women stand it may quite simply be impossible to preserve a viable society. Men generally have played, in western culture at least, the aggressive roles of explorer, innovator, entrepreneur. Women have played an affective, relational role. That is not necessarily good if it leads to the *supermadre* approach alluded to many times in this study. Both roles are needed. Men's roles have been overly emphasized, and to bring a needed balance into society, women must begin to play a part. To do so would require them to modernize their ways of working and to harmonize traditional feminine values with attitudes of achievement and universalism. (Chaney 1979:164)

What I defined, in the terms of those times, as "feminine" were those issues

> crucial to [women's] lives [and] . . . related to the family, children and the old, food prices and inflation, peace, moral questions. . . . Such issues are, however, usually defined by the male power structure either as "non-political" ("male" issues revolve around questions of authority, power, war, arms, monopoly over resources, economic policy) or "conservative." (Chaney 1979:164)

What women needed to do, or so it seemed to me, was to hang onto "their" issues for dear life and to note that even in 1979 some of "their" issues—abortion, equal pay for equal work, daycare, even sharing the housework—were beginning to enter mainstream politics (Chaney 1979:164).

The final question asked in my study was whether or not women would finally begin to enter the political arena:

> Will women seek political power in increasing numbers as they become aware that their contribution is essential to the finding of solutions to the great problems perplexing humankind? Will women finally be admitted to the political arena as full-fledged power contenders, or will men simply co-opt women's issues and attempt to solve them on a masculine "power" basis

(as they have largely done with population control, and as they appear to be doing in the quest for solutions to the problem of world hunger)? (Chaney 1979:165)

I believe the answer to this question still is pending. Women's entry into the formal political arena in Latin America, after some gains, appears again to be waning, despite the opening to democracy in many countries. Moreover, many of those who entered political life in the period about which I wrote are now the older generation. The answer will need to come from their political daughters.

Notes

1. Most Latin American countries gave women the right "to elect and to be elected" only after World War II. In Chile, national woman suffrage came in 1949; in Peru, in 1955.

2. In 1969, only four women held cabinet-level posts in all of Latin America. However, there were (and are) many women at lower levels in government bureaucracies all over the world, doing extremely responsible, often highly technical work.

3. This was a worldwide phenomenon: In the political ferment of the post–World War II period in France, for example, there were 40 women in the assembly of 630 members and 23 in the senate; by 1970, the numbers had dwindled to 8 and 5. In Italy, there were 45 women in the immediate postwar parliament; by 1970, only 25.

4. After World War II, for example, men in the United States moved into such feminine fields as primary teaching and social work and soon moved up to head schools and social agencies, even when the bulk of the workers remained female.

PART TWO

Women in
the Mexican
Political Arena

❀ 6 ❀

Women and Power in Mexico: The Forgotten Heritage, 1880–1954

Carmen Ramos Escandón

The current debate on the characteristics of women's movements in Mexico and their contribution to a strong civil society with more egalitarian forms of political participation has failed to consider, until now, the historical precedents of women's participation and their contributions to the formation of a polity in which women have gained the full rights of citizenship. In this chapter I review three instances during which women opened for themselves a space in the political life of Mexico. The effort to recover those historical events is needed in order to construct a feminist memory capable of correcting the notion that feminism and the political activity of women in Mexico are of recent vintage.

The chapter covers the developments in the complex relations between women and political power in Mexico for a period that spans over fifty years. The three periods and developments I have selected are (1) the relationship between women and the power structure in the Porfiriato, reflected in the legislative actions affecting women's family rights between 1880 and 1917; (2) the spontaneous political participation and the breakdown of barriers between public and private spaces in the armed conflict of the Revolution; and (3) the coalition of women's organizations with diverse political orientations that joined to form the Frente Unico Pro Derechos de la Mujer (Sole Front for Women's Rights, FUPDM) during the decade of the 1930s. In each case and in each of the different periods we find innovative relationships between women and the state and new forms of political participation that respond to the specific interests of women.

The Liberal Oligarchic State, or
the Preeminence of the "Good Families"

Political life in Mexico during the government of Porfirio Díaz has traditionally been described as the government of an economic and political
elite. Political life was restricted to a few, and the elitist control of the political structure was consolidated and perpetuated not only through economic control but also, and perhaps more effectively, by the systematic exclusion of new political groups for whom there were no channels for
participation. The rarefied political space of the Porfiriato was controlled
almost exclusively by a small minority whose interests were frequently
managed as a family matter. Politics did not appear to be regimented and
organized as a space that was separate from the family interests.

The strong interconnection of the Porfirian elite is well documented, and
if the family is a channel of oligarchic power, what we are interested in
demonstrating is that, beyond the web of power of the "good families," the
family organization that was considered the basic social unit was legally
defined during this period so as to promote a single line of inheritance and
to regulate the rights of women. The legislation implemented beginning in
1870 substantially modified the rights of women within the family and is
crucial to explain how the Porfirian state helped to establish a family paradigm in which women found their personal rights diminished. The political paradigm of the elitist liberal oligarchic state featured a clear economic
and political inequality. However, the relationship between social and political inequality and gender inequality is less well known or clear. The key
to deciphering this relationship can be found in the reordering of women's
family rights implemented during the Porfiriato.

If we consider that the first form of relation between the individual and
organized political power is the relation with the state apparatus and its
concrete forms of expression in the regulation of individual life, the reforms to the family codes take on a different significance. To the extent
that the state defines and also guarantees the individual rights of a person, a modification in the regulation of those rights implies a different relation between the individual and the state apparatus.

In this sense, toward the end of the last century in Mexico we find a
state still bent on legitimizing itself as a power structure that can also
guarantee and define individual rights. At that time the Mexican state was
attempting to establish the forms that would allow it to exercise an effective control over civil society. The well-defined Porfirian discourse on the
importance of the family as the basic cell of the social body and of the
submission of women within it finds its fullest explanation within this
context. The redefinition of women's rights within the family in the Porfiriato is not an accident. The curtailing of women's marital property

rights and the submission of women in the domestic sphere are concomitant with the political project of social control.

The first form of regulation of social relationships occurs in the family environment. In effect, the reforms to the civil code enacted in 1870 and expanded in 1884 reduced a woman's personal rights upon entering into a marriage in that she lost her capacity to contract, litigate, alienate her property, or be represented in a trial. Moreover, separation—without divorce—of the spouses in cases of adultery stipulated a series of requirements that were clearly different and unequal based simply on whether the spouse involved was the man or the woman. Adultery by a woman was a cause for dissolution of the marriage in all cases, whereas adultery by a man was cause for divorce only if it was committed in the family residence, if the lover became a concubine, or if the lover mistreated the wife (1879 Civil Code Art. 241–242; 1884 Civil Code Art. 227–228).

This consolidation of male rights at the expense of female rights in marriage is based on a broad political project that recognizes the family as the basic social unit on which the entire social apparatus rests. By regulating the rights of married women, the liberal oligarchic state subsumed women's individual rights and restricted them, making the family the first sphere in which the state exercised control over women, be it through the father or the husband. The regulation of women's rights within the family reinforced and redefined a turn-of-the-century Mexican paradigm of female behavior that included submission, the idealization of maternity, and the repeated equating of femininity with a disinterest in political life or in politics. Most sociologists of the period agreed in describing the "brazenness" (read boldness and initiative) of lower-class women as a form of contempt for good manners and for the ideal of feminine behavior.

Of all the forms of "brazenness," none was more criticized than an interest in political life and action. Writing in *Revista Positiva* in 1909, Horacio Barreda, the son of the founder of the National Preparatory School, declared that feminism, by preaching the equality of rights for men and women, was a "theory that threatened to uproot the very foundation of the family and of society" (1909:8). From his perspective feminism was aberrant to the extent that it was a struggle for political rights. Francisco Bulnes persisted in the judgments critical of feminism when he wrote in 1916 that

Feminism has penetrated in Mexico like a disturbing auxiliary force. It is well known in Latin countries that only unattractive women, desperate widows and indigent dressmakers, when they are susceptible to hysterical emotions, devote themselves to social causes. A well or only moderately educated woman, gifted with a modest or great talent, poor, old, ugly or simply embittered is a great social danger if her energies are not employed in religious or charitable activities. These reformist women are the generators of a hatred against society more dangerous than that of a Barcelonian anarchist. (1916: 142; my translation)

Many other examples could be cited, but rather than highlighting the antifeminist refrain of Porfirian discourse, the point I wish to underscore in this first period is the following: Both in the discourse and in the legislative regulation of the relations between women and public power, women suffered the effects of the state through regulations that reinforced their submission and control. Women were excluded from politics even to the extent of being denied access to the most basic form of political participation, the vote, and were subjected to forms of control by the state over which they had no say. Women were outside of formal politics but not outside the exercise of the state's power.

Off to War, or the Subversion of Everyday Life

The Mexican Revolution is another significant moment in the relationship between women and the state. Official discourse about the revolution excluded women. The Revolution, viewed as the founding myth of the Mexican state, led to the organization and constitution of a state that does not include the differences in the forms of participation of men and women. Although it has been stated that the Mexican Revolution was not a revolution for women (see Macías 1974, 1980), anyone who examines their situation during the Porfiriato and compares it with the 1920s cannot help but notice an enormous difference and cannot ignore the perception that women themselves had of the importance of the Revolution, especially for the generation that moved from the gun to the desk.[1]

The relationship between women and power was different at different times and in the different regions of a Mexico in revolt (1910–1920), but it is clear that the struggle itself modified the gender-based roles and spaces, subverting everyday life and erasing the boundaries between the spaces of public action and private life. Everyday life was subverted by the war itself, but the space of female power was also expanded and redefined in the heat of the struggle and by the effect that the collapse of the state apparatus and of the hierarchical power structures had on individuals, families, and groups. Women participated in the countryside, in cities, and in all the revolutionary factions, but the forms of participation varied by region, class, and political times.

The revolutionary *caudillos* (chiefs) had different attitudes toward women, most of them spontaneous and at an immediate level. Thus, Pancho Villa had to tolerate the presence of *soldaderas* (female soldiers) in his army because otherwise the soldiers refused to fight (Lau and Ramos

1993:44; Knight 1990:143). In the area controlled by Emiliano Zapata the daily life of the peasant relied on the presence of women, and it is in this area where we might say that the tasks of the revolution and of domesticity were most mixed and joined (Cano 1988:23; Lau and Ramos 1993:42; Womack 1969:167). For Venustiano Carranza, on the other hand, women represented a space for legitimization. By recognizing pensions and ex-combatant rights for many women, Carranza sanctioned the participation of women in the Revolution. The fundamental change that Carranza made in family law was another way of integrating the concerns of women into the revolutionary program, as it had been women themselves who had expressed at the Feminist Congress of Yucatán in 1916 the need for new regulations in marital relations based on the sexual needs of women. Hermila Galindo, a leading feminist, took to the 1916 Constituent Congress the demand that the vote was a right that women could and should have. Although the congress refused to consider women's suffrage, this does not negate the fact that women participated actively in the Revolution, both in a spontaneous personal manner as well as in the many women's clubs and organizations that were formed during those years.

In the subsequent generation, Mexican women had greater visibility in the political, economic, and cultural life. Beyond the examples of the exceptional women, the tone with regard to the political life of women in the 1920s was given by the increase of women in the labor force, in the newly created government agencies, in teaching, and, above all, in the women's organizations that fought for political rights. Women were particularly visible in those government agencies that are a continuation of traditional female tasks, welfare and education.[2] In terms of political participation, for women in Mexico the 1920s were the first opportunity to participate in electoral activities as candidates for public office.[3] Women's associations in which the common goal was the struggle for women's rights also appeared at that time (Macías 1979).

In terms of women who stood for elected political office, the case of Elvia Carrillo Puerto is the most important. The sister of a progressive governor of Yucatán, Elvia Carrillo Puerto is an example of a new type of woman, modern and innovative in her life and in her personal and political attitudes. Widowed at twenty-one, she remarried and then divorced, surviving as a rural schoolteacher. In her political life she was likewise innovative, founding in Mérida in 1919 the Rita Cetina Gutiérrez feminist league, an association of women devoted to promoting the political participation of women and to supporting local candidates for government positions. The league also promoted educational activities, rewarding women who participated in the literacy campaigns (Soto 1990:87). Her political participation was not limited to promoting other candidates, and she, along with Beatriz Peniche, Raquel Dzib, and Guadalupe Lara stood as candidates to the local legislature of Mérida (Cano 1991:283). In 1924, when Carrillo Puerto's brother was assassinated and she was forced to leave her elected position in Yucatán, she moved to San Luis Potosí. There, along with Hermilia Zamarrón, she ran for state office and won, although her victory was not recognized by the electoral college of the local Chamber of Deputies and thus she was never sworn in (Morton 1962:10).

The presence of Alejandra Kollontai, a socialist feminist and Soviet ambassador in Mexico, also served to motivate the feminist organizations, and Mexican feminists frequently debated and exchanged ideas with her (Tuñón 1992:28). The Consejo Feminista Mexicano (Mexican Feminist Council, CFM) and the Mexican section of the Pan American League for the Advancement of Women are examples of outstanding women's organizations of that period. The council was founded in 1923 by Elena Torres and Refugio (Cuca) García, both members of the Mexican Communist Party from its inception in 1919. The CFM was intended to be a broad organization orienting the women's movement toward socialism (Tuñón 1992:26).

The Mexican section of the Pan American League, founded by Margarita Robles de Mendoza, sought to promote the civil rights of women and to establish contacts with women's organizations in other countries. Representatives of the Mexican section of the Pan American League and of the CFM attended the Pan American Women's Conference held in Baltimore in April, 1922, and in 1924 the first congress of the Pan American League of Women was organized (see Nava de Ruiz Sánchez 1922).

By the end of the 1920s the issue of women's suffrage had become part of the political agenda of the political parties. In its 1929 statement of principles, the Partido Nacional Revolucionario (National Revolutionary Party, PNR) included the need to stimulate the access of Mexican women to the activities of civic life. For its part, the Partido Nacional Antireeleccionista (Antireelectionist National Party), which ran José Vasconcelos for president in the 1929 elections, included women's suffrage in its political platform and had a large number of women supporters, including the prominent Antonieta Rivas Mercado, Vasconcelo's close collaborator (Skirius 1978:124).

Although the 1920s were important in the participation of women in political life, the beginning of the women's movement in the country was difficult and was plagued by unsuccessful attempts by women to participate individually or as a group in the national political arena. In the following decade the organized presence of women became more significant. The most important moment for feminism and the organized women's movement was the creation of the FUPDM. Structured in 1935 as a broad organization to bring together various women's groups, the FUPDM eventually incorporated over 50,000 members grouped in eighty-eight women's organizations throughout the country. The FUPDM fought openly for official recognition of the political rights of women, particularly suffrage. However, this demand was not exclusive to the FUPDM. In effect, the political parties had already included the suffragist demand in their political platforms, and although they agreed in recognizing the importance of women in political life, the differences concerning the form that women's political participation was to take were significant.

Although the militants of the PNR and of the Communist Party had a common origin in the Antireelectionist Party and the Vasconcelos campaign, they had important differences that divided the women's movement in Mexico during these years. The women members of the Mexican Communist Party, who frequently followed the guidelines of the sixth congress of the Communist Party of the Soviet Union, categorically opposed an autonomous women's movement and proposed instead a position that did not recognize a gender struggle within the class struggle. In other words, they held that the central struggle is the class struggle, not the gender struggle, and accused the women of the PNR of fostering a bourgeois struggle because they placed women's interests above class interests. For their part, the members and supporters of the PNR fought to gain a political space within the ranks of their party and for recognition of their specific demands. The party leaders and, particularly, the governments of the Maximato[4] opened some areas to capitalize on the political action of women. This accounts for the PNR pronouncements in favor of women's suffrage and their sponsorship of the national congresses of women workers and peasants held in October 1931, January 1932, November 1933, and September 1934. At these congresses, both the Communist women and the women of the PNR expressed their ideas concerning women, stressing different aspects. The Communists spoke about the situation of women workers and peasants and proposed specific solutions to improve their situation, whereas the militants of the PNR chose to present papers pertaining to women's suffrage and to the need to have an organization specifically for women.

The congresses reflected the political situation of the period, and therefore an analysis of them helps us understand the relationship between the organized women's movement and the political situation of the country in general. Thus, the 1931 congress was clearly anticlerical. Participating groups included the Mexican Anticlerical League, the Liberal League of Reformist Women, the Feminist League of Yucatán, and the Revolutionary Feminist Party. Participating women insisted that men attending the conference should have a limited role and that they not express their opinions out loud, so as not to impress the delegates (Ríos Cárdenas 1942:39). The congress came out in favor of the creation of the Confederación Femenil Mexicana (Mexican Women's Confederation) to face "those problems that are exclusively their own" (*El Universal*, October 8, 1931).

The effects of this first congress were important, and in January 1932 the PNR responded to women's demands for suffrage by stating that "the Constitution does not deny a woman's right to vote, but considering that the State wants to introduce women gradually to civic life, it is not advisable to precipitate this matter" (Ríos Cárdenas 1942:57). In the opinion of the PNR, women needed to be incorporated gradually to civic life so they could be divested of their "inherent religiosity and prepare politically." These notions provoked the reaction of PNR women, who through María Ríos Cárdenas argued that if it was true that women could be influenced by the candidates, the same was true of men, that is, it was not only women who could be politically manipulated. She also noted the inherent injustice in the fact that the right to vote had been granted to men without restrictions, even to illiterates and delinquents, whereas even university-educated women were denied suffrage (Ríos Cárdenas 1942:74).

The Second National Congress of Women Workers and Peasants in November 1933 was better attended, but the differences between the Communists and members of the PNR continued. The Communists insisted on the need to engage first in a class struggle, not a gender struggle, and criticized the isolation of the PNR women. The PNR women, for their part, resorted to the organization of parallel congresses and, in 1934, called the Third National Congress of Women Workers and Peasants in Guadalajara, Jalisco, where the PNR women had greater support. This congress featured the call for support of single mothers, punishment for men who abused women, easier divorce proceedings, and, above all, the creation of jobs for women in general and for prostitutes in particular. The most serious rivalries in this congress were between the PNR women, who were accused of supporting the government, and the Communists, who accused their adversaries of carrying firearms and other weapons in the sessions (Ríos Cárdenas 1942:118). This rivalry was finally overcome when the permanent commission responsible for organizing the fourth congress in Chihuahua in 1935 was formed both by Communist and PNR women. This tactical alliance marked the beginning of a collaboration among women that was well used by the ensuing FUPDM.

United We Will Win, or
the Sole Front for Women's Rights

The rise of Lázaro Cárdenas to power in 1934 represented a change in the form of political confrontation in Mexico. Cárdenas sought to increase his political support and, at the same time, eliminate as much as possible the factional confrontation that had characterized the Maximato governments. In this new partisan climate the organized women's movement was one area in which *cardenismo* sought support, needed to build on the basis of a stronger link with the masses and to secure a vertical control of them. Within this scheme, organized groups, including the women's movement, were a constant concern for the Cárdenas regime.

For its part, acting within the context of a broad mass mobilization, the women's movement moved from confrontation among its different groups to cooperation and the formation of a unified front (Tuñón 1992:53). In 1935, Communist women and the women of the PNR joined to form an organization that could represent them as militant women rather than as members of political parties. This organization was the FUPDM. Officially constituted October 11, 1935, it fell within the context of the broad fronts being created in other parts of the world, although on the local level it also reflected the politics of masses favored by Cárdenas.[5] This new organization united feminists from the left and right, liberals, Catholics, and women from the women's section of the PNR, *callistas* and *cardenistas* (supporters and followers of Presidents Plutarco Elías Calles and Lázaro Cárdenas, respectively)(*El Machete*, September 14, 1935).

The FUPDM's agenda concentrated on practical measures to improve the daily life of women and on political demands. It advocated lower electricity rates, lower rents, lower taxes for women who sold in the markets, the establishment of schools for the children of employees of foreign companies, books for schoolchildren, and so on. Politically it sought the liberation of Mexico from foreign oppression, particularly U.S. imperialism; social and political equality for peasants and indigenous populations; opposition to fascism and war; and, most important, "the broad right of women to vote" (*El Machete*, October 19, 1935). The political platform of the FUPDM went beyond purely feminist interests and promoted a broad program of political reform and democratization. In fact, the only exclusively feminist demand was for women's right to vote, but it was this demand that gave the organization its cohesion and political character. Despite class, regional, and ideological differences, the FUPDM constituted a political organization with specifically feminine interests that was broad based and led by lower-class women in grassroots organizations. Adelina Zendejas, a militant of the period recalled:

> The activities centered on born leaders (some 150) who had begun the struggle and had become leaders by the respect and recognition of their reason and logic. There were many rural schoolteachers of peasant extraction who were the leaders of agrarian leagues in the states. The centers of these leagues were at the municipal and *ejido* seats, but they radiated out, and mobilization meant that the league reached not only the women who were members, but to all those in the region.[6]

In view of the broad feminist mobilization by the FUPDM, the organized parties began to recognize the importance of women as a political factor. Thus, *El Machete*, the official organ of the Communist Party, stated in an issue dated October 12, 1935: "The fact that for the first time women are uniting and forming organizations that group women from the most diverse ideological and religious tendencies poses for all Communists and for the revolutionary movement in general the task of lending all its help and support to this organization."

The internal structure of the FUPDM gives some idea of the breadth of its composition and effectiveness. Refugio (Cuca) García, a Communist who was widely respected among other women's groups and even by the most powerful revolutionary generals of the period—such as Francisco J. Mújica, Jacinto B. Treviño, Andrés Figueroa, Gabriel Leyva, and Lázaro Cárdenas—was the secretary general of the FUPDM. As the national leader, Cuca García had the support of the collective coordinating committee formed by twelve prominent women who discussed jointly the proposals that, when approved, became working directives. Adelina Zendejas recalled:

> The surprising thing is that the work directives emerged from the exchange of opinions, because there were workers, peasants, artisans, homemakers who also worked, but they did not decide by themselves and the directors were not the brain of the organization; this was the greatest virtue of the FUPDM, the coordination for solving problems and the ties with popular demands. (in Tuñón 1992:76)

The broad nature of the FUPDM provided room for diverse and even contradictory definitions of feminism, from the egalitarian feminism of Margarita Robles de Mendoza, whose demand for legal equality for women supported the official position of the PNR and of Cárdenas, to much more radical positions such as those held by Cuca García. Robles de Mendoza sought conciliation with other factions and attempted to "unite all the powerful forces of the country for the purpose of achieving an effective realization of the postulates of the revolution" (1931:15). Matilde Rodríguez Cabo, another Communist member of the FUPDM and the wife of the influential *cardenista* general Francisco Mújica, proposed a much more orthodox Marxist feminism that stressed the class struggle, which, for Rodríguez Cabo, was more important than the gender struggle. In a lecture delivered in 1937, Rodríguez Cabo stated that "women, considered as a whole, form part of the oppressed and their position of inferiority has a dual aspect: one economic, by the fact of being workers within and outside their homes, and one social, by the biological fact of being women" (1937:9). Catholic women, through their numerous charitable and social organizations, also collaborated with the FUPDM because of their common interest in social programs.

In spite of the diversity of its positions, the FUPDM achieved a significant political presence because it appealed to unity based on specific efforts to improve everyday life. However, its central demand, women's right to vote, was the group's most important political demand during the *cardenista* regime. Beginning in October 1935, the official party began a campaign to attract women. This campaign was consistent with Cárdenas's efforts to consolidate the support of mass segments of the population in the wake of his break with Calles (see Córdoba 1979; Hernández Chávez 1980). In pursuit of this policy, in his State of the Nation address on September 1, 1937, President Cárdenas spoke of "the need to reform the nation's Code in the most adequate way so that women, an integral half of Mexican society and of its citizenry, may be rehabilitated as is proper and convenient to the dignity of a people." In his search for political bases of support, Cárdenas spoke out in favor of the political activities of women and publicly lamented that women were denied the most basic political right, the right to vote.[7]

The PNR, Cárdenas's party, also included a platform for women that incorporated Mexican women into political and civic life, granting them rights equal to those of men, enabling them to develop their abilities to the fullest, and promising equal rights for men and women in civil, social, economic, and political legislation.[8] The party, and more important, the president himself, accepted the importance of the women's struggle and their programs. Thus, on November 19, 1937, President Cárdenas sent to the Senate a bill that reformed Article 34 of the Constitution to include women in the definition of citizenship and, hence, grant them the right to vote. Although the bill was sent to the Senate, it was never published in the *Diario Oficial*, and consequently the measure never became official (Hidalgo 1980:31). Again, in his *Informe* of September 1, 1938, Cárdenas stated that "if Mexico truthfully aspires to strengthen its democratic system, one of the most appropriate ways to achieve this is obviously women's suffrage" (ANFER 1984:31).

The fact that this presidential initiative did not become official is an anomaly in the Mexican political system, where the president's voice traditionally prevails over that of the legislators, and therefore leads us to examine the relationship between the women's movement and the government at this time. The Cárdenas government needed the support of organized groups, and the women's movement had evolved to the point where its political presence could not be overlooked. This accounts for the *cardenista* pronouncements in support of the feminist movement, especially in those aspects that coincided with the policies of social improvement such as training for technical and university professions and recognition of conjugal and maternity rights. It was a matter, in short, of incorporating women as allies into the regime's political scheme. On July

6, 1938, the Chamber of Deputies approved the political rights of women but, inexplicably, the official ratification and publication of the notice in the *Diario Oficial de la Federación* did not follow (Ríos Cárdenas 1942:176).

In a speech given on November 1, 1939, Cárdenas insisted on the need to grant women the vote, but at the same time he expressed his fear that the exercise of this right by women could bring antirevolutionary conflicts (Ríos Cárdenas 1942:185). This new presidential statement should be interpreted in the context of the period. Cárdenas was in the last years of his tenure as president, and the national political scene was complicated by the problem of the presidential succession, which meant a possible conflict between the party factions. In this context the president's withdrawal of his support for the feminist cause is explainable to the extent that women's suffrage was still a subject that could provoke a division among the group in power. Cárdenas thought that women's political participation could favor the conservative forces of the country.[9]

For its part, the organized women's movement fragmented again. The Comité Nacional Femenil (National Women's Committee) came out, in February 1940, against independent candidate Juan Almazán (Ríos Cárdenas 1942:194) while the Alianza Nacional Femenina (National Women's Alliance) sought justice for women. Most of its members belonged to the middle class, had a certain level of political and technical training, and participated in the political life of the country in different areas. Amalia Caballero de Castillo Ledón, for example, was noted for her participation in international women's congresses and for her ties with other organized women's movements in Latin America. Adela Formoso de Obregón Santacilia was the founder of the Mexico Women's University, where middle-class students were taught to be teachers, secretaries, administrators, decorators, and other intermediate professions that were considered at that time proper fields for women.

The Federal Deputation, for its part, declared in March 1940, that "women's suffrage cannot be approved because the spiritual values represented by feminine virtues would be lost. Besides, women have not embraced enthusiastically the idea of participating in the political life of Mexico" (Ríos Cárdenas 1942:195). The official candidate, Manuel Avila Camacho, who had clear conservative tendencies and was sympathetic to the church and to the submission of women, stated that protective laws for women were needed and that if he became president he would promote maternity institutions and institutions to help needy women. Since this program agreed with some of the demands from women, one could say that Avila Camacho did not directly antagonize the women's movement but sought, rather, to integrate it into his political campaign by creating a National Women's Committee for the PNR to support his candidacy (ANFER 1984:16). The measure proved effective only at a symbolic level, for although contingents of women were present at the polling places on July 7, 1940, their presence did not modify the central fact that women could not exercise their right to vote. The 1940 elections were hotly contested, and the opposition candidate, Juan Almazán, claimed electoral fraud. The mute presence of women at the polling places was a reminder by women that their demands for political participation had not been satisfied and added more tension to the country's already tense political situation.

With Avila Camacho's rise to power, the FUPDM lost its belligerence and political visibility. It can be said that during his presidency (1940–1946) the women's movement set aside the political objectives of increasing women's power and concentrated more on social programs, as demonstrated by the demands presented to the newly elected president: expansion of maternity leaves, production cooperatives for working women and indigenous women, legislation for domestic servants, and reduced taxes and rents. The political and civil rights of women were mentioned only in passing.[10]

The 1940s marked a regression in women's ability to organize, reflecting the conservative characteristics of Avila Camacho's regime. It should also be noted that World War II had an impact on the national situation and affected the women's movement. The FUPDM became the Committee of Women for the Defense of the Nation, which was very supportive of the soldiers of Squadron 201 sent by the Mexican government to the war (ANFER 1984:16–17). In addition, although the postwar opening of the government of Manuel Alemán (1946–1952) to a new economic scheme allowed women to enter certain labor sectors, at the same time it disarticulated the organized movement with predominantly feminist political demands.

This does not mean, however, that women's organizations disappeared. On July 27, 1945, the Unidad Femenina pro Miguel Alemán (Women's Unity for Miguel Alemán) held a meeting in support of the then-presidential candidate. This organization, headed by Aurora Fernández, sought to rebuild the organized women's movement. In his speech, which made a clear reference to the war, Alemán indicated that the historical forces "open a path for women in all those occupations that formerly belonged exclusively to men."[11] Alemán referred in this speech to the importance of women in the industrialization process in Mexico and promised to promote constitutional reform so that women could occupy a popularly elected position within the Municipio Libre (free municipality). The candidate stated: "If we consider that for popularly elected positions the *Municipio Libre* is the basis of our political organization, women have a place that is waiting for them; because the municipal organization is the one that cares most about the interests of the family and must pay most attention to the needs of the family and of children, we will promote, to this end, opportunely, the proper constitutional reform" (ANFER 1984:32). The same tone prevailed in the candidate's platform, presented to the public on September 30, 1945, in which he stated that he was proud that in Mexico women were "by tradition immemorial incomparable mothers, abnegated and industrious wives, loyal sisters and chaste daughters" (ANFER 1984:42).

Thus, in his public speeches Alemán advocated the political participation of women at the municipal level (which, one must remember, had already been done in Yucatán during the time of Carrillo Puerto) on the one hand, that is, he advocated a limited political participation at the local level. On the other hand, in terms of the parameters of feminine behavior, Alemán favored the traditional scheme of subjected women.

Nonetheless, Alemán kept his promise and on December 10, 1945, women's suffrage was approved by the Senate through the reform of Article 115 of the Constitution, according to which, from that moment forward, women could vote and be voted for; in other words, they could now participate fully in municipal elections (Hidalgo 1980: 46, 51; Morton 1962:51). The political participation now open to women by this reform was limited, however, to the local level and did not extend to the national arena. Alemán also appointed outstanding women to the Department of the Federal District and established schools for civic and political training in major cities to instruct women in the exercise of their newly acquired right. Social welfare clinics and agencies, devised to train women, were also established (Morton 1962:57–58).

The recognition by President Alemán of women's right to participate politically at the local level served to integrate women gradually into political life, legitimizing the regime at the local level and gaining the support of women voters at a time when the massive exodus of migrant workers made this necessary (Tuñón Pablos 1987:187). This new space for the political participation of women should be explained in relation to the process of political restructuring that led to the organization of a new party, the PRI, to replace the Partido de la Revolución Mexicana (Party of the Mexican Revolution, PRM). The PRI was organized in January 1946 with the motto of Democracy and Social Justice. The new party inherited from its precursor the need to offer greater participation to women in the ranks of the party and, in keeping with this idea, named Margarita García Flores as women's director of the National Executive Committee of the PRI (ANFER 1984:17).

The next step, women's suffrage at the national level, was to a great extent the work of organized groups of women, especially of the Alianza de Mujeres de México, headed by Amalia Caballero de Castillo Ledón. She interviewed Adolfo Ruiz Cortines, the 1952 presidential candidate, and obtained from him the promise to grant women's suffrage if she could garner the signatures of one-half million women (ANFER 1984:18). In a country of 30 million inhabitants this task was not difficult, and Castillo Ledón obtained the required signatures. Ruiz Cortines's presidential initiative proposing the vote for women was read in the Chamber of Deputies on December 9, 1952. Ester Chapa, a Communist militant and founder of the FUPDM, disagreed and asked that the procedure begun in 1937 be concluded. Her petition was not accepted, and on October 17, 1953, the *Diario Oficial* published the constitutional change that recognized for women in Mexico the right to vote and to run for office in national elections.

Conclusion

These three historical moments illustrate three different forms of the relationship between women and political power in Mexico. Beyond the difference in these forms—resisting the restrictions on their family rights, breaking down the rigid spaces that separated the public from the private sphere, or constructing interparty alliances that placed gender interests above the interests of political groups—what must be noted is the fact that women sought and exercised alternative forms of organization and action that allowed them to open new spaces and effect changes in the relationships between women and political power in Mexico. The contemporary women's movement has a heritage that deserves to be remembered.

Notes

1. Among the women who wrote on the importance of the revolution are Robles de Mendoza (1931), Ríos Cárdenas (1942), and Saez Royo (1954).

2. This is the case of Guadalupe Zuñiga, Alura Dias, and Josefina Vicens. For an oral history of these outstanding women, see Cano and Radkau (1989).

3. Although women were not granted the right to vote nationally until 1953, they did have the right to vote in local elections. The first states to grant women the right to vote locally were Yucatán, in 1922, and San Luis Potosí, in 1923.

4. Maximato refers to the political arrangement that followed the presidency of Plutarco Elías Calles (1924–1928). Calles was founder of the PNR and kept effective political control after he stepped out of the presidency. For further information, see Córdova (1995).

5. Tuñón (1992:66). On *cardenista* politics, see Córdoba (1979) and Hernández Chávez (1980).

6. Interview with Adelina Zendejas, cited in Tuñón (1992:72). See also Adelina Zendejas, "El movimiento femenil en México," *El Día*, June 21, 1975. Hereinafter all translations are mine.

7. Cárdenas, *Informe Presidencial,* September 1, 1937, quoted in Ríos Cárdenas (1942: 147).

8. See *Primer informe anual que rinde el CEN del PNR a todos los sectores sociales del país* (1936).

9. Interview with Soledad Orozco, in Tuñón (1992:110).

10. See *Llamada de atención a la conciencia nacional* (1940:3).

11. See Miguel Alemán Valdés, "Discurso a la Convención de Mujeres," July 27, 1945, reproduced in Hidalgo (1980:35–39).

❈ 7 ❈

De la A a la Z:
A Feminist Alliance
Experience in Mexico

Marta Lamas

Private Interest and Public Action

The multiple differences within the feminist movement in Mexico, especially those generated by the different political identities of its constituents (regardless of whether they have a partisan affiliation or not), not only summon theoretical interest but also generate a profoundly practical preoccupation: Will the feminists be able to overcome their political differences and promote those demands in which they are in agreement? Will it be possible for the feminists to establish an alliance in order to introduce their proposals in the democratic agenda and obtain representation in politics? The dilemma is of an urgent nature, since political parties do not seem very willing to accommodate the content and values that feminism has proposed for years.

The rise of the De la A a la Z group in the Mexican political panorama is a very new experience of feminist alliance and political representation that intends to consolidate a pact between feminists of different positions. As a member of this group, my reflections in this chapter presuppose uncomfortable risks that are related to one another: protagonism, lack of objectivity, narcissism, excess of subjectivity, and so on. However, remembering the splendid reflection about private interest and public action made by Albert O. Hirschman (1986), I could not resist the challenge of speaking in the first person and trying to show that difficult link.[1] Like Hirschman, who doubted his book should be considered as belonging to the social sciences since at times he had "the sensation of writing a conceptual outline of a *Bildungsroman* (with certain autobiographical touches here and there, as it always occurs in novels)" (1986:9), I am also suspect about my reflections. However, even though I do not wish to compare my resulting thoughts with his brilliant discourse, I do establish a parallel as to the desire to allocate more importance to autocritical evaluations of personal experiences. According to Hirschman, when transformations in collective behavior occur, a great part of the responsibility is attributed to external events. He, however, questioned the endogenous factors, "those neglected driving forces that can be found behind the changes observed in behavior and which can shed new light on the important turning points" (1986:13–14).

It is from this framework that I attempt to relate in this chapter the development of an experience of feminist alliance and representation in Mexico, underlining the importance of the practice of *affidamento*.[2] For the group of Italian feminists who introduced this concept—a mixture of having faith and trust in other women—*affidamento* renews the historical experience of women who have looked to other female figures in order to assert, defend, and inspire themselves. Historian Gabriela Cano has taken Sor Juana Inés de la Cruz's famous reply to Sor Filotea (the pseudonym of the bishop of Puebla) as Mexico's historical example of *affidamento*. In that letter, Sor Juana defended her rights (and those of all women) to think, study, and give her opinion in public, and she constructed a genealogy of symbolic reference to the women who had preceded her.[3]

The Italian women's concept of *affidamento* also introduces a significant difference with our predecessors: a recognition of the disparities among women. Feminism, whose identity policy favors the feeling that "we are all equal," has been especially blind in this respect. At the Fourth Latin American Feminist Congress held in Taxco in 1987, a small group of "historical" feminists, myself included, met for two mornings to debate about "Latin American Feminist Politics Today" and to rethink certain analytical categories and political practices we had been carrying out. Reflecting on the external and internal obstacles to the Latin American feminist movement's political activities and comparing our experiences in the different countries, it became evident that certain interrelated myths that constantly appeared generated a vulnerable and ineffective political practice. These myths are the following:[4]

1. Feminists are not interested in power.
2. Feminists practice politics differently.
3. Feminists are all the same.
4. There is a natural unity by the simple fact that we are women.
5. Feminism exists only as politics of women and for women.
6. The small group is the movement.
7. The spaces of women guarantee a positive process on their own.
8. Because I as a woman feel it, it holds.

9. Personal matters are automatically political.
10. The consensus is democracy.

Even though the validity of these myths has eroded, at that time they operated in our imagination as the "endogenous factors" to which Hirschman referred. Our questioning sessions in Taxco were very useful to me, especially the criticism of the denying and victimized way we feminists handle power and the denouncing of the idealization of our activism, which—even though we may pretend to be "different"—in reality most of the time is done in an outmoded, arbitrary, and manipulative fashion. My conscience was priced by the nasty weight of the third myth, "Feminists are all the same." Even though feminism recognizes ethnic, class, and age differences among women, it implicitly denies any differences in intellectual capacity, ability, and sensitivity. It is as if the simple fact of being women has given us all the same potential, and it is only life's circumstances that have placed us in different positions with different possibilities of developing certain attributes. This militant egalitarianism has led to a paralyzing practice that diminishes the effectiveness and political presence of the movement. The myth fuels womanism, which idealizes and mystifies the relationships among women and hinders leadership. And because of this myth, very often the small feminist groups become "asphyxiating ghettos in which self complacency halts criticism and development" ("Del amor a la necesidad" 1987:16). The internal discussion in Taxco helped me define more clearly my desire to build alliances, while fully recognizing the differences, in a movement in which sectarian dynamics make very difficult any confrontation with other women who have other ideas and other ways of practicing politics.

When we met in Taxco for the Feminist Congress, Viviana Erazo had just arrived from Italy and brought with her a fresh issue for debate: relationships among women are born not out of love but of necessity. According to this thinking, it is love that has made women significant to the world: to be for others. This way of thinking was transferred by feminists to the activities of political and social life, to the feminist movement, to women's groups. Thus we feminists had developed a loving logic—we all love each other, we are all equal—that did not allow us to accept the conflicts and differences among us. In order to disentangle this web of self-complacency—to stop being identical, as Celia Amorós (1987) suggests—it was essential to eliminate that loving logic and move on to a relationship of need: We women need each other to assert our gender. Thanks to the logic of necessity we recognize our differences and give each other support, strength, and authority. Highly motivated by those ideas, we produced our text, *Del amor a la necesidad* (see "Del amor a la necesidad" 1987).

The ideas and words that came from Italy were about *affidamento*: When
we accept the fact that another woman possesses something we do not—
better organizational skills, greater intellectual capacity, superior ability for
some type of work—we give her our trust, we value her, and we invest her
with a degree of authority; in her strength we find our strength, and we
value ourselves as women. Our Taxco document, which finished with an
exhortation—"Let us not deny our conflicts, contradictions, and differences"—had taken the spirit of *affidamento*, instilling in us the hope of bringing to reality the statement, "in the strength of each feminist lies the
strength of the feminist movement" ("Del amor a la necesidad" 1987: 17).

From Recognition to Action

In mid-1993, a little desperate and tired of the dynamics of the feminist
movement in Mexico, its internal conflicts, jealousies, and poorly resolved
competitions, as well as its difficulties in arriving at agreements with minimal political efficacy, I dreamed of another option: an organized group
made up of a few feminists, representing no one but themselves, but with
enough political weight to have, at the very least, a symbolic impact.

At the same time, and even earlier, some other colleagues of mine had
expressed their frustration at the difficulties in establishing alliances and
consensus between feminists and women politicians. Attempts at unity[5]
had not endured, in spite of the fact that *priísta* feminists (that is, members
of the PRI) and government officials had been excluded. This failure may
have been due to the alliances' internal dynamics themselves, as in the
Coalición de Mujeres Feministas,[6] or to the explicit pact with opposition
parties, as in the Frente Nacional por la Liberación y los Derechos de las
Mujeres (National Front for Women's Rights and Liberation, FNALIDM),
in which some feminist groups[7] associated themselves with unions, the
Partido Comunista Mexicano (Mexican Communist Party, PCM), and the
PRT. Or failure may have been due to the insistence on political purity, the
result of which was that the Coordinadora Feminista of Mexico City had
little life and no repercussion.

Perhaps this sectarianism was a reason the groups that configured the
new wave of Mexican feminism in the 1970s, although playing an important role in the integration of a new political culture and a critical cultural
discourse, were not able to sustain their initial political impact in the
1980s. Even though the advent of a women's popular movement after the
earthquake of 1985 revitalized the feminist movement and began to show
signs of a possibility of a broad women's movement,[8] the exclusionary
identity practices of the feminists did not allow for the consolidation of a
broad alliance in the 1990s.

This behavior is related to the absence of a collective entity that fosters assembly and discussion for the Mexican feminist movement, an absence that hinders an organized reply to key issues that require a rapid reaction and at the same time generates resentment when initiatives arise. Some attempts at alliances surrounding key issues have been criticized because of their "individualistic" origins, even though they have had a positive impact. For example, during Holy Week in 1989, some judicial agents went to a clinic that provides clandestine abortions and arrested the medical personnel and some women who had just had abortions. The agents took them to the police facilities of Tlaxcoaque and tortured them. A few days later, one of the women detained decided to denounce what happened. The violation of human rights became the central element, which automatically created a different reaction: Society expressed its indignation in defense of the victims of the police. In light of these events, and thinking that the incident also demanded a public pronouncement on the penalization of abortion, I took the initiative to collect signatures for a newspaper spread with the help of several of my colleagues. This was possible because of the existence of an informal network of communication among the various feminist groups and also because of the personal relations of some of my colleagues with top women politicians and artists. The spread, whose main characteristic was the plurality of its adherents— government officials, artists and intellectuals, politicians of the PRD and the PRI—was published in three national newspapers.[9] Even though the publication of the spread generated a wave of external support, it also provoked harsh criticism within the movement. What was questioned most was the invitation extended to *priístas* and government officials. However, if the spread had an impact,[10] it was precisely because it included nonfeminist women, public officials, women of the political parties, artists, and so on. In the end, the events surrounding the newspaper spread meant for me a personal rupture with the sectarianism and the closed dynamics of the feminist movement, which resents sharing its causes and has serious difficulties in defending them with political efficacy and assuming them responsibly.

Building Alliances: De la A a la Z

In spite of the fact that the challenges and potential of alliances have been raised and analyzed very little in the movement, the will to build alliances has been expressed repeatedly by myself and by other feminist colleagues. In the early 1990s, a pact among feminists, government officials, and women of the political parties had a notable success when it won approval for legislation concerning victims of sexual crimes and reforms to such law.[11] Especially important were the efforts of persuasion and negotiation that Amalia García, then congresswoman for the PRD, made with congresswomen from all political parties. Almost singlehandedly, she put together an alliance among women politicians never seen before in Congress. The support from Grupo Plural and from several popular organizations of women helped to press for approval in 1991 of the legislation presented by all the congresswomen united.

With these precedents, the unanimous wish of those of us who make up De la A a la Z was that of creating a group of feminists who were capable of engaging in dialogue and serving as reference points and who would compose the wide center-left spectrum of feminism. An alliance with *panistas* was impossible for me, since the dogmatic and moralizing ideology of the PAN is totally opposed to feminism. Those of us without a party affiliation wanted to mix, as independents, with the women from the political parties, and vice versa, just to see how things worked out among us, with all our differences and likenesses.

The need for political equilibrium and for agility in reaching agreements forced us to be very selective. In addition, respect and political trust in each other were indispensable. The seven feminists who formed and conformed De la A a la Z (A/Z) were Laura Carrera (PRI), Amalia García (PRD), Teresa Incháustegui (PRI), Marta Lamas (*Debate Feminista*), Cecilia Loría (Grupo de Educación Popular con Mujeres [Group for Women's Popular Education, GEM), Patricia Mercado (Mujeres en Acción Sindical [Women in Action in Unions, MAS), and Rosario Robles (PRD). As can be observed, the group consisted of three independent feminists and four feminists who belong to a political party (two from the PRI and two from the PRD).

All seven of us were able to establish a pact, without denying that there were conflicts, contradictions, and differences among us, under a basic rule: Decisions were to be made by consensus. Our experiences had made clearly evident the need for *affidamento*. The element of trust was crucial, since the alliance of A/Z could potentially incur negative costs for the colleagues of the parties; the political scenario brought about by the events of 1994 heightened this risk because the PRI-PRD polarity widened even more. Internal partisan differences were added to that, accentuated more in the colleagues of the PRI, who had aligned themselves separately with different presidential pre-candidates: one with Luis Donaldo Colosio and one with Manuel Camacho.

In line with the principles of *affidamento*, we chose to come into the open in a symbolic way, with a recognition. October 1993 was the fortieth anniversary of Mexican women's suffrage, and we decided to pay a public homage to the women who fought for it. We asked historian Gabriela Cano to write a document about women's struggle for franchise. Thus, the first official appearance of De la A a la Z was an act to celebrate "forty years of female citizenship," which was recognized with the decree of October 17, 1953, that granted Mexican women the right to vote. At the ceremony, which took place on Saturday, October 16, in the Casa de Cultura Reyes Heroles with an attendance of more than three hundred, an engraved plaque was awarded to surviving suffragettes and to those who represented the deceased ones in acknowledgment of their struggle. In addition to the historical account presented by Gabriela Cano of the feminist mobilization that preceded the vote (which contradicts the official story about the supposedly generous concession of President Ruiz Cortines—that is, the government did not *give* us the vote, we *conquered* it), Benita Galeana and Carlos Monsiváis also spoke. It was moving to see women who had actively participated in the struggle for suffrage at the ceremony. Even though the *priístas* were in considerable minority, since most of the public was of the PRD, the ceremony took place in an atmosphere of respect and with enjoyable expressions of sorority.

By choosing this "social debut," the A/Z group not only showed its gratitude toward the colleagues who fought for the political rights of women (a clear example of *affidamento*) but also showed to a group of women preoccupied with democratization the face of a new feminism prepared to build alliances across political ideologies.

A New Political Culture:
Neither to Represent Nor to Lead

If the spirit that inspired the composition of A/Z was the yearning for a posture of feminist solidarity among women with a certain political trajectory, the concrete objective was to introduce a new political style, which we tried to make explicit in our first document, a flier distributed that Saturday (October 16, 1993). In it we stated that "we women still have an important path to follow together, beyond the political differences that identify each one of us," and we proposed, very much in the same vein as Alessandra Bocchetti (1990), to "recognize the 'fierce bond' that links all us women, notwithstanding the differences in culture, political position or age that divide us, so we can make our social and political presence visible and viable in today's Mexico."

Notwithstanding the differences, our concerns and interests revolved around one basic preoccupation: "How do we generate a new political culture that incorporates the recognition of differences and at the same time aims to eliminate inequality?" In the political practice that we proposed, our rationale was

> neither to represent nor to lead, but to incite, convene, build bridges and make alliances, and therefore to originate a new relationship between women and their organizations and their problems, demands, and proposals

in order to generate political and cultural transformations, and thus to reno-
vate the traditional statutes of politics, which are the key to representation,
from the practice of power and discourse, so they will allow increasingly for
the life and vision of women in the building of society and in the direction of
the state. (Taken from the flier of October 16, 1993)

When the event ended, and upon seeing so many women from different
political persuasions sharing the general enthusiasm, I felt that through
those symbolic and unifying acts we were taking the right steps to generate a new form of doing politics.

Perhaps the concept of "neither leading nor representing" had much to
do with the initial success of our assembly. For our second public appearance, we chose a truly feminist celebration: International Women's Day.
Our convocation in the press read:

WE ARE FED UP WITH BEING AN ELECTORAL BOOTY AND WITH THE
FEMINIST PERSPECTIVE BEING ABSENT IN THE CANDIDATES'
HEADS, IN THE PROGRAMS OF THE PARTIES, AND IN THE CANDI-
DATE LISTS FOR DEPUTIES AND SENATORS.
     We have many questions:
     To what point can a political project that does not integrate a perspective
of gender be democratic?
     How can that perspective be integrated? Through increased participation,
with mechanisms that will guarantee spaces and representation; through
programmatic changes in the platforms; or including certain demands?
     With whom can we ally ourselves? Are women "natural allies"? To what
point does a woman's body guarantee a feminist compromise?
     We have more questions and we want to hear yours.
     If you have any questions concerning the feminist participation of women
in the project of democratic transformation in the nation, attend the session
"Thinking Out Loud", which will take place on Tuesday, March 8, International Women's Day, at 6:00 PM in "El Hábito", 13 Madrid, Coyoacán.[12]

In addition to the novelty of putting forth questions instead of answers,
or the incitement in the heading "We are fed up!" (*¡Estamos hartas!)*, or the
strange mixture of PRI and PRD affiliates and independent feminists
making the rallying cry, the truth of the matter is that when more than 150
women attended the session "Thinking Out Loud," it was because we appealed to a need for public debate. We did not expect such a crowd; we
expected an attendance of twenty at most to whom we were going to present the proposal outlined already in October:

Faced with the upcoming 1994 elections, we want to promote the creation of
a feminist agenda from where we can evaluate and critique the candidates'

(male or female) proposals, and which will lead to a new way of looking at politics and life. We wish to support those candidates who have a real pre-occupation with basic questions about people's everyday life, and who will commit to recognize and promote participation, pluralism, and democracy in public policy. (Taken from the flier of October 16, 1993)

The discussion was long and intense. The unifying element of those present was our spread in *La Jornada*, but the variety of ages, social classes, education, occupations, and political positions confirmed our feminist hypothesis: Before other political differences separate us, we have a long path to follow together. The hot issue was the August elections. We had less than six months to incorporate the interests and demands of women as a part of the programs of the parties and as an expression of national interest.

About 30 percent of those present militated with the PRD, 50 percent were PRD sympathizers who intended to vote for Cárdenas, and the remaining 20 percent were *priístas* or sympathizers of Colosio. In spite of being a minority, the *priístas* were outspoken and critical. I am convinced that the plural makeup of the group favored a debate that could have easily turned into a confrontation. Feeling very enthusiastic, we called for a second meeting in two weeks, as we wanted to promote the mobilization of all groups of women in the country.

Exactly two weeks later, Colosio was assassinated. The group could not break away from the political crisis that shook the country. In addition, even if the Chiapas uprising had not been a disruptive element in the group, the election campaigns made our joint work in public more difficult. We were getting near to what we had feared so much: the possibility that the parties' agendas would make a political consensus among us impossible.

There was, of course, the heavy weight of personal considerations. The death of Colosio, a close friend of Laura Carrera, affected her profoundly and paralyzed her for some time. Teresa Incháustegui, who had aligned herself with Camacho, had withdrawn somewhat from the PRI because of the party's attacks on Camacho. Cecilia Loría was heavily involved in the citizens' movement in support of Chiapas. Amalia García struggled internally in the PRD for a more democratic designation of candidates through opinion polling and internal voting and was paving the way to run for president of the party. Rosario Robles was running for Congress. And Patricia Mercado and I were heavily involved in the arrangements for the Cairo conference and in the Latin American campaign for legalizing abortion. The difficulties for undertaking collective actions in the group seemed to grow.

In addition, one must not forget that the political practice of women itself presupposes ambivalence, as proposed by Italian feminist Maria Luisa Boccia: "Keep together participation and strangeness with respect to politics." Bringing together participation and strangeness implies struggling to have a presence as well as continuing to question that presence—that is to say, neither believing in it completely nor ceasing to act on it. Despite the importance of making visible that "position of eccentricity" of women in the sociopolitical order, a deep ambivalence was also invading us.

Notwithstanding the external obstacles to our work, the need for internal discussion and the affection for each other sustained us. The cost of abstaining from actions that might put any of our colleagues at risk had the benefit of preserving our alliance. Of course, the latent question was whether an alliance that does not express itself in the public arena is worthwhile politically. With a pragmatic political criteria, A/Z ceased to have any efficacy in mid-1994: We did not appear in public or make declarations again. However, the group's transgressive nature was sustained symbolically; its impact derived from the radical nature of an alliance of that kind, capable of shattering some of the more deeply rooted myths about Mexican and Latin American feminism.

Conclusion: The Impact of Our Alliance

For me A/Z constituted, above all, a political exercise of feminists who dared to be different. Showing the unity among feminists of the PRI and of the PRD and independents had a substantial symbolic effect, since it made visible the existence of a feminist perspective and a feminist compromise. This type of alliance shatters the existing and widely accepted symbolic order—each party militant with her party and the nonmilitants having nothing to do with them—and confronts the existing cultural or political codes, offering new elements that forecast another order: the utopia of conceiving feminism as a political force capable of altering the balance of institutionalized political power.

In the search for political coherence, a fundamental point to recognize is that we are constantly changing, even though our objectives and our principles may remain the same. From that perspective, A/Z, in addition to reaffirming the importance of the movement's actions and negotiations earned through confrontations with the world, made it clear that it is essential for feminists to legitimize symbolic forms of a female social authority. A/Z is one of very many that should arise to make a true promotion of that authority.

Hirschman spoke about "the haziness of the dividing line between effort and accomplishment, characteristic of actions performed in behalf of the public interest" (1986:11). My self-reflection has led me to conclude that since A/Z was not established in order to support any candidate or particular party, but rather was initiated as a form of feminist legitimization and political responsibility, in one way or another it meant a different kind of loyalty to feminism. I admit that internally I privileged and enjoyed the utopic quality of A/Z: a "non-place" from which to have a symbolic influence. In that sense, for me the metapolitical achievement of the group was strictly of a symbolic order: breaking the political code of political party/feminist group confrontation and PRI/PRD party confrontation, thus opening the possibility of being publicly identified as allied feminists cutting across political ideologies.

For me, the practice of *affidamento* has been very liberating, but I do not want my personal enthusiasm to cloud excessively with optimism a rather somber fact: the limited symbolic impact of A/Z in the world of *realpolitik*. The main purpose of our political project was to propose a new form of practicing politics, but the tragic political events of 1994 very much hindered the development of one of the initial objectives: putting together a shared feminist agenda and presenting it to the candidates. That proposal, which would have also served to debate certain items publicly and to spread our positions to other sectors, could not be carried out. From our political forecasts, which were completely surpassed by reality, in 1994 we were going to utilize our strategic positions to ensure that the presidential candidates, at least the one of the PRI (Colosio) and the one of the PRD (Cárdenas), would respond to feminist concerns. The closeness of Laura with Colosio and of Teresa with Camacho, as well as the high positions of Amalia and Rosario in the PRD, made our aspiration plausible. But who was to imagine what happened that year?

With our demobilization and the conflictive political situation under which we arrived at the elections, I was struck by the recognition of the persistence of the rigid *machismo* of the Mexican political class, which did not even take notice of the profound political questioning of the A/Z experience. Obviously, and in spite of the efforts of the feminist movement during the last twenty-five years to erode it, that sexist blindness persists. Despite the disappointment that this situation represents, I hope it will serve as a warning about the risk of once again investing our energies "inside" the movement, with little or no impact on the outside world.

Notwithstanding the rubble of the difficult times we faced, we must also accept a responsibility on our part for the lack of consolidation as a group. In order to be truly viable, an initiative of united leadership such as the one of A/Z requires that the group's work be sustained for a longer time and with more consistency. For that reason, if we are going to advance in our objective, we as members of this alliance should be more self-critical about the issues we have criticized in the feminist movement, especially the lack of structure and internal coordination. In retrospect, it seems that perhaps A/Z reproduced internally some of the Taxco myths.

Notes

This chapter was written with the support of the Ford Foundation.

1. Alicia Martínez, a researcher at the Facultad Latinoamericana de Ciencias Sociales (Latin American Faculty for the Social Sciences, FLACSO), recently expressed her concern about the invisibility of the different actors of the new Latin American feminism. Her thoughts reminded me of how uncomfortable I have felt on several occasions in my double position as protagonist and analyst, and I became aware of how frequently I have opted to "erase" myself or to use an all-encompassing "us." For this reason I have decided to write this chapter in strictly personal terms, incorporating individual references.

2. For a broad explanation of *affidamento*, as well as its theory and practice, see Librería de Mujeres de Milán (1991). Several references to *affidamento* also appear in *Debate Feminista*, no. 2, September 1990, devoted to feminism in Italy.

3. The quote Cano refers to is the following: "En fin, a toda la gran turba de las que merecieron nombres, ya de griegas, ya de musas, ya de pitonisas; pues todas no fueron mas que mujeres doctas, tenidas y celebradas, y también veneradas de la antigüedad por tales" from Sor Juana Inés de la Cruz, *Comedias, sainetes y prosas*, vol. 4 of *Obras Completas* (Mexico City: Fondo de Cultura Económica, 1957), pp. 460–462 (see Cano in *Debate Feminista* 7 [March 1993]:288).

4. The myths were analyzed in the document *Del amor a la necesidad*, signed by Haydée Birgin (Argentina), Celeste Cambría (Peru), Fresia Carrasco (Peru), Viviana Erazo (Chile), Marta Lamas (Mexico), Margarita Pisano (Chile), Adriana Santa Cruz (Chile), Estela Suárez (Mexico), Virginia Vargas (Peru), and Victoria Villanueva (Peru). The editing was done by Viviana Erazo, Marta Lamas, and Estela Suárez, and the document was published in *fem* 11 (60):15–17 in December 1987.

5. For an account of these attempts from 1970 to 1993, see Lamas (1994).

6. Even though participation in the coalition was supposedly on an individual and personal basis, the oppositionist stance of the majority of its members made the participation of female government officials or *priístas* extremely difficult. I recall how several sympathizers of the PRI, faced with the internal dynamics of strong rejection toward the government and that party and finding themselves in a very small minority, chose to leave.

7. Not all groups agreed to associate with the political parties. The two extremes of the feminist gamut, Movimiento Nacional de Mujeres and La Revuelta, were opposed and did not participate in the FNALIDM. See "Se forma el FRENTE," *fem* 4 (17), February-March 1981.

8. This process is analyzed in Lamas, Martínez, Tarrés, and Tuñón (1995b).

9. It appeared in *Excélsior, La Jornada,* and *El Día* on April 5, 1989.

10. As a result of the spread, the secretary of health invited some of those who signed the petition to talk with him. Even though the meeting was nothing more than a ritual act ("famous" women were invited but not the experts), confirming as it did the government's lack of interest in approaching the problem as one of public health, it was indicative of the impact of the spread.

11. In the late 1980s the group Movimiento Nacional de Mujeres (National Women's Movement, MNM), which since its beginnings was suspect because of

its interest in establishing relationships with women of the PRI and women in government in order to effect public policies, prepared and presented (in conjunction with a female official of the Ministry of Justice) a project for the creation of agencies specializing in sexual crimes, convinced that the problem of attention to rape victims could not be assumed by the movement and required the attention of the state. When the initiative became public knowledge, some members of the MNM, especially Esperanza Brito and Anilú Elías, were confronted with a wave of verbal aggression and were questioned about their *"priísmo"* and their "collaborationism." Once the first Agencia Especializada en Delitos Sexuales was open, this initiative, which was highly criticized and misunderstood by the majority of the feminist groups in its initial stages, opened a channel for the supervision of its operations and for reforms in the laws concerning sexual crimes. The Ministry of Justice itself called for the creation of the Grupo Plural, formed by feminists, women politicians, and government officials from several parties, so they could work on the projects to reform the law.

12. See *La Jornada*, March 8, 1994, p. 20.

❀ 8 ❀

Everyday Struggles: Women in Urban Popular Movements and Territorially Based Protests in Mexico

Vivienne Bennett

Women have engaged in social activism at the grassroots level in Mexico in a multitude of ways. Their actions can be grouped into the following six categories: territorially based organizations (such as communal kitchens and neighborhood loan organizations located within individual neighborhoods), territorially based protests (such as protests within individual neighborhoods over public services), urban popular movements, rural social movements, human rights groups, and guerrilla movements. In this chapter I examine the everyday struggles of poor women in urban Mexico by focusing on the incorporation of social activism into their everyday tasks. The role of women in urban popular movements and territorially based protests in Mexico exemplifies the place that social activism has come to have in the everyday lives of Mexico's urban poor.

Urban popular movements are formally constituted organizations that consist of the voluntary confederation of numerous socially active neighborhoods within a given city. These confederations are based on the fact that member neighborhoods have a commonality of goals and a shared place within Mexico's political and social structure. Being formal organizations, urban popular movements have consolidated leadership, rules of organization and decisionmaking, and continuity over time. In contrast, territorially based protests are moment and issue based. They arise within individual neighborhoods and are directed at solving immediate problems. Some territorially based protests are carried out by groups of neighborhoods, but these are usually contiguous neighborhoods that experience similar problems, and the protests do not lead to the creation of lasting partnerships or overarching organizations. Territorially based protests arise and subside as needed; as a result they are both more flexible than urban popular movements and more lacking in continuity.

Both urban popular movements and territorially based protests have become more and more prevalent in urban Mexico over the last twenty-five years in response to the critical and growing inadequacy of the means of social reproduction: housing, water and sewerage services, transportation, and health care. At the same time, women's participation in these two forms of social activism has been fundamental: Women vastly outnumber men in urban popular movements across Mexico, and women carry out the bulk of territorially based protests as well.

Women as Social Activists

The theoretical groundwork for understanding women's social activism was laid out by Molyneux (1985), who distinguished between women's practical and strategic gender interests. Molyneux suggested that when women organize from their practical gender interests, they focus on practical issues and do not link their immediate problem (water, finances, child care, and so on) to the characteristics of patriarchy and social class that structure the unequal relations shaping their lives. Women's actions that stem from their practical gender interests are centered in the sphere of reproduction—that is to say, in their household and neighborhood, or around household and neighborhood issues. The fact that poor urban women do not have interlocutors representing their interests within the formal political structure has forced them either to use public protest as their channel of communication with government decisionmakers or to create urban movements that can represent their collective voice.

Beyond women's practical gender interests are their strategic gender interests, which are based on an explicit recognition of the gendered nature of power. Once women understand that their daily lives are structured by gender inequality—in the jobs available to them; the wages they are paid; their working conditions; in their relationships with their husbands, their fathers, their male bosses; and in the unequal distribution of household work between women and men and of positions of political and economic power—then the focus of organizing changes or expands. At least part of the objective of women's actions becomes the transformation of gender relations.

Sometimes, women participate in protests or popular movements for practical gender interests, but their participation leads to an awareness of their strategic gender interests. For example, numerous studies show that when women become militant, they encounter strong resistance within their households, particularly from husbands who oppose their wives' moving into spheres of action beyond their control or beyond the traditional housewifely roles (see Stephen 1989, 1997; Jelin 1990a). The contact with other women facing the same problems at home can lead to enhanced gender consciousness and the consequent need to forge a new identity other than passive wife and citizen (Caldeira 1990). Even when participation in collective action based on practical gender interests does not lead to an awareness of strategic gender interests, it can lead to an intermediate step that could be called an enhanced sense of citizenship (Massolo 1988:80–81). This includes the construction of a panorama of rights, including the right to have basic services, shelter, health care, and education. Practical gender needs are thus transformed into the right of every citizen (Jelin 1990b:206), challenging government paternalism and the selective nature of government planning.

Women become social activists because they are confronted by problems that cannot be resolved in any other way. A woman's gender role includes being the manager of the process of social reproduction: shopping for food, cooking, cleaning, doing laundry, child care, caring for sick family members, or managing the household help who carry out all the above tasks. Increasingly in Mexico, being the manager of social reproduction is to be the manager of poverty. After fifteen years of economic crisis, the ranks of the poor and extreme poor have swollen to include as much as half the country's population.[1] All of the tasks of social reproduction are constrained by poverty, so a woman's job becomes much more difficult (Bennett 1995a:110–111, 1995b). For example, most poor neighborhoods in Mexican cities do not have homes with in-house water service or even neighborhood faucets with continuous water supply. Cooking, cleaning, bathing children, laundry—all are tasks that are much more difficult and even sometimes impossible to carry out if there is irregular water service. As managers of poverty, women also assume the responsibility and stress of stretching insufficient budgets to somehow feed, clothe, and shelter their families (Benería and Roldán 1987).

Because women are the managers of social reproduction, they are the most affected by the living conditions imposed by poverty. As a result, when there are particularly dramatic problems with any of the elements of social reproduction—for example, loss of water service, elimination of a bus route, reduction in electrical service, threat of eviction—women are usually the first to respond. In urban Mexico there have been two principal responses to these types of problems: urban popular movements and territorially based protests.

Urban Popular Movements

The first wave of urban popular movements in Mexico occurred in the early 1970s in response to the burgeoning urban crisis. High rural-to-urban migration combined with vastly insufficient government and private sector investment for low income housing and public services led to an urban crisis by the late 1960s: There were extreme shortages of housing, inadequate water and sewerage services, insufficient transportation services as well as lack of schools and health care for outlying neighborhoods (Bennett 1992:243).

During the 1970s, of all the above problems, the most urgent one was housing (Gilbert 1989; Pozas 1990). In response to the lack of affordable housing, multitudes participated in land invasions. In a typical land invasion, a group of families would occupy a vacant lot at the edge of the city during the middle of the night (when they could do so without being seen). In the first few hours they would mark out lots and hastily put together shelters out of cardboard and tin. Often, word of mouth was so effective that while the invasion was in progress other families would arrive and join in. At some point in the first few days land invasion communities could expect to face some sort of aggressive response by the state because land invasions by necessity occupied land they did not own. If they survived the state's attempts to evict or dislodge them, and many did (because after all the state had no alternative to offer them, and there simply was no other housing available), they went on to become neighborhoods that were much more highly organized and structured than "normal" city neighborhoods. This too was by necessity. Whereas an ordinary neighborhood is planned by developers from its inception, in the case of land invasions the "developers" were the families who participated in the invasion. They had to decide on their own how to lay out their new community, how to allocate lots, and how to go about acquiring the necessary public services such as water and electricity. This meant that groups of poor families who were all struggling just to survive had to work out, in addition, the modus operandi for every detail of their new neighborhood, and they had to do this with each other. However, in some of Mexico's most important cities there were land invasion neighborhoods that were organized to an even greater degree, and these were neighborhoods that were led by student activists.

After the 1968 student massacre by the federal government put an end to the student movement (Hellman 1983), it became very difficult and dangerous to organize openly in any sort of opposition capacity in Mexico. In response, several radical groups that had been based at the Universidad Nacional Autónoma de México (National Autonomous University, UNAM) decided it was time to leave the ivory tower and move out among the people, to help the masses organize, and to carry out "revolution from below." Clandestinely, cadres from left wing political organizations in Mexico City were sent out to other states to try to help the peasants and urban poor in their struggles. In the provincial cities where they were successful (Durango, Chihuahua, and Monterrey at first), these cadres quickly saw that the most pressing problem for the urban poor was housing, and they joined poor families in carrying out land invasions (Haber 1992; Quintana Silveyra 1991). At the same time, land invasions became places where the students could guide residents in setting up the community's organizational superstructure as well as help them shape their vision of a just community. Once a land invasion was successful, it became a base from which to support other emerging land invasions.

The presence of the student activists was critical because they had a vision of a new society, and they came to see the first building block of that new society as the land invasion neighborhood itself. As a result, in cities across Mexico we find land invasion neighborhoods with nearly identical forms of organization (because the student cadres who joined the poor urban families came from the same guiding political organization in Mexico City). These neighborhoods all had an assembly form of decisionmaking, with commissions constituted to address particular issues. The leaders of these neighborhoods were the student activists, but issues were resolved in consultation with the commissions and ratified and discussed by the community at large in neighborhood-wide assemblies. In addition, each block in the neighborhood had a block leader, and groups of block leaders reported to an intermediate leader, and so on up the ladder, so that in principle there was a mechanism in place for every family's voice to be heard by the leadership of the neighborhood.

As the 1970s wore on, two phenomena occurred. One was the formation of citywide coalitions of land invasion neighborhoods (Ramírez Saiz 1986). The second was that women increasingly became the most active members of the land invasion neighborhoods. During the 1970s, the number of land invasion neighborhoods in Mexican cities multiplied, and the number of city residents living in land invasion neighborhoods reached into the hundreds of thousands. In some cities (Monterrey and Durango were the first) groups of land invasion neighborhoods came together under umbrella organizations, usually led, once again, by the same student activists mentioned above. The umbrella organizations (such as the Frente Popular Tierra y Libertad in Monterrey, and the Comité de Defensa Popular in Durango) began to have great visibility and therefore local power because of the sheer numbers they represented (Bennett 1992; Haber 1992). These umbrella organizations represented consolidated land invasion neighborhoods whose very existence challenged one of the fundamental principles of Western society: the principle of private property. The land invasion neighborhoods—which by the late 1970s consisted of communities with clearly laid out streets, neat cinder-block homes, schools, health clinics, shops, and so on—were all built on illegally occupied land, on land that had been appropriated by the occupants and not paid for. As a result, the formation of confederations or coalitions of such neighborhoods represented a threat to society and certainly to the power of the state as the enforcer of the prevailing rules of the society (such as the right to private property).

The confederations of land invasion neighborhoods in Mexican cities became known as urban popular movements. All the early urban popular movements (from the 1970s) continue to exist today, with some about to turn twenty-five years old. However, the last twenty-five years have seen an evolution in goals and strategies of the older movements as well as an evolution in the development of new urban popular movements.

Although land and shelter were the first concerns of the initial land invasion communities, as the neighborhoods consolidated other needs rose to the top: water, electricity, paved streets, street lights, clinics, public transportation, and so on. Acquiring these public services took two forms. On the one hand, the new neighborhoods could simply appropriate some of the services, just as they had the land. In particular, water and electricity could sometimes be directly appropriated, with wires strung clandestinely from an electrical pole to the neighborhood or with pipes attached clandestinely to a water main. On the other hand, some of the services required long negotiations with the city and state governments. In these cases, neighborhood committees had to be formed to petition the government for a bus route, for paved streets, for a medical clinic, and so on. The majority of the committee members were often women.

When negotiation did not work, the committees had to escalate their strategy to one of disruption. Urban popular movements have been particularly effective at organizing tactics of disruption because they are able to mobilize large constituencies. Thus actions such as marches and protest rallies can have the numerical size needed both to cause a disruption (of traffic, of work at government offices, and so on) and to gain the attention of the relevant government authorities. The majority of those participating in disruptive actions are women. Thus it has become a common sight in Mexican cities to see masses of women marching through central downtown streets or standing at government office buildings holding a rally demanding help for neighborhood problems (Ramírez Saiz 1986).[2]

Over time, in the radical land invasion neighborhoods even the assemblies began to have majority female participation. The reason for the strong female presence in the committees, the marches, the rallies, and the assemblies is the same. One very important set of issues addressed by the urban popular movements had to do with the elements of social reproduction, and social reproduction was the terrain of women. After the first precarious period of a new land invasion neighborhood had passed, the men sought work while the women continued to organize around improving life for their community (even if they also had waged work).

Thus even though the leaders of the first urban popular movements were all men, the movements were central to the evolution of women as political actors in Mexico because they were the first groups where women began to have a voice (Massolo 1994c).

By the late 1970s, urban popular movements consisting of coalitions of land invasion neighborhoods existed in a number of cities, including Acapulco, Mexico City, Durango, Chihuahua, Monterrey, and Juchitán (Ramírez Saiz 1986; Tirado Jiménez 1990; Rubin 1990). In 1981, urban popular movements from across Mexico joined together to form a national confederation of urban popular movements, which came to be known as the Coordinadora Nacional del Movimiento Urbano Popular (National Coordinator of the Urban Popular Movement, CONAMUP). The purpose of CONAMUP was to support the continued evolution of urban popular movements throughout Mexico, and it did so in several ways. It provided an umbrella structure that organized yearly meetings in different cities, where individual movements could exchange information and discuss direction; it mediated between the government and local movements; and it disseminated information on the status of active movements across Mexico through its publications (Bennett 1992:251).

In 1983 the Women's Regional Council of CONAMUP was created to address a wide range of women's issues that were not satisfactorily being addressed by CONAMUP itself. The Women's Regional Council emerged from a discussion about democracy in which it became clear to men and women alike that although women constituted the majority of CONAMUP members, they did not have much of a voice at the leadership level (Stephen 1997). The Women's Regional Council is a striking example of the coming together of women's practical gender interests with their strategic gender interests. The council focuses on a combination of issues, including domestic violence, sexuality, women's participation in politics, and strategies for coping with urban poverty. The Women's Regional Council is located in Mexico City, housed in a building it was able to purchase after substantial petitioning led to government support. Its collective kitchen distributes over 16,000 government subsidized breakfasts to children daily. In addition, the council offers services to the elderly and runs a school for women, a health clinic, and ongoing workshops for women (Stephen 1997).

During the decade of the 1980s, there was a shift both in the nature of new urban popular movements and in the goals of the older movements. The massive earthquakes that struck Mexico City within days of each other in September 1985 served as catalysts for the formation of new urban popular movements. The catastrophic destruction of downtown housing and sweatshops—150,000 made homeless, 150,000 jobs lost, 1,326 garment factories destroyed—followed by highly inefficient and corrupt government handling of the crisis forced citizens to come together to address the major issues of replacement housing and work. The new movements in Mexico City were no longer based in land invasion neighborhoods, although they also dealt first with issues of housing. These were pan-neighborhood movements, representing a multitude of downtown neighborhoods that had been seriously affected by the quakes. For the first time not only was the membership of the urban popular movements majority female but women were actually leaders as well. As a result, not only immediate practical needs were addressed (such as housing, work, water service) but strategic gender needs as well (such as spousal abuse, division of labor in the home). One of the most significant new urban popular movements, the Comité Unico de Damnificados, had as its slogan Democracy in the City and in the Home (Massolo 1994c:422).

The older urban popular movements made a transition in the 1980s from challenging the social system through the formation of land invasion neighborhoods, building citywide coalitions, and defending their right to exist to accessing resources directly by entering the arena of electoral politics. Although movement leaders once believed that participating in electoral politics was to achieve reform at best, and never revolution, in the 1980s they took the position that formal political power would gain them access to resources, resources that could be used to strengthen their movements (Bennett 1992). As a result, leaders of the older urban popular movements ran for public office and were actually elected to Congress and even to mayoralties.[3] Younger members of the movements were able to assume secondary positions of leadership, but women were still generally excluded from the leadership of the older movements. In these movements, traditional gender roles were replicated within the power structure so that women might do a lot of the actual organizational and logistical foot work, and women certainly constituted the mass base of the movements. However, men continued to hold tightly to positions of power or control.

Territorially Based Protests

Urban popular movements were created to help meet the needs of their affiliated neighborhoods, but plenty of low-income neighborhoods that were not part of an urban popular movement also suffered (and continue to suffer) from equally deficient public services. These neighborhoods did not have neighborhood organizations or umbrella organizations to represent them, and traditionally they have been very poorly represented at the decisionmaking levels of the Mexican government, so residents have had to take matters into their own hands. Although low-income neighborhoods may actually be criss-crossed with differentiation when it comes to income and education, or even in terms of race, ethnicity, and linkages to a rural past (Schild 1991), when it comes to urban services they are homogeneous. Women who may be different in terms of their income, education, or race are brought together by the living conditions created by the public services provided to their neighborhoods. Because women are the managers of the process of social reproduction, inadequate public services have a greater impact on them than on men. Thus it is the women of low-income neighborhoods who have added to their workload the job of confronting their neighborhoods' public service problems.

When women confront public service problems in their neighborhoods, they have to create strategies that will get the authorities to resolve the problem, and their selection of tactics is both class and gender based. Without mediating organizations or representatives to turn to, housewives must deal directly with the institutions and bureaucrats who can resolve their problems, that is, city and state government agencies, city and state government officials. The overarching strategies chosen by women across urban Mexico have been negotiation and disruption. When a public service problem first arises, women will usually try negotiation. This takes the form of neighborhood committees formed to meet with appropriate government bureaucrats to ask for help. However, if and when the problem is not resolved, women from low-income neighborhoods have consistently escalated their strategies. If negotiation does not work, low-income women have to create some sort of disturbance or disruption in order to get attention and ultimately get help (Bennett 1995a:116–122).

Women in low-income neighborhoods in Mexico have found many tactics that create enough disruption of ordinary life to insure that they be heard. For example, in Monterrey, where water services had deteriorated to the point where many neighborhoods only had a few hours of water service per day with unreliable hours of service, women used a variety of tactics (Bennett 1995a, 1995b). In neighborhoods that were located along major roads, housewives blocked those roads with tubs and buckets, then formed a human chain across the road, demanding water service for their neighborhood. Several times over several years women were successful at blocking the entire downtown of the city in this manner. For days at a time no vehicular traffic could pass through the central business district of Monterrey. Many other times the blockades were along the major roads leading to industrial complexes. This created massive traffic jams for workers (on buses) and for factory deliveries. Another creative tactic was for women to seize water authority vehicles and their drivers as they passed through the neighborhood, holding vehicle and driver hostage until water service was improved.

The most ubiquitous tactic by women in Mexican cities, however, has been protests and rallies on public space.[4] Women have been successful at organizing protests in front of mayors' offices, governors' offices, and other political or institutional buildings. To dramatize the problems of water shortages, women have done their laundry in public fountains and bathed their children in fountains in front of politicians' offices (Bennett 1995a). They have camped out in hallways in government buildings and in plazas in front of these buildings.

The protests, rallies, street blockades, and kidnappings all have one goal in common: They are tactics aimed at disrupting the normal flow of city life or the normal workday of government officials. As stated by Tarrow (1989:6), "The power of the protest is in its power to disrupt the lives of others, and this it does through its drama, its symbolism, and the uncertainty it creates." By creating a disruption, women are able to get attention drawn to the problems of their neighborhood, and that is usually the *only* way low-income women can get the attention of government authorities who have the power to solve (whether temporarily or permanently) the public service problems that beset low-income neighborhoods in Mexican cities.[5]

We call the kinds of protests and disruptive activities described above territorially based protests because they emanate from individual neighborhoods. Public service problems affect individual neighborhoods and may affect one neighborhood and not its neighbor, even if both neighborhoods are basically at the same income level. Participation in and support for territorially based protests comes from residents of the neighborhoods themselves and from nearby neighborhoods *only* if they suffer from the same problems. These protests and disruptions are issue specific, meaning they are focused on solving a particular problem, not at transforming society or changing the political economic system that generated the problem. The duration of the protests is therefore also linked to the duration of the problem. Territorially based protests may occur throughout a city over the same issue, organized in discrete neighborhoods with no effort to link the neighborhoods in a citywide movement. Therefore, territorially based protests are to be differentiated from urban popular movements in that there exists no formal organization to coordinate protests across the city and there are no overarching leaders who orchestrate the protests in different neighborhoods across the city.

In those cases where a multitude of neighborhoods are using similar tactics to address the same problem, this is testimony to the widespread nature of the problem and not evidence of the existence of a formal organization to coordinate the protests. For example, in Monterrey, dramatic water shortages led to territorially based protests that peaked in 1978, 1979, 1980, 1982, and 1983. During those years, as many as sixty to seventy neighborhoods from all parts of the city protested the shortages, repeating similar tactics over and over again. However, each neighborhood acted on its own, and there was never any attempt to coordinate the protests or to use them as a launching pad to create some sort of urban movement. When the water service problems were addressed satisfactorily by the government, the protests ended (Bennett 1995a).

What led to the use of similar tactics by different neighborhoods was not the existence of a leader or coordinating body (which did not exist) but the fact that the tactics were gender based. Women did what other workers do when they have work-related problems: They responded in their workplace or at the offices of the relevant authorities. A housewife's workplace is her neighborhood. When women chose tactics they could carry out within their neighborhoods, they had to do something that would be visible outside their neighborhood—otherwise they would not catch the attention of bureaucrats who could respond to their complaints. Hence the widespread use of tactics such as blockading streets or kidnapping government vehicles. The other locus for voicing territorially based problems was at government offices. Again, women had to use tactics that would catch the attention of officials at their offices. Hence the use of protests and sit-ins. Whether the issue is water service, bus routes, or street lights, women use variations of the tactics described above.

Conclusions: Urban Popular Movements
Versus Territorially Based Protests

There are some obvious similarities and some not so obvious differences between urban popular movements and territorially based protests. In terms of strategy there are key similarities, whereas in terms of tactics there are some key differences. Both forms of social activism share a tendency to try negotiation first, then escalate to disruption if negotiation does not succeed. Occasionally both will resort to disruption without having first tried negotiation. However, when it comes to tactics, the nuances of negotiation by urban popular movements is quite different from that of territorially based organizations. Urban popular movements usually have fairly large memberships, which can give their leaders a certain amount of power when they try to negotiate with government bureaucrats. Urban popular movements can effectively mobilize huge groups in rallies, marches, and protests. Because urban popular movements are formal organizations, over time their leaders may develop direct connections with government officials. Negotiation that occurs between a government official and a leader of an urban popular movement who represents a large and loyal constituency and who has an ongoing relationship with city or state officials is very different from the process that occurs between a government official and a commission of low-income women who have no formal organization behind them and who, in all likelihood, have no connection to any government officials.

When disruption is the strategy, urban popular movements can draw upon their existing organizational structure to plan the activity and to get participants. Territorially based protests do not have the advantage of a formal organization when it comes to planning and carrying out activities, but that does not mean they start from scratch every time. Even without a formal organization, participants in prior protests have acquired experience that can be drawn upon. On the other hand, it is much harder for the government to stop territorially based protests by repression and co-optation than it is for the government to co-opt or repress urban popular movements. Because territorially based protests do not have overarching leadership, there are no individuals who can be co-opted or physically intimidated. It is also hard to repress these protests because they are usually carried out by masses of women, and there is (in Mexico at least) strong moral pressure not to carry out violent repression against groups of women. Conversely, it is permissible to carry out acts of repression against the leadership of urban popular movements, who almost all happen to be men. Thus, leaders of urban popular movements have been jailed and attacked, and entire movements—especially in their earliest land invasion stages—have been attacked by police or military units. In contrast, territorially based protests have traditionally been allowed to proceed without repression whether they are blocking streets, kidnapping government vehicles, or holding protests rallies.

In the case of Monterrey, urban popular movements and territorially based protests have had substantially different histories. In the early 1970s the shortage of low-income housing in Monterrey was so acute that land invasions became commonplace and were very successful. The fact that one of the successful land invasion neighborhoods was led by a small group of cadres from one of the clandestine political movements out of Mexico City (discussed earlier) led to the formation of one of Mexico's most significant urban popular movements, the Frente Popular Tierra y Libertad (Tierra y Libertad Popular Front, FPTyL). At the time of its formation in 1976, the FPTyL consisted of thirty-one neighborhoods, sixteen tenant groups, three *ejido* associations, and various working-class collectives (bus drivers, street vendors, and so on) (Pérez Güemes and Garza del Toro 1984:42). The neighborhoods that belonged to the FPTyL worked to achieve better living conditions and to achieve security while the leadership at the top of the movement worked both at the local level to help individual neighborhoods with their needs and at the national level to develop the long-term goals and the political direction of the urban popular movement system nationwide.

The FPTyL was successful in using land invasions as a strategy to create a new political actor in Monterrey and in the state of Nuevo León: Whereas individual land-invading families would have had no power vis-à-vis the government, their absolute number and their relatively large weight within the population of the city as a whole, combined with the leadership of the cadres from Mexico City, made them a force to be reckoned with. After several years, the land invasion neighborhoods that belonged to the FPTyL were never threatened with eviction, and they lived in consolidated neighborhoods that looked from the outside just like any other low-income neighborhood in Mexico. The government had been forced to accept their existence on "stolen" land.

Although the leadership of the FPTyL was key to the consolidation not only of the neighborhoods but of the movement as a whole, no less key was the work of women from the neighborhoods. After the early formative stages of the land invasions was over, it was the women of the new neighborhoods who became the backbone of the movement. They filled out the rosters of neighborhood committees (mostly led by men); they made up the majority of those who attended neighborhood assemblies (held by the male leaders); they were majority participants in the marches, protests, and rallies called by the leadership to punctuate demands for services and to protest various government actions or lack of action (ranging from protesting state government attacks on other land invasions to protesting federal government food price policies). Without the consistent presence of the women, without their willingness to put themselves on the line to fight for what they thought was right or what was their due, no urban popular movement would exist today in Mexico.

Although women did not hold top leadership positions in Monterrey's urban popular movement, they were the leaders of its most important territorially based protests. The most significant protests that Monterrey has ever seen occurred over the issue of inadequate water service in the late 1970s and early 1980s (Bennett 1995a). Because the protests over water in Monterrey took place without the creation of a formal organization to guide them, there was little opportunity for men to take over the leadership roles. The protests occurred primarily when women got fed up with the hardships of their jobs as housewives when water service became patently unreliable and insufficient. As women stood endlessly in line at common water faucets that dribbled out miserable streams of water, as they waited day after day for a water delivery truck to appear that was way behind schedule, as the piles of dirty clothing mounted up, as their children went to schools that had no water for the bathrooms, they reached the point where they had to take action. Since they were the ones most affected by the problems, they were the ones to act. In the Monterrey protests, as in most territorially based protests in Mexico, women were the organizers, the spokespersons, the negotiators, and the protesters (Bennett 1995a, 1995b). Thus, by their nature, territorially based protests offer women the opportunity to become leaders as well as participants.

Even though the protests over water service in Monterrey did not evolve into a lasting and more generalized social movement, they did succeed in constituting the women who protested as a political actor. The protests challenged the distribution of water services organized by the state. After the state government tried numerous tactics to stop the protesters, the federal government had to reverse decades of neglect for Monterrey's water system and infuse the region with resources to expand its hydraulic infrastructure. At the same time, it had to bypass the national policy of not providing home water service to poor neighborhoods and create a program just for the city of Monterrey that indeed brought individual home water service to every home in every poor neighborhood of the city (Bennett 1995a). The impact of the protests, and thus the impact of the poor urban women who protested, was the equal of any other effective political actor: They were able to wrest changes in federal spending and federal policy—albeit if only for their city.[6]

In conclusion, in Mexico, social activism has become a part of the everyday life and the everyday struggles of poor urban women. Whether they are the most active members of urban popular movements led by men, the leaders themselves of new urban popular movements, or the organizers of territorially based protests, women are making themselves the "active subjects of social change" (Arizpe 1990:xvi) instead of the passive objects of decisions made by their husbands, their movement leaders, or their government. Whether or not individual women are striving for this, the fact of their participation in popular movements and protests is contributing to a reformulation of their identities as citizens, so that citizenship has come to include the right to decent living conditions and the right to a voice—a voice in the home and a voice in the public domain.

Notes

1. Hernández and Boltvinik (1995, cited in Cornelius 1996:106) claimed that 66 percent of the population lived in poverty in 1992, up from 48.5 percent in 1982. A United Nations study (1993, cited in Cornelius 1996) claimed that 43.8 percent of the population lived at or below the official poverty line.

2. In this chapter, the term *strategy* refers to a general method or plan for obtaining a specific goal, and the term *tactic* refers to the specific steps taken to execute that method.

3. For example, one of the leaders of the Frente Popular Tierra y Libertad in Monterrey was elected to the federal Chamber of Deputies in 1988, and one of the leaders of the Comité de Defensa Popular in Durango was elected mayor of the city of Durango in 1992.

4. In this chapter, the term *public space* refers to a city's streets, parks, and squares. Key government buildings in Mexico are usually situated on public squares or parks.

5. Higher-income women have individual power more or less in proportion to their higher income level. Through contacts or through their own family networks, they can get action by making phone calls directly to the powers that be at whatever government agency handles the public service problem they are facing. In contrast, low-income women have no personal power as individuals and thus must act in groups in order to be heard.

6. The Frente Popular Tierra y Libertad in Monterrey did not take on the water issue as a cause in and of itself. Although its affiliated neighborhoods also suffered (as did the entire city) from inadequate water service, this was simply one among many issues they contended with. One of the original leaders of the Frente told me that in retrospect he could see that they had missed the boat in terms of an organizing opportunity. They did not see the protests over water in other neighborhoods for their larger organizing potential and did not get involved with them.

❀ 9 ❀

The Role of Women's Nongovernmental Organizations in Mexican Public Life

María Luisa Tarrés

I used to fight for others, the poor, the peasants, the Indians, the marginalized. Today, when I fight for women, I include myself, and this has a profound meaning not only because of its motivational force but also because it allows me to transcend. It is something selfish: a struggle for my own self that becomes a struggle for all women and all of society.

—**Mexican NGO activist**

In Mexico, women's participation in public life has traditionally taken place in social spaces that are very similar in form and function to those carried out by nongovernmental organizations (NGOs). This pattern is so common that one could argue that women are pioneers in this type of organizations if their experience is compared to that of males, whose participation has overwhelmingly been in the institutionalized political systems.

Until 1953, the year in which women were granted the right to vote and therefore came to be recognized as citizens, women were excluded from exercising formal politics. Today, notwithstanding that there has been some progress, they are still excluded. Even though nowadays women are elected and appointed to public office, their contribution to the common good takes place mostly in noninstitutional spaces where the practice of politics acquires another style.

These exclusionary practices have caused women's participation in public life to be closer to the type of activities that take place in both NGOs and in the new styles of practicing politics in contemporary societies (Eder 1993). Women influence the decisions that affect their society

131

from their own spheres of action, from where they define demands, form organizations, and generate projects that appear in the institutional scenario only in crisis periods or in very specific moments in national history (see Tarrés 1991, 1993). The integration of women into NGOs thus occurs smoothly, as it is rooted in the link between women's historical experiences of subordination and collective action (Tilly 1978).

The formulation of agendas and the activities of these organizations, however, are permeated by the vast transformations that have taken place in Mexican society in the last years and given a voice to new actors, such as women and Indians, who had not been recognized as legitimate by the political system. In this sense, NGOs differ from traditional groups and associations of women that participate in public life under traditional values. NGO activities are directly or indirectly influenced by the demands of the feminist movement, which are aimed at reverting the subordinate condition of women and at offering new models of gender relations.

With the passage of time, NGOs have become a center of power independent not only from the government but also from the groups in which the previous activist experiences of their participants were developed. From this perspective, one can argue that these organizations represent the culmination of a process in which women become independent from the tutelage of traditional public actors and are able to generate an agenda that vindicates them and suits their own organizational objectives.

In this chapter I offer a profile of the universe of NGOs dedicated to women in Mexico, based on an analysis of the information provided by members of a sample of organizations in a series of in-depth interviews. The discussion focuses on the characteristics of the members, the sociocultural resources that facilitate their participation, and the meanings they attach to their participation in NGOs. The chapter concludes with some thoughts on the role of NGOs in the uncertain sociopolitical scenario of contemporary Mexico.[1]

The Creation and Establishment of NGOs

The creation and development of NGOs dedicated to women have been underlined by the emergence of social movements and by the presence of a series of groups, associations, and networks in civil society that since the 1980s have been steadily organizing in spaces parallel to those allowed by the official political system. This general mobilization has occurred in the midst of a legitimacy crisis of the governmental elite and the need to redefine the role of the state in the economy and in social life. Women's NGOs are thus created in a changing and political context that defies the popular perception of the state as the depository of social welfare, populism as a form of political relationship, and Marxism as the political alternative of the popular sectors. This changing context in turn leads to a different set of demands, which instead of falling within the general category of "social justice" are presented as a set of citizens rights that in order to become effective presuppose the existence of a democratic government.

It is perhaps for this reason that the feminist discourse, whose impact was limited until the 1980s, becomes generalized and serves as a symbolic reference point for the most diverse social and political women's groups, who reelaborate it according to their own particular ideological postures and preferences. An example is the indigenous women of the Zapatista army in Chiapas, who vindicate women's political equality with men as well as a woman's right to choose her spouse and the number of children (see Chapter 10). The women of the conservative and Catholic PAN, also, on diverse occasions have condemned their male colleagues' *machista* mechanisms of candidate selection that preclude women from the opportunities of being elected to public office (see Chapter 14). One of the most conclusive proofs of this generalization of feminist discourse is the formation throughout the country of countless organizations that center their activities around gender issues and are directed by women.

NGOs dedicated to women, like other nongovernmental organizations, began developing in the 1990s, after the groups involved in their creation showed they were able to propose solutions to concrete social problems, for instance, during the earthquakes of 1985 in Mexico City and in the aftermath of the fraudulent presidential election of 1988.

Mexican NGOs have a rather different profile from NGOs in other countries because their composition and activities tend to be different from those of popular or social organizations that represent a wider social base. By and large, NGOs in Mexico are professional groups that offer aid to diverse social groups from the popular sectors or to specific populations. This characteristic is probably the outcome of a tradition that relates to the support groups *(comunidades de base)* of the Catholic Church as well as to the vanguard of the left. Thus, students, professionals, or activists establish relationships with the popular sectors and offer their technical, organizational, or ideological support. The presence and activism of a great number of NGOs in the country are thus based on a wide variety of political and organizational experiences.

The life span of groups that associate in a voluntary fashion and that slowly become institutionalized is unpredictable because their durability depends upon numerous factors. The greatest obstacles are found in the process of institutionalization. The transition from a utopic project to concrete collective action entails a process of maturation and profound commitment to a cause or project. It is perhaps for this reason that there are many failed attempts when it comes to trying to form these organizations among activists of the feminist movement and of the women's movement.

Once they are created, NGOs serve as small spaces where alternative procedures for overcoming the subordination of women can be practiced and where women can experiment on their relationships with the public-political world, since these function as platforms of action. These spaces, however, are fragile. They appear and disappear so quickly that it is difficult to state accurately how many NGOs exist in the country or what their characteristics are. It is also difficult to analyze the groups of women that get involved in these activities; the internal logic of the organizations; their projects, networks, and conflicts; and their forms of participation in public life. The sections that follow offer a glimpse into the universe of women's NGOs in Mexico.

The Profile of NGOs: A Heterogeneous Universe

In Mexican society, it is common to find expressions of disenchantment and disappointment with the established order. What is less common is for social groups, in addition to questioning that order, to propose new alternatives or projects to replace it. The feminist movement and the women's movement are among those rare exceptions, since they not only reject the established order that subordinates women but also propose specific practices for implementing alternative sociocultural models to the traditional relationship between men and women (Lamas et al. 1995a).

If the presence of feminists and women was limited for many years to denouncing the established order that imposes such limitations on them, it is essential to recognize that various interpretations on gender relations were always discussed and that several actions aimed at transforming them were developed. NGOs thus became a privileged space for debating the demands of this social movement, and their work has been able to offer new proposals and practical solutions to a variety of problems related to women's interests.

NGOs have thus become the institutionalized space from which women can voice their demands and needs as well as the forum from which they can propose public policies related to the interests of women from a gender perspective.[2] Many individuals from all over the country have participated in the creation of these groups. However, not all of them are able to establish themselves permanently, since voluntary associations usually find numerous obstacles to their development as social needs constantly change.

At the end of the 1990s there were ninety-seven established NGOs in the country working around gender interests. This figure,[3] which comprises the NGOs that worked actively, has not always been the same. During the 1970s, the rhythm of growth of women's NGOs was slow and steady: Ten organizations were created, at an average of one per year. Since 1980, and especially since 1984, that rhythm has accelerated, which has meant not only a quantitative but also a qualitative change, since there were years (1984, 1987, and 1990) in which ten organizations were created during each one that are still active today. This time period coincides with a critical moment in the women's movement, characterized by an approach of feminism to women from the urban popular sectors and in some cases to indigenous and peasant women, who expanded their struggles to incorporate the specific interests of women. All this seems to indicate that in a similar sociopolitical context, the problems shared by different sectors of the women's movement tended to produce similar solutions.

NGOs have thus become a specific mechanism for responding to the needs of women in different groups and regions of the country, since they are independent of male control, political parties or groups, and the government. But they also present innovative features insofar as they search for fresh resources and professionalize the activities that for many years depended on volunteer work.

Notwithstanding the fact that NGOs share common features in their formation period, their growth has been unequal throughout the country. Almost half of them are located in Mexico City and the rest in state capitals and other important cities, such as Tijuana, Baja California, and San Cristóbal de las Casas, Chiapas. In the rest of the country, NGOs are found in small urban areas, and there are very few in the countryside with a gender perspective.[4] The distribution of NGOs in the country seems to follow a certain logic, if one takes into consideration that the women's movement has developed more strongly in large cities and in urban areas. Urban life is where new opportunities are developed for women but also where they experience the dilemmas and hardships produced by their expanding roles. It is also there that they have greater possibilities of relating to other women who share the same experiences and therefore of coming to realize that their problems are not individual but collective.

Thus, the creation of women's NGOs tends to go hand-in-hand with the strength and development of feminist movements and women's movements and to be more common in large cities. Only when their principles become broader and more generalized is it likely for them to appear in smaller cities and in the countryside. With this in mind, it is then possible to establish a relationship between the development of women's NGOs and the urbanization and modernization processes, given that most women living under conditions of urbanization and modernization experience an expansion of their roles and the consequent conflicts. It is also here that women have more opportunities to organize themselves with the purpose of changing a system that does not favor them.

Areas of Activity

Women's NGOs are organized around a variety of issues related to the subordination of women, and each one of them aims to develop specific strategies and mechanisms to eliminate this subordination. The diverse issues that determine the areas of activity (health, political participation, human rights, and so on) are intertwined with an analysis of power structures, which to a large extent determine the specific mechanisms that each NGO develops to deal with women's subordination. Thus, for example, the groups that locate women's subordination in the physical body of women direct their activities toward problems of sexuality, reproductive health, public and domestic violence, abortion, or voluntary maternity. Other groups privilege the exercise of power in public life and work for more recognition of female contributions to domestic life, social struggles, and the labor sector. Among them are the NGOs that are concerned with opening opportunities for women in the areas of employment, politics, and education and that demand their participation in nationally relevant decisionmaking bodies.

At the national level, the most popular area of activity for women's NGOs is health, which includes reproductive health, family planning, and mental health (see Table 9.1). This is followed in importance by violence and human rights, which are considered jointly as the two sides of the same coin. It is worthwhile to point out that these two areas are the areas of activity of 53 percent of the NGOs in the country, whether as their main activity or as a secondary project. In addition, a large number of the more established and specialized NGOs tend to center their activities around health and violence.

The organizations oriented to the integration of women in the areas of production, education, or politics are not as abundant, and neither are those that struggle for legal reforms or for improving the condition of women as citizens. This is noteworthy when one stops to consider the huge number of mixed organizations aimed at participating in electoral processes or other civic matters.

Areas such as the environment, regional development, and housing are not common among women's NGOs. However, what we have called gender theory, which includes the study, discussion, and dissemination of feminism or activities oriented to the construction of a new identity, is dealt with by 25 percent of them, regardless of the main area of activity of the organization.

NGOs tend to work on several areas, with different levels of depth. More than 70 percent of them cover between one and five fields, and the remaining 30 percent are active in more than six; fourteen is the maximum. Working on several areas does not necessarily mean that these

TABLE 9.1   Areas of Activity of Women's NGOs

Areas	%
Health	49
Violence	28
Human Rights	25
Gender Theory	25
Labor Rights	19
Law (Legal Issues)	6
Political Participation	3
Education	18
Environment	14
Housing	14

In this table the total corresponds to the areas of activity covered in the 97 cases. The percentage is higher than 100, since some organizations are active in more than one area.

NGOs are scattered, since some of these areas are complementary. Such is the case, for example, of health, sexuality, and gender theory. However, in other cases the absence of a shared project can lead to a set of loosely structured areas of activity, often born from the preeminence of individual interests over collective ones, or to the utilization of the NGO as an umbrella for scattered activities with little structure.

If the variety of areas NGOs work on is taken as a criteria (see Table 9.2), then it becomes apparent that they are not, as a whole, very specialized organizations. The principal area of activity of half of the organizations in the sample is health, yet only 10 percent of the organizations work exclusively on health-related issues (this proportion increases when adding the 19 percent that devote more than half of their activities to this area). Even NGOs that work on violence, an area highly rooted in the history of the national feminist movement, tend to be scattered, considering that only 34 percent of them dedicate half of their activities to that field. In contrast, organizations that work on less common areas, such as political participation, environment, or housing, tend to be more specialized. Human rights, rights in general, and education tend to be complementary subjects in organizations structured around other areas of activity.

The huge presence of NGOs dedicated to health and violence is distributed similarly throughout the country. We found no significant differences in relation to the fields of activity and an NGO's date of creation. Only the area of gender is more commonly found in Mexico City and in the state capitals than in the smaller localities, probably because in the former there is more access to university centers and libraries, which tends to stimulate the discussion and dissemination of this subject. This is also partly due to the nature of the demands that NGOs in small cities and lo-

TABLE 9.2 Level of Specialization in the Areas of Activity in Women's NGOs

Level of Specialization as % of Activities	Health		Violence		Human Rights		Labor Rights		Legal Issues
	N	%	N	%	N	N	N	%	%
No specialization	13	27	8	29	14	7	3	35	43
Average	21	44	10	37	9	7	4	35	57
Specialized	9	19	4	15	–	2	–	10	–
Very specialized	5	10	5	19	2	4	–	20	–
Total	48	100	27	100	25	20	7	100	100

Level of Specialization as % of Activities	Political Participation		Gender Theory		Education		Ecology		Housing
	N	%	N	%	N	N	N	%	%
No specialization	1	33	19	33	8	6	4	40	28
Average	–	–	24	41	8	5	3	34	22
Specialized	–	–	6	10	–	2	–	13	–
Very specialized	2	67	9	16	2	2	7	13	50
Total	3	100	58	100	18	15	14	100	100

calities have to deal with, which often revolve around an urgent pressure to respond with services and direct attention to a public composed chiefly of female peasants and Indians living in poverty, very often extreme.

The Public They Serve

A cursory examination allows us to observe a certain homogeneity in the public to which NGOs direct their activities, since the majority are oriented to the popular sectors. In Mexico City, NGOs channel their efforts first and foremost to the urban-popular sector, followed by women in general, indigenous and peasant women, and men and women. In both large cities and smaller localities the most common clienteles are indigenous and peasant women as well as women in general. Thus, the majority of NGOs promote activities that favor the development of women from the poorest sectors. In this sense, women's NGOs share with other NGOs dedicated to other areas of activity in the country an autonomous character and an eagerness to contribute to improved life conditions for the popular sectors, to which they offer alternative models to those of the established order.

Organizations that privilege other clienteles are scarce. However, it is essential to underline the existence of other women's NGOs that, because of the nature of their functions, tend to serve a very clearly defined public. These are, for example, those that deal with women and other victims of violence (including men, children, and the elderly); those that work around a single subject, such as the citizenship of women and their relationship with social and political democratization; or those that attempt to influence public policy in a specific sector, such as health. In these cases there is a greater variety of clienteles because what matters is getting women involved in civic activities, regardless of their socioeconomic background. Other organizations try to influence groups of people with positions of political power or in strategic posts in the bureaucracy, such as physicians and paramedics in the health sector, who make decisions on matters that affect women. But even in these cases, the discourse of the members of women's NGOs indicates that their principal clientele is the vast population stuck in poverty and marginalization.

In addition to offering an alternative model to the popular sectors, women's NGOs seek to offer women an avenue for controlling their condition and destiny as women. The point of departure is the assumption that, in addition to being poor, women are dominated by a cultural system that defines them in negative terms. Thus the programs dealing with health, violence, and rape, as well as other projects that promote the integration of women into formal employment and production or those aimed at political participation, are overwhelmingly aimed at overcoming the hierarchical relationship between men and women.

Services and Activities

NGOs offer a vast array of services, and their members devote a great deal of time to undertaking activities that contribute to the attainment of the goals as well as to the functioning and growth of the organization. On average, NGOs provide five services, plus an additional three extra activities, all of which are indispensable in order to ensure the supply of services and the fulfillment of objectives.

The amount of work invested by the members of NGOs in maintaining these activities is very large and to a certain extent makes up for the scarcity of economic and human resources that characterizes these organizations. An initial examination of NGO activities confirms this. In fact, in addition to fulfilling their basic purposes, most NGOs conduct diagnostic or evaluation research in order to define, plan, or improve their services. Indeed, 60 percent of the organizations studied maintain a Documentation and Information Unit open to the public, and a large percentage support and provide counsel to groups and organizations with objectives similar to theirs. Only 30 percent spend time on lobbying activities and exercising pressure in political or bureaucratic spaces where decisions related to their fields of activity are made.

These latter activities may not be terribly productive, and many organizations do not even include them in their programs. It is nevertheless clear that they could be advantageous in the long run, whether to diversify the generation of material resources or to promote support for their activities among people who work on similar areas in decisionmaking arenas.

It is within this organizational framework that the members' high degree of commitment to the organization's collective project becomes a basic resource for accomplishing the group's objectives. More than 90 percent of NGOs offer direct services to their public. In half of the cases these services take the shape of Talleres de Capacitación (Training Workshops), which are oriented to self-help groups in the areas they request, even though in practice they tend to be directed to the general areas of health, violence, and gender. In 23 percent of the NGOs, services are offered as Atención Médica, Psicológica, y Legal (Medical, Psychological, and Legal Assistance), and 21 percent support and promote Proyectos de Desarrollo (Development Projects) directed to the women in the indigenous and peasant sectors, urban residents and workers, women in general, and specific groups such as adolescents, lesbians, the elderly, and prostitutes.

The principal investment capital of NGOs is the commitment and loyalty of their members. They are also blessed with the presence of very active women leaders who have the ability to organize women around different interests and to obtain resources and support for the fulfillment of the goals they set. Several of these organizations (56 percent) have obtained sufficient resources to maintain a body of both full- and part-time paid personnel. This implies an institutionalization of practices and a professionalization of the members of the groups, who must constantly search for external support and resources in order to reach the objectives of the organization.

The dependence on external financing often leads to conflicts over the control of material and nonmaterial resources, both internally within organizations as well as among kindred organizations. Since what is at stake in these conflicts is the survival of the organization's collective good and often the employment of several people, it is essential to act strategically if the organization is to survive and continue to secure resources from the outside.

Commitment and loyalty, as was seen earlier, are critical resources of NGOs because organizational goals coincide with the goals and demands of the members. It is indispensable that these groups, as they become institutionalized, give prime importance to this nonmaterial resource, as it has been a key ingredient in the formation of these organizations. Moreover, the promotion of activities that strengthen the esprit de corps makes every organization unique, since they bring into play every individual member's identity and background.

In sum, even though material and financial resources are indispensable for maintaining organizations that, like these, are linked to a social movement, it is essential to foster the commitment and loyalty of the members toward their group and their movement, since material resources are not sufficient for safeguarding organizations of this nature.

The Background and Resources of Women in NGOs

Organizations are not born out of thin air. Their creation and development are based upon the previous experiences in social, political, or religious participation of the members that make them up as well as upon their educational, cultural, and sometimes economic resources. In this fashion, the majority of people who build organizations and contribute to their development have a personal history of participation, even though there are a few who join an organization of this kind for the first time. Overwhelmingly, the members of these NGOs are women who have been critical of the political system since their youth and rebelled against the socioeconomic inequality of Mexican society by participating in arenas that allowed for dissidence, militating directly in opposition parties or other opposition groups, or contributing to resolve problems they perceived as unjust through their affiliation with the Catholic Church.

The information provided through the research questionnaires indicates that women who search for opportunities to organize independently possess special characteristics. Overall, they come from the middle-class, educated sectors of Mexican society. The education levels of these women are very high when compared to the national general averages or to the average education of women, given that 81 percent of the members have a bachelor's degree, 4 percent a master's or doctorate, and 12 percent the equivalent of high school. Thus, we are dealing with a highly educated elite, since these levels of education can only be observed among women of high income or among those working in positions that demand them, such as universities. This dimension grows further when one considers that many of these women work in the provinces and that some of them with a master's or a doctorate degree are researchers and university professors or high-level officials who join these organizations as a form of contributing to the women's cause and to the development of society.

Thus, the members of women's NGOs bring with them a variety of educational and cultural resources that they place at the service of a cause. Nonetheless, it is fair to speculate that at least some of these highly educated women, often fluent in other languages and with rich experiences living abroad, have perhaps not found the position they searched for in the formal employment market or a position that would allow them to exercise their professional authority in an autonomous fashion. Their high level of education, coupled with a lack of social and professional recognition, may have created ill feelings and increased their interest in creating an organization or joining an NGO.

In practice, 65 percent of NGO members receive compensation for their work with the organization. Of these, however, only one-third are able to devote themselves full-time to the organization. In addition, it is important to point out that the other 35 percent of the active personnel in women's NGOs are volunteers and have other employment outside the NGO. This voluntary contribution replicates traditional female patterns; in NGOs dedicated to human rights the rate of volunteers is reduced to 6.6 percent, and in those dealing with environmental issues to 3 percent (Aguayo and Tarrés 1995). Whatever the reason, it is clear that in NGOs women find a public arena of personal fulfillment where their contributions are recognized, unlike what happens in political parties and other social organizations.

Previous Experiences of Activism

High educational levels, however, are not sufficient to explain why these women seek to build a space for themselves. As pointed out earlier, previous participation experiences facilitate the decision to create or join an NGO. Without any doubt, this decision is affected by a rupture with the organizations in which they were activists or militants. This rupture, coupled with the attractiveness of the feminist discourse, mobilizes these women to the point of stimulating them to undertake an endeavor as risky as the creation of an NGO.

Even though the biographies of NGO members are very diverse, all women share a pattern of previous experiences of activism. This is a key factor in explaining not only the creation but above all the permanency of NGOs. In fact the majority of the members, if not all, participated or were socialized in four very specific sectors before becoming part of their NGO. The first sector is the Comunidades Eclesiásticas de Base (Ecclesiastic Base Communities) linked with the Catholic Church's Liberation Theology, and the second is the semiclandestine leftist groups such as Línea de las Masas (Line of the Masses), Grupo Espartaco (Spartacus Group), Asociación Cívica Revolucionaria (Revolutionary Civic Association), Democracia Proletaria (Proletarian Democracy), and so on that were active politically until the late 1980s. The third sector is the leftist political parties such as the PCM, the Partido Mexicano de los Trabajadores (Mexican Workers' Party, PMT), the Partido Socialista Unificado de México (Unified Socialist Party of Mexico, PSUM), and especially the PRT, which recognized feminism since very early on and provided an important group of leaders to the feminist struggle. The fourth sector is the discussion groups of the feminist movement, often simultaneously with their activism in political or religious organizations.

As can be easily observed, this is a group of rather special people, not only because their activism leads to the opposition or the Church but also because they are very active people who in previous occasions participated in more than one organization or group preoccupied with influencing the direction of national development.

The road that NGOs have to follow in order to become established is so rocky and so filled with obstacles that usually the initiatives to form organizations fail. One of the key factors that contributes to an NGO's stability and permanency is undoubtedly the previous activism experiences of its members, since it helps to ease the creation and development of the new organization in its different stages.

In fact, the previous experiences of these women make their decision to participate in an NGO easier, influence the organization's projects, and are a social and political asset because its members have access to social and political networks to which they previously belonged.

Conclusion

The presence of NGOs dedicated to women in Mexico's national public scene is a novelty, and therefore we are still far from being able to evaluate the consequences and impact of their activities. The sample of organizations analyzed in this chapter provides us with only a superficial knowledge, and therefore the conclusions presented here must be discussed further.

It is important to consider, however, the experience of women's NGOs in the context of the critical period of the country's political system. For that reason, one can tentatively say that the members of women's NGOs, perhaps even unintentionally, are practicing politics beyond politics. This is not only because they have managed to build a new public presence after having militated in political parties or other political organizations, but above all because they have created a community where subjects of general interest are debated. The existence of NGOs illustrates how society produces its own self as much as it illustrates the will and initiative of its individual members. NGOs are interesting because they provide a rather nomadic space, with very little institutionalization when compared with the more traditional arenas. An NGO conducts research without the need to become a university and debates issues of national interest without the need of becoming a parliament.

NGOs also practice politics because they articulate the interests and initiatives of the popular sectors' organized groups and take them to other groups that possess the technical and professional abilities to offer them solutions (e.g., for legal, sanitation, accounting, and economic matters). In this sense, NGOs also contribute to the generation of public policies. In light of the country's political and economic crises, however, it is also likely that these different functions undertaken by the NGOs are a response of the middle classes to the lack of representation found in political parties and to the legitimacy problems of a system that, notwithstanding its constant attempts at reform, has not been able to make a full transition to democracy.

The visibility and political importance of NGOs in the last years are probably a consequence of the fragility of the country's political institutions. If the democratization of the national political system were to be strengthened—which assumes popular representation in political institutions; a legal system that is institutionalized, respected, and obeyed; and the existence of a large group with real decisionmaking powers—it is likely that the stature of NGOs would decline.

Democracy presupposes, above all, the existence of a public space where the conflicts and issues that affect society can be debated. NGOs cannot encompass these functions. Just as the overload of demands on the political system can contribute to a loss of governability, the deviation of public functions to other arenas that are barely in a process of institutionalization (such as the NGOs) can lead to an even larger legitimacy crisis. But regardless of what functions NGOs may perform in contemporary Mexican society, it is clear that those dedicated to promoting the interests of women are contributing to the democratization of society and to the building of public platforms that facilitate the access of women to a political system that up until now has excluded them.

Notes

1. The information upon which the analysis that follows is based was obtained in various stages. In the first phase my interest was to focus on the largest number possible of NGOs dedicated to women in order to form a sample that included only those with the following characteristics: independent of other institutions (government, universities, unions, political parties), aimed at improving the condition of women, and willing to answer a basic questionnaire conducted over the telephone. The second stage consisted of selecting ten organizations that had a degree of stability over time and a certain public presence, that worked on women's issues, and that were located in several regions of the country. The organizational history and the individual characteristics of the persons involved in these ten organizations were researched more deeply through interviews. What follows are the first findings of that research.

2. In the feminist movement there were, and still are, the so-called reflection groups that discuss these subjects. The women's movement has also made room for this discussion. However, these are places of discussion and debate whose function is to generate individual self-consciousness about women's subordination.

3. It is important to point out that this sample does not include all NGOs but only those that met the criteria set for the sample. This sample is larger than that in PIEM (1993) and smaller than that in PUEG (1995). The sample upon which PIEM (1993) is based consisted of fifty-seven NGOs; the sample upon which PUEG (1995) is based included guilds and professional and political associations constituted by women as well as NGOs managing some project having to do with women.

4. Rural NGOs are often confused with social organizations. There are hundreds of organizations of women formed around a specific productive activity or financial credit, but there are very few with a perspective of gender and perhaps even fewer acting as independent NGOs according to the criteria utilized in this research. See Aguirre, Carmona de Alva, and Alberti (1995) for an interesting account of the experiences of female peasant groups that have organized around and debated gender and feminist issues.

10

Gender and Grassroots Organizing: Lessons from Chiapas

Lynn Stephen

During the past twenty years, Mexico has seen the emergence and continued existence of significant social movements, including human rights, rural and urban movements for improved living conditions, land reclamations, student movements, relatives of the disappeared, labor unions, feminist movements, abortion and reproductive rights movements, movements demanding the democratization of political systems, and more. Women were and are a major presence in these movements. The participation of women in these movements and their increased importance in Mexican political life is a critical factor in cultural demands for increased democratization in all spheres of life, including formal political systems.

Although only one out of fourteen prominent Mexican politicians has been female (Camp this volume), women have played significant political roles through their presence in social movements as well as in political parties. The type of activism they represent—articulated by increasing numbers of women's organizations in Latin America—often integrates a commitment to basic survival for women and their children with a challenge to women's subordination to men. Their work challenges the assumption that the issues of rape, battering, and reproductive control (for example) are divorced from women's concerns about housing, food, land, and medical care. In part the integrated nature of their demands is a result of their historical location. The emergence of a clearly articulated feminist movement in Latin America that gained strength in the 1980s was an important ideological influence in how women's demands were framed in grassroots movements. Feminism as well as dominant cultural ideologies about women's proper place in the home and family influenced the public discourses and individual interpretations of the goals, strategies, and results of these movements.

Central American women's organizing, particularly that of El Salvador and Nicaragua, represents another distinct model of development. Most Salvadoran and Nicaraguan women's organizations were created as part of the clandestine political-military organizations and parties that made up part of the Frente Sandinista de Liberación Nacional (Sandinista National Liberation Front, FSLN) and the Frente Farabundo Martí de Liberación Nacional (Farabundo Martí National Liberation Front, FMLN). Unlike national women's organizations in Cuba and Nicaragua that remained linked to revolutionary parties that came to head governments, however, some of El Salvador's women's organizations declared their autonomy from the parties that founded them before or shortly after these revolutionary parties entered into the formal political process (Stephen 1997).

In Mexico, the Zapatista Army of National Liberation that publicly emerged in January 1994 provided a different model of women's organizing from that associated with the revolutionary left of Latin America. In this chapter I tell the story of how the Zapatista women built on an existing base of women's grassroots organizing in Mexico that increasingly emphasized democratization, political participation, and the integration of what have often been called feminine versus feminist demands into something called popular feminism (Lamas et al. 1995a; Stephen 1997). After first outlining what the experiences and demands of the Zapatista women were, I will go on to discuss how the resulting political opening created by the Zapatistas, and specifically by Zapatista women, helped to build new sets of social and political relations between women from different social sectors, often cutting across ethnic and class divides through the Chiapas Women's Convention and the Convención Nacional de Mujeres (National Women's Convention, CNM).

The Meaning of Democratic Political Culture

A preoccupation with internal processes of democracy found in many women's organizations and in the participation of women in mixed organizations in Mexico highlights the importance of negotiating differences among women. The issue of democratization was certainly a major political concern in Mexico, and it is quite logical to think that national political concerns have a significant influence on the internal processes of social movements. At the same time, however, a significant preoccupation with processes of internal democratization also indicates the necessity of mediating, not erasing, difference—of asking a common set of questions but not demanding that everyone have precisely the same answers.

The term *participatory democracy* is used here to denote widespread citizen participation. It is not confined to electoral democracies in which the primary exercise of citizenship is voting. Politics as participatory and citizenship as the active engagement of peers in the public realm assume a notion of democracy that is not the negative liberty of noninterference or the legitimization of every individual interest (Dietz 1992). Democracy "takes politics to be the collective and participatory engagement of citizens in the determination of the affairs of their community" (Dietz 1992:75).

The issue of internal democracy has arisen for the women in Mexico through a variety of avenues. First, it has come through the sometimes brutal treatment of opposition organizations by various agencies of the state as well as by groups such as the White Guards (Guardias Blancas) sponsored by large landowners in Chiapas. Second, it has arisen through exclusion and marginalization of women within opposition organizations, often of the left. In many cases, a fairly obvious contradiction emerged between the calls from independent labor, peasant, and revolutionary organizations for the democratization of national politics and their reproduction of vertical structures of decisionmaking within their organizations. For example, the Women's Regional Council of the CONAMUP emerged because of women's exclusion from the structures of power within the CONAMUP (Stephen 1997; Mogrovejo Aquise 1990).

In order to understand the importance of internal democratization in the Chiapas examples explored here, it is useful to define the term *political culture*. As described by Alvarez, Dagnino, and Escobar, political culture is the "domain of practices and institutions carved out of the totality of social reality that historically comes to be considered properly political" (1997:10). Internal democratization efforts by women in the Regional Council of the CONAMUP, for example, consist of creating alternative forms of political culture and process that do not reproduce the marginalization they experienced in mixed organizations (Stephen 1997; Bennett this volume). Alvarez, Dagnino, and Escobar (1997:10) write that:

> The cultural politics of social movements unsettle the dominant political culture. To the extent that the objectives of contemporary social movements go beyond perceived material and institutional gains; to the extent that social movements shake the boundaries of cultural and political representation and social practice, calling into question even what may or may not be seen as political; to the extent, finally, that the very cultural politics of social movements enact cultural contestations or presuppose cultural difference—then we must accept that what is at stake for social movements, in a profound way, is a transformation of the dominant political culture in which they have to move and constitute themselves as social actors with political pretensions.

Described as such, social movements have truly radical potential. And perhaps one of the longest-lasting social legacies of the Zapatista movement as a whole will be its attempt to transform the larger Mexican political culture. But at the same time, the explicit participation of women in the Zapatista army and civilian movement has brought a particular gendered version to the model of democracy advocated by the Ejército Zapatista de Liberación Nacional (Zapatista National Liberation Army, EZLN) and its adoption and modification by other organizations throughout Mexico involved in carrying out work with the Zapatista women.

As pointed out by Lamas et al. (1995a:344), the "hallmark of the women's movement in the 1990s is the creation of forums for public debate and alliance building among women with differing ideologies and party affiliations." This model of coalition and alliance building that marks Mexican women's movements in the 1990s is also the basis of Zapatista organizing among so-called civil society in Mexico. Perhaps the most outstanding feature of the varying Zapatista strategies to build support in civil society has been the capacity to bring together sectors of Mexican society that have had difficulty in relating to one another. Because the women's movements of Mexico already had considerable experience in doing this beginning in the late 1980s, the connections that Mexican women have forged from a variety of regions and sectors of Mexican society with Zapatista women and others in Chiapas have been particularly illuminating, bringing together indigenous and peasant women with working-class, middle-class, and urban intellectual women in new ways.

The presence of Tzeltal, Tzotzil, Chol, Zoque, Mam, and Tojolobal women and girls among the ranks and to a limited extent among the leadership of the Zapatistas who emerged with a revolutionary law of women also spoke to women throughout Mexico. The issues articulated in the revolutionary laws—domestic violence and rape, reproductive control, political participation equal to that of men, and rights to education, medical care, and economic justice—resonated with those of many women's grassroots organizations.

The EZLN and the Revolutionary Law of Women: Origins and Context

When the EZLN burst onto the international scene on January 1, 1994, a few observers noted that there were significant numbers of women among their ranks and that the temporary takeover of San Cristóbal had been directed by a woman whose *nom de guerre* was Major Ana María. It was not until sixteen days after the now-famous "Declaration from the Lacandón Jungle" was released that the newspaper *El Financiero* made mention of the "Women's Revolutionary Law" that was distributed simultaneously with the Lacandón declaration (Castellanos 1994:4). It states:

First, women have the right to participate in the revolutionary struggle in the place and at the level that their capacity and will dictates without any discrimination based on race, creed, color, or political affiliation.

Second, women have the right to work and to receive a just salary.

Third, women have the right to decide on the number of children they have and take care of.

Fourth, women have the right to participate in community affairs and hold leadership positions if they are freely and democratically elected.

Fifth, women have the right to primary care in terms of their health and nutrition.

Sixth, women have the right to education.

Seventh, women have the right to choose who they are with (i.e. choose their romantic/sexual partners) and should not be obligated to marry by force.

Eighth, no woman should be beaten or physically mistreated by either family members or strangers. Rape and attempted rape should be severely punished.

Ninth, women can hold leadership positions in the organization and hold military rank in the revolutionary armed forces.

Tenth, women have all the rights and obligations set out by the revolutionary laws and regulations. (*Doble Jornada* 1994:8).

The wide-ranging set of issues discussed in the laws points to the importance of the EZLN as a political organization and suggests an underlying conception of democracy that includes women's rights to full political participation and control over all decisions that affect their lives, whether in their sexual lives, raising children, work, politics, or their participation in a revolutionary organization. The issues highlighted in the Revolutionary Law of Women did not emerge spontaneously in the wake of armed struggle but come out of a sustained organizing context in which women slowly articulated the need for attention to their life experience as well as that of male *campesinos*. As stated by Comandante María Alicia in an interview carried out in June 1996:

The organizational process that we went through didn't just involve the core of the Zapatistas. We involved everyone in our process. We asked everyone, "What are we going to do." We also said, "We have to consult with the women." If we Zapatistas are going to do something, then everyone has to be in agreement. This process is critical for us because in the past, in our communities, no one ever took what we thought into consideration. We have to take the opinions of people in the communities very seriously. . . .

We women have accomplished a lot. Now a lot of women have rights they never had before because of this law. People are obliged to guarantee women these rights now. That is why we made the women's law—to guarantee the rights of each of us to participate. Thousands of women participate in the decisions that we make now.

The process of how thousands of women came to be incorporated into decisionmaking structures in Zapatista communities as well as in approval of the Revolutionary Law of Women is bound up in the history of colonization and religious and political organizing in the region.

The Cañadas region of Chiapas, which is the stronghold of the EZLN, is one of the most diverse areas of the state. The region is largely populated by migrants from other parts of Chiapas and elsewhere in Mexico who were encouraged to resettle in the Mexican frontier as part of colonization programs. The area includes Choles from Palenque, highland Tzotziles pushed out of San Juan Chamula by traditional *caciques* aligned with the PRI, Tzeltal and Tojolobal Indians who were plantation workers or lost their land to local elites in the northern and eastern highlands, and landless *mestizo* farmers from a variety of states (see Collier 1994; Harvey 1994:27; Ross 1994:256; Rus 1994). This ethnic diversity was further complicated by grassroots organizing efforts promoted by Liberation Theology under the direction of Bishop Samuel Ruiz, by Protestant evangelization, and by independent peasant organizations and *ejido* unions promoted by Maoist activists of varying political lines (see Harvey, 1994).

The work of Bishop Ruiz and his team of priests was critical in laying the foundations for the First Indigenous Congress, referred to by many as a landmark event in the contemporary movement for autonomous multiethnic regions in Chiapas. Before the 1974 congress, local and regional congresses and meetings to prepare for the congress were run in a style characterized by "planting and harvesting the words of the people *(sembrar y cosechar la palabra)*" in which all issues were discussed first in small groups of six to eight people that worked by consensus (García de León 1994:ii). After small discussion groups reached consensus, democratically elected leaders would make a periodic synthesis of what had been decided in small groups and call for a larger-level consensus. The teams that led these meetings were made of up indigenous leaders and put together largely by the church. They also included advisers from the Maoist group Unión del Pueblo (The People's Union, UP) who were invited by Samuel Ruiz to help prepare for the congress (Harvey 1994:29). Methods used by UP and then later by other Maoist organizers were designed to decentralize and democratize decisionmaking.

The demands of the congress and the platforms given and published in Tzotzil, Tzeltal, Chol, and Tojolabal focus on land and land conflicts; labor rights, including provision of the minimum wage; issues in indigenous education, including language instruction, problems with teachers, and a demand for an indigenous newspaper to be published in four languages; credit and issues of commercialization of coffee and other products; and health issues, including the preservation of traditional medicine, the establishment of clinics, and eradication of chronic diseases (García de León

1994:iii–viii). Women's issues were not directly addressed at the congress, and although there were some women delegates, their numbers were few.

Following the congress, grassroots organizing efforts took off in several directions supported by the Church and leftist activists, although the two groups did not always see eye to eye. In 1976, three regional *ejido* unions were formed bringing together two or more communities in the municipalities of Las Margaritas and Ocosingo. Organizers from the Maoist-oriented Proletarian Line were active as advisers in each of these *ejido* unions.

In 1980, a different statewide effort to improve the terms of coffee marketing resulted in the unification of the three *ejido* unions as well as other smaller producer groups to form the Unión de Uniones (Union of Ejido Unions and Solidarity Peasant Organizations of Chiapas, UU) (Harvey 1994:30, 1992). UU focused primarily on peasant appropriation of the production process. As described by Harvey, it was "the first and largest independent campesino organization in Chiapas, representing 12,000 mainly indigenous families from 170 communities in 11 municipalities" (1994:30). In 1983 the organization split. One part of the split plus two other *ejido* unions later formed another organization in March 1988, called Asociación Rural de Interés Colectivo (Rural Collective Interest Association, ARIC)—Unión de Uniones.

Another important regional peasant organization that developed in the 1970s was the Central Independiente de Obreros Agrícolas y Campesinos (Independent Central of Agricultural Workers and Peasants, CIOAC), which organized Tzeltal and Tzotzil agricultural workers into unions on coffee and cattle ranches in the municipalities of Simojovel, Juitiupan, El Bosque, Pueblo Nuevo, and Solistahuacan in Chiapas. Its documents reflect an awareness of indigenous identity and politics through the acknowledgment of indigenous claims to lands historically denied, defense of indigenous languages and forms of government and religion, and the need to struggle against efforts to assimilate indigenous peoples. Although indigenous identity within the CIOAC was still framed by "class struggle," CIOAC organizing efforts brought indigenous peoples together across ethnic boundaries, resulting in a multiethnic organizing model that forced participants to break down the cultural barriers of particular ethnic and linguistic boundaries. Again, women were part of the organizing efforts at the grassroots base but were seldom in positions of leadership and were not automatically included in decisionmaking processes. They did, however, participate in large numbers in marches, demonstrations, and other actions.

As outlined in Harvey (1994), many other sources of independent peasant organizing emerged in the 1970s and 1980s. The Coordinadora Nacional Plan de Ayala (National Coordinator Plan de Ayala, CNPA), which takes its name from Zapata's 1911 plan to redistribute land, was founded in 1979 with ten regional peasant organizations. Their principal demands included "the legal recognition of long-standing indigenous land rights; the distribution of land exceeding the legal limits for private property; community control over and defense of natural resources; agricultural production, marketing, and consumption subsidies; rural unionization; and the preservation of popular culture" (Paré 1990:85). CNPA participants included indigenous peoples with communal land or no land, *minifundia* peasants, peasants who were soliciting land, and some groups of small producers and agrarian wage workers. The CNPA had twenty-one member organizations in the early 1980s, many of whom were involved in bloody disputes with ranchers over land. Twelve different ethnic groups were represented within the CNPA, and the organization was explicit in its defense of indigenous land rights. Like some other independent peasant organizations and particularly those in Chiapas, the CNPA began to respond to ethnically based demands within a framework of multiethnic politics.

During the 1980s, the CNPA began to experience debates about whether or not it should organize an autonomous women's presence within its ranks. The first effort to organize a women's presence within the CNPA came in 1981. The national organization decided, however, that an autonomous women's presence would be an invitation for internal division. A second attempt in 1984 during a CNPA congress resulted in the creation of a women's commission whose charge was to organize a national meeting of peasant women in 1986. Women in the CNPA were mobilized around organizing to create jobs, obtain social services, lower the cost of basic goods, health, and educational issues. The official report from the 1984 CNPA meeting reflected considerable dissatisfaction by the women's commission about the role of women in the organization. It stated that women had had little participation in official negotiations with the state, had received little political training, and had not participated in choosing authorities or reached positions of authority themselves within the CNPA. The commission enumerated particular problems related to women and asked for financial support, child care, and other resources that would help them to participate more fully in the CNPA. The official report also encouraged the inclusion of women's specific demands as part of those adopted by the organization, requested that women be given *ejidal* plots regardless of their marital status, and urged that the CNPA include at least one woman in its directorate (Documentos del Movimiento Campesino 1984:123–126).

Another important source of organizing of all people, but particularly of women, that is little discussed in Chiapas is the role of Protestant evangelization. Citing the work of Rosalva Aída Hernández Castillo (1989,

1994), George Collier wrote of how Protestantism in eastern Chiapas provided those who migrated to the region with new ways of forming community and was particularly important to women (1994:58–60). In Protestant churches in Chiapas and elsewhere, women can hold official public
roles that they may be denied in highland communities. They learn to
speak in public, attend regular services and meetings, and get more public recognition for skills they may have manifested at home and in ritual
settings. Protestant communities also seem to have higher literacy rates in
Chiapas, which also positively affects women and girls (Collier 1994:
58–59). Through learning to read and by participating in public events
and organizational meetings, women and girls in Protestant communities
have gained an important set of skills in the past twenty to thirty years
that has shaped their participation in larger community politics. More
than anything, their experience with the Protestant church as well as that
of Liberation Theology may have socialized them to expect to be included
in public events and discussions in some communities.

Collier's discussion and my own experience in several Lacandón communities with significant Protestant populations contrast with the findings of Christine Eber, who worked in the highland Tzotzil community of
San Pedro Chenalho. Rather than enhancing women's possibilities, Eber
found that women's participation in Protestant sects was limited.

> During services women take offering on the women's side of church, one
> woman prays out loud, and several women sing in choruses, but no women
> fill cargoes as deacons or pastors. Wives assist husbands who are deacons
> and pastors, much as couples serve traditional cargoes, but women have no
> voice in decision-making and do not represent their people in public meet-
> ings (1995: 222–223).

The role of Protestantism in the eastern Lacandón is no doubt different
because of the history of colonization in the region and the presence of
other types of organizing, primarily of peasants. Thus the particular con-
stellation of circumstances that gave rise to the EZLN also affected the ways
women participated in it. As Collier suggested, migration from the highlands to the Lacandón may have been particularly hard for women who
were not accustomed to being away as were men who migrated on an annual basis to perform agricultural work. In communities built in the Lacandón, women had to build new bonds with new organizational forms, which
may have resulted in their taking on roles distinct from those they held elsewhere (1994:59–60). The organizing work done by Protestants, Liberation
Theology Catholics, and peasant organizations was all part of the political
terrain the Zapatistas encountered in the 1980s.

Subcomandante Marcos has acknowledged that when he and a few
other organizers first arrived in the Lacandón jungle, they had traditional

leftist ideas about how to run a guerrilla organization. They viewed themselves as organic intellectuals in the revolutionary vanguard who would educate others. One of their biggest mistakes was to question the existence of God and the authority of Bishop Samuel Ruiz. They had chosen an area with over twenty years of varied organizing experience by different strains of Maoism as well as by the church. They had to adjust their organizational style to the political culture that had already been established by the church and a variety of peasant and indigenous organizations. This organizing style emphasized consensus and inclusion of everyone in the process including women and children. As described by Guillermoprieto:

> The Maya communities' notion that no one person should be above any other, the Church's goal of empowering all members of a community and the secular organizer's belief in political mobilization—all translated into a working, if cumbersome democracy. Women were brought into discussions, children were given a voice. So successful were these efforts that decisions took hours, or weeks, or months of debate . . . (1995:38).

According to the Zapatistas, the Women's Revolutionary Law went through a long process of discussion and consensus decisionmaking before it was adopted. It was not an easy process and made many people uncomfortable. The significant presence of women in the EZLN is attributed to the presence of two women in the original group. Major Ana María says of the role of women in the small original group of armed combatants:

> At first there were only two women in the Zapatista Army. Ten years ago it was very small, made up of only eight to ten people. . . . They told me and another *compañera* who arrived with me that if we hadn't been there [from the beginning] that other women would not have joined us. We were the first two women who came to form part of the first ranks of the Zapatista Army. Because of our participation they saw that we were capable of being in the army and because of this other women joined up . . . We protested that there were no laws specifically for women among the Zapatistas. This is how it started. We wrote the law and brought it to a meeting where there were men and women representing all of the communities. (Rovira 1994:215, 224–225)

Spanish journalist Guiomar Rovira (1997) has published the only in-depth account of Zapatista women based on interviews between 1994 and 1996. Her interview with Maribel, a Zapatista insurgent, focused on the process of organizing the Women's Revolutionary Law. Maribel, who is from the Tojolobal region, described to Rovira how the core of Zapatista women insurgents grew, how they recruited entire families, and then worked specifically to establish women's committees in each community and to guarantee that women participated in Zapatista community assemblies (1997:109–110). This is consistent with descriptions I received from young women insurgents about how they entered the Zapatista ranks. Once the women's committees were established as well as study groups, they were integrated with other community and regional organizational structures. According to Maribel, the creation of organizational spaces just for women, but also articulated with wider community organizational committees, created the room for women to begin to discuss their specific needs.

> When the discussion about the women's law began, the *compañeras* in the communities understood very well what they needed to fight for, what were their specific needs which were different from the general demands. The *compañeras* said, "We can see here among ourselves that within our communities there are injustices that exist because the ideas of the rich have affected the men here so that they want to dominate women. These kinds of ideas are not in our interest." So the women began to discuss this. They said that they had a lot of things that they needed to struggle for, apart from the general demands of all of the communities. (Rovira 1997:110)

According to subcomandante Marcos, the passage of the women's law was not easy. It created a lot of tension among the Zapatista ranks, particularly among men. "The delegates from the Women's Day Committee, the 8th of March, were unhappy with things and we began to hear rumors about their disagreement. The Tzeltales told their *compañeros* that they shouldn't tell anybody what was going on with the women because it was going to be a big mess . . . " (Rovira 1994:225).

Women combatants interviewed in 1994 indicated that there was widespread discussion and exchange about the women's law within the EZLN.[1] Captain Maribel stated:

> The laws are about women's rights to participate in organizations in accordance with their skills. No one is obligated to participate. The law also talks about how women should be paid a just wage. Sometimes women are paid less than men. This isn't fair if they do the same kind of work. . . . If a *compañera* is raped, then this rapist has to be punished. The *compañeras* from the small villages were the ones who insisted that this point be included. These are laws for women here. Not everyone has to adopt them. Other kinds of women can make other kinds of laws. Like women who are students. They can make their own laws. These are ours.

Men interviewed also spoke of the importance of respecting women according to the rank they had and as individuals. Major Eliseo explained: "We have to obey women who are our commanders, even if we don't want to. Of course that is hard for some men, but they have to learn." Not all of the women felt that the laws were easily adopted by men. Lieutenant Ana responded to a question about how well men obeyed the women's law: "Well, they are supposed to obey, but it takes some men a long time to learn to obey women. I had a hard time with some of them."

For women who are combatants in the EZLN, making a commitment to the armed struggle entailed many changes in lifestyle. Lieutenant Norma talked about changes in her life upon entering the EZLN:

> I joined when I was 12 years old. My whole family is part of the EZLN. I started working in social projects, in farming, and in health. Probably the most striking part of participating is the education you get. Especially for women. We were taught about our bodies, about reproduction, and about different diseases. As a young woman where I grew up we never learned about these things. We even heard about condoms. That is not something you hear about in most villages.

According to EZLN combatants, women are integrated into many different levels of the EZLN and into local councils. As detailed by EZLN members, those called insurgents live in military-style camps and go into communities to carry out political education and social welfare projects such as those mentioned by Norma. The militia members or *milicianos* continue to live in their communities, receive military training, and participate in coordinated local militias. Coordination between local militias appears to have been the first step in building a larger army to fend off the attacks of the White Guards (Guardias Blancas) of local landowners. Each community sympathetic to the EZLN organizes its own Consejo Clandestino Revolucionario Indígena (Clandestine Revolutionary Indigenous Council, CCRI), which incorporates local militants. The local CCRI then organizes local committees and elects officers in local assemblies who are responsible for communal safe houses, education, and health. These officers meet regionally to coordinate plans. Local CCRIs also elect representatives to four regional CCRIs, which in turn choose delegates to sit on the CCRI-General Command, well known for the communiqués it sends out (Ross 1994:287).

EZLN representatives have consistently stated that women are about 30 percent of the insurgents and are also representatives on local and regional CCRIs. The CCRI-General Command has two women out of its eleven members who specifically represent women. If local governance operates as it is described by the Zapatistas, then this is a significant change in communities where women do not participate actively in local politics and community assemblies. According to Captain Maribel:

> It has been very difficult to integrate indigenous women into the movement. It is very different than a group of students. They need a lot of support. What

we are trying to establish is that women don't have to just work in the kitchen. Women are also capable of leading society and not just leaving this up to the men. They also have the capacity to govern. What happens is women aren't trained to do this. In the EZLN we have this opportunity. In all of the towns that we control there are women with local positions of responsibility and authority. Slowly things are changing. We have to start in each community and with young people. Most of the women in the EZLN are between 17 and 20 years old.

Although it is difficult to assess the degree to which such changes have permeated society in the Lacandón, the example of the female Zapatista combatants, the dissemination of the Women's Revolutionary Law, and the dedication of local women to the EZLN do suggest some significant advances in women's self-confidence, ability to participate in their communities, and public acknowledgment of their important roles. When the Mexican military invaded communities held by the EZLN in February 1995, women took an active role in driving out and controlling the military in many communities and in representing their community's defense efforts to the press and the media. On several occasions women who are EZLN supporters from La Realidad have told me about how they drove the military outside of the boundaries of the community and continue to monitor their activities. Lucía told me her version in June 1996:[2]

> The army arrived on the ninth of February in 1995. We withdrew to our *ejido* lands behind the town. Then the army came again. They said, "We have come for peace." But that isn't true. We drove them out of town. We got together a group of women and shouted at them, "Get out. Get out of here! We are in charge here, not you. Go back to your barracks. Don't come here to frighten the women." . . . We kept on screaming at them. This is still going on. They come here all the time. We have coffee groves where we can't go to work alone because they are there. We have to constantly be on the lookout for them because we never know when they will try to take advantage of us.

The significance of these testimonies is not only that women in La Realidad physically confronted the army but that they now think of themselves and represent themselves as defenders of their community to each other, the press, and to international delegations. They have taken on an important public role and will tell anyone who asks about the key role that organized women play in the community. This is certainly a confirmation of the strong community role that women play and of the importance of their inclusion in local politics—a key element in creating a participatory democracy that includes women.

The vision of democracy projected by women in the EZLN demands democratization not only of formal political systems and political organizations but also of the daily-life arena of marriage, family life, and work. These are perhaps the most difficult spaces to democratize and, as elsewhere in Mexico, continue to be arenas of intense struggle. In the state of Chiapas, many of the issues underlying the Women's Revolutionary Law have been taken up in a state-wide coalition.

The Chiapas Women's Convention

The issue of rape received significant attention when three young Tzeltal women were raped by a group of soldiers in a military check point in Altamirano in June 1994. After the women were raped, they were set free and threatened with death if they did anything to prosecute the perpetrators of their crime. After rumors were spread in the community that they "were not worth anything anymore," they left and spoke first to a representative of the Comisión Nacional de Derechos Humanos (National Human Rights Commission), who did nothing to help, and then finally with NGOs in San Cristóbal, including the Coordinación de Organismos No-gubernamentales por la Paz de Chiapas (Coordinating Committee of NGOs for Peace in Chiapas, CONPAZ), Chiltak, and the Grupo de Mujeres de San Cristóbal (Lovera 1994a:109–110).

The case set off a series of local and regional organizing activities that were important in building regional solidarity around women's issues and pulling in supportive advisers from elsewhere in Mexico. On June 17, CONPAZ initiated an urgent action alert around the world. Two other indigenous groups, P'as Joloviletik and the Organización Independiente de Mujeres Indígenas, discussed sexual abuse in peace times and under militarization. The case of the Tzeltal women was part of their exchange. On June 30, CONPAZ and the Grupo de Mujeres de San Cristóbal made a formal report about the case to the Ministerio Público Federal de Chiapas (Lovera 1994b:115–116). On August 5, indigenous women from Chiapas along with others marched in support of the three Tzeltal rape victims after the termination of the First State Convention of Chiapas Women. The case thus served to bring together the issues of racism, poverty, and lack of democracy that were part of the EZLN women's agenda with the issues of rape and domestic violence.

The Chiapas Women's Convention was first formed in July 1994, in preparation for the historic first meeting of the Convención Nacional Democrática (National Democratic Convention, CND) in Aguascalientes, Chiapas, called by the EZLN. The call for the convention came from the Zapatistas in mid-June after they rejected the government's thirty-four-point peace plan. The plan was widely discussed in base communities in the Zapatista area of support and rejected by a majority because it did not adequately address questions of political democracy that came to form the centerpiece of the convention platform. The convention focused on a range of themes, including the peaceful transition to democracy, the construction of a new nation, ways to implement the eleven points of the "Declaration from the Lacandón Jungle,"[3] the structure and direction of a transition government, and the establishment of a constitutional congress and a new Mexican Constitution (see Stephen 1995). Each state in Mexico held statewide conventions before the national meeting and elected delegates.

In order to ensure that women's issues were not diluted in the convention, women from twenty-five NGOs and peasant and indigenous organizations came together to articulate the needs of women in the state of Chiapas. The women's program demanded an end to violence against women, including rape, used as ways of intimidating the civilian population by large landowners, their white guards, and the army; demilitarization of the state of Chiapas; respect for human rights; economic justice; an end to discrimination against women; democratic processes and practices that include women in all levels of politics and representation; economic programs and training that allow women to take care of their families; equal rights under the law; the right for women to marry whom they please; equal rights with fathers and children; the right to decide how many children to have; the right to inherit property; and punishment for men who disrespect women and who rape and mistreat them and don't meet their obligations to their families.

The women elected five delegates to the CND who attended subsequent meetings of the convention. The CNM continued to meet on its own and to provide a statewide network for women who work within mixed organizations (the majority of peasant and indigenous organizations) and in explicitly women's organizations.

On November 25, 1994, on the Día Internacional contra la Violencia hacia las Mujeres, 700 women and 180 men from thirty-six different communities and ten different organizations participated in a march in San Cristóbal to protest the rape of the Tzeltal women and to call for the end to all forms of violence against women. According to reporter Sara Lovera, who was at the event, women shouted, "We are human beings, we have feelings, and we demand social justice and democracy . . . enough of domestic violence and abuse" (Lovera and Morquecho 1994:122). Better than anything, the march visually confirmed the regional organizing process in Chiapas that had exploded since the Zapatista uprising—joining together indigenous women both in and out of the Zapatista struggle with other women from a wide range of sectors in Mexican society focused on linking participatory democracy with other issues challenging the subordination of women, such as domestic violence. The Chiapas Women's Convention also developed linkages with feminists in Mexico City and organized workshops on health, violence, and economic survival (see Convención Estatal de Mujeres Chiapanecas 1994).

The Chiapas Women's Convention met again in October and November 1994 and also in January 1995. At the third national meeting of the CND, held in Querétaro in February 1995, the example of the Chiapas Women's Convention was followed at the national level. Before the meeting of the CND, hundreds of women from all over Mexico from "diverse ideologies, personal histories, ethnic groups, sexual preferences, religions and different political tendencies" met in the first CNM (Convención Nacional de Mujeres 1995:1). Their manifesto called for a transitional government that would reject

> all forms of discrimination and oppression. A government that results from the coming together of free will, where women have the right to propose, decide and to represent themselves. The government of transition will not be democratic if it does not include the knowledge, ability, and sentiments of women. This government should be a space for the reformation of politics which considers generic democracy in all of the fields of public and private life. (Convención Nacional de Mujeres 1995:1)

The resolutions of many of the working sessions reflected concerns raised in the Women's Revolutionary Law and by the Chiapas Women's Convention. They included issues of women's control over reproduction, violence against women, rape, representation at all levels of government and in formal terms in the constitution, and equal working conditions and pay.

The CNM was one of the few sections of the CND, along with the Convención Nacional Indígena (National Indigenous Convention, CNI), to take the disparate politics, alliances, and ideologies that continually threatened to divide the CND and forge them into a unified platform that was discussed locally and regionally. Although the CNM does not represent a majority of Mexican women, its presence and the content of its manifesto have opened up critical space in the national discourse on women's rights, democracy, and the meaning of political participation.

In 1998, neither the CND nor the CNM formally exists, but they have given way to new organizational forms such as the Frente Zapatista de Liberación Nacional (Zapatista Front of National Liberation, FZLN) formed to launch the Zapatista movement into public political life and the first National Meeting of the Indigenous Women held in Oaxaca.

Democracy and the Integration of Public and Private Spheres

The discourse on democracy inspired by the Zapatista women and their revolutionary laws is featured front and center in the manifestos and documents of the Chiapas Women's Convention and the CNM. Democratization is proposed as a critical ingredient in improving the lives of women at all levels, both in participation in community, regional, and national politics and decisionmaking and at home.

Women in Chiapas have also used the theme of democratization to legitimize their right to self-determination in both public and private spheres, defying the idea that they will only operate in one sphere properly defined as feminine or masculine. By arguing for the democratization of all spheres of Mexican social life in terms of gender equity, they have refused to recognize the dichotomy between public and private life that for so long has relegated women to what is called "the home" and been used to exclude them from participating in a wide range of public institutions often seen as "male."

Underneath the dichotomy of "feminist/strategic" needs versus "feminine/practical" needs is an assumption of a universal division between the public world of politics that is assumed as male and the private/domestic world that is seen as female. Feminist anthropologists—including, for instance, Michelle Rosaldo (1980)—who proposed the existence of a universal male public and female private dichotomy to explain the universal subordination of women later recanted and noted that universal dichotomies (including that of the public and private) reinforce the tendency to naturalize gender and for theorists to declare that women's present lot derives from what in essence women are. If gender and gendered behavior are social constructions, then neither women nor men can be intrinsically bound to particular spheres or sets of behavior. These categories tend to reflect more about the social and cultural world of social theorists than of their subjects. The neat division between public and private is a historically bound construction relevant to industrial societies at particular points in time. The daily-life world of many sectors of Latin American society is not built around such a division (Stephen 1991).

If women in Mexico are demonstrating the irrelevancy of public-private dichotomies, it makes no sense for observers of their movements to continue this false division and repackage what they do as either "feminine," that is, demanding women's traditional rights linked to the private concerns of mothering, being a wife, and raising families, or "feminist," that is, challenging women's gender subordination and breaking into the public sphere. What they are doing is, in fact, both. Rather than trying to pigeonhole the actions of women according to a fixed structural framework, it seems more fruitful to look at the contributions their movements are making toward larger social change in Mexico.

Notes

An earlier version of this chapter was published in Spanish as "Género y la democracia: Lecciones de Chiapas" in Tarrés (1998).

1. Combatants and supporters of the EZLN were interviewed by the author in August 1994 in and around Guadalupe Tepeyac; in La Realidad in April 1995 and June and July 1996; and in San Cristóbal in July 1996. Captain Maribel's statements are from an interview conducted by Eduardo Vera in October 1994. All translations here and elsewhere in this chapter are by the author.

2. Pseudonym given to woman interviewed. No names were given at the time of the interviews conducted in La Realidad in July 1996. Women preferred to remain anonymous. At that time, the army was coming through the community on a daily basis in a convoy of humvees and tanks to photograph and videotape all community residents and anyone who was visiting.

3. The "Declaration from the Lacandón Jungle" was distributed by the EZLN on January 1, 1994. The eleven points were work, land, housing, food, health, education, independence, liberty, democracy, justice, and peace.

PART THREE

Women in Politics: Government and Political Parties

❖ 11 ❖

Women and Men, Men and Women:
Gender Patterns in Mexican Politics

Roderic Ai Camp

Little is known about the ambitions, values, and experiences of women in Mexico.[1] Even less is known about women who have sought out professional careers. Among professionals, politically active women, because of their public visibility, have attracted some scholarly attention, but little serious analysis has resulted. In this chapter I provide a comparative analysis of women's access to political careers, both with Mexican men and, to a lesser degree, with women elsewhere in the world of politics. Consequently, I will examine what type of women emerge in national public office, what paths they pursue to reach the apex of the political system, and what opportunities lie ahead. It is essential to understand the characteristics of the recruitment process because it is not a lack of political ambition, but access to officeholding, that is a decisive variable in explaining the level of female representation (Carroll 1985:1241).

Women generally are placed at a disadvantage in their pursuit of political careers compared to men, given differences in their level of interest in politics. Mexican women are no exception to this pattern. The 1990–1993 World Values survey data clearly demonstrate that women share less interest in discussing politics than men.[2] On the other hand, Mexicans generally, and Mexican women specifically, report higher levels of frequency in such discussions than occurs in many other countries, among them Italy, France, and Britain. Mexican women are almost exactly on par with those in the United States in terms of the frequency with which they discuss politics. But when queried specifically about their level of interest in politics, only three out of ten women show somewhat or strong interest, two-thirds the level of Mexican men. More significantly, among citizens who responded to the question: "How important is politics in your life?," only 35 percent of Mexican women compared to 46 percent for men deemed it important. That response still placed Mexican women above French and Italian women but well below U.S. women.

The reason why level of interest in and frequency of discussion about political matters are significant is that socialization studies generally, and my own work on Mexican leadership specifically, suggest a relationship between a family environment in which politics is an important topic of conversation and the decision of a teenager to explore political issues and politics.[3] The backgrounds described by Mexican politicians from earlier generations suggest that initial interest in politics was stimulated by a family member (Camp 1984).

Female Representation in National Political Offices

The recruitment of Mexican politicians and other leadership groups has come under increasing scrutiny since the 1970s. But among all the major variables within the recruitment literature that deserve examination, gender is the least studied. This omission may be explained in part by the historical context in which women politicians have operated and by the fact that their presence, and consequently potential influence, has been limited. Indeed, women made no appearance in Mexican national public office until 1940.[4] Since that date, only one out of fourteen prominent Mexican politicians has been female. Nevertheless, as my own data clearly illustrate, the percentage of female politicians from the Manuel Avila Camacho administration (1940–1946) through the Carlos Salinas de Gortari administration (1988–1994) doubled from 1946 to 1958, again from 1958 to 1964, and a third time from 1970 to 1982.

Women have been represented in all branches of the Mexican government. In fact, comparatively, higher levels of female officeholders can be found in some branches than in their counterparts in the United States. Mexican women have been most successful in the judicial and legislative branches of government and in the national leadership of political parties. For example, in 1994, women accounted for 19 percent of supreme court justices, 15 percent of federal magistrates, and 24 percent of judges. Among the three major parties, in 1991, women were best represented in the PRD, with 22 percent, followed by the PAN, with 18 percent of leadership positions, and the PRI at a distant third, with only 12 percent. These institutions, however, have exercised the least influence over policymaking.

The executive branch, which has dominated Mexican decisionmaking, has not been characterized by strong female representation, which at its highest levels has typically averaged about 5 percent. Furthermore, if we make a qualitative distinction among influential and less influential agencies within the executive branch, it is clear that women are not found in the most powerful agencies and that they sometimes concentrate in certain types of agencies. These findings are significant not only for what they reveal about access by gender to the decisionmaking apparatus but also because executive branch careers are critical to upward political mobility within the system as a whole, having exercised an overwhelming influence on recruitment criteria and practices in the Mexican political model.

Specifically, the first female cabinet officer headed the tourism secretariat during the José López Portillo administration (1976–1982), a post currently occupied by a woman in the Ernesto Zedillo government (1994–2000).[5] Other female cabinet secretaries in the initial years of the current administration included ecology (a newly constituted agency) and the controller general (also of recent origin).[6] Then, in the cabinet reshuffle of early 1998, a woman was appointed for the first time as head of foreign relations. Since 1982, women have headed the following cabinet-level agencies: attorney general of justice for the Federal District (1), secretariat of fisheries (1), secretariat of tourism (2), controller general (2), ecology (1), and foreign relations (1). Women at the subsecretary and *oficial mayor* levels (second- and third-ranked positions) have been found most frequently in public education, labor, government, and foreign relations. Of these latter agencies, only foreign relations can be said to have had more than a token representation.

The first major question we can attempt to address is why women are better represented in the legislative and judicial branches. What sets women apart from men in terms of their credentials for public office? An examination of all first-time national officeholders in Mexico from 1934 to 1993 and into the present (see Camp 1995a) suggests the following unique characteristics. First, women are much more likely to have pursued careers within their respective parties. Members of the governing party, the PRI, which has controlled most of the national political offices during this time period, were much more likely to have held party offices at the state or local level. In fact, only a fourth of all men in PRI have held any party office, compared to half of all women who reached national political posts.

Second, women tended to become politically involved through two major channels: unions and grassroots organizations. Women often entered political life through their membership in local organizations, a pattern apparent among women politicians in the United States (Martin 1989:166). These organizations, in turn, led them to become active in politically affiliated groups, particularly women's umbrella associations attached to the PRI. An older generation of women also pursued political careers related to their professional careers: teaching at the primary and secondary school level. A fifth of all female politicians were trained as teachers, compared to only 5 percent of their male counterparts. Teachers' unions were an important affiliate of the PRI, specifically incorporated into the popular or middle-class sector of the party. Because public education at this level was controlled by the federal government, teachers were in a sense federal workers. Of the three original party sectors— agrarian, labor, and popular—the latter dominated both the leadership and the rank-and-file choices of party candidates for elective office. Consequently, women could use their union careers as a stepping stone to party positions and then to national elective office, typically in the Chamber of Deputies.

Women have also become strongly involved in grassroots organizations independent of the government, contributing to both their awareness of and interest in politics (see Tarrés, this volume). In Mexico City alone, for example, from 1986 through 1989, they accounted for 27 percent of the leadership positions in NGOs. Among Mexican human rights organizations in 1993, women directed nearly a third. Their involvement in the rapid growth of autonomous organizations since the mid-1980s enhances their potential influence and their potential to become political actors in the future.

Women have also obtained stronger representation in the judicial branch. Their leadership in this branch is more difficult to explain, but two variables probably are significant. In the first place, as some analysts have argued elsewhere (see Chaney, this volume), women in their initial forays into professional careers are often directed into less influential posts. Of the three branches of government in Mexico, the judicial is the weakest. Second, women have done better in those agencies or branches where some semblance of meritorious promotion criteria takes precedence over other, more informal criteria, the essence of most political appointments in Mexico.

Recruitment Variables Affecting the Selection of Women

Two of the most important variables in the recruitment process in Mexico are education and family background. One of the initial characteristics that has held women back in obtaining equal access to political office is their comparative lack of formal education, specifically at the college level. Younger, politically ambitious women are keeping pace with men in achieving similar levels of graduate and undergraduate education. In the earlier years, however, only half of all women politicians were college graduates, compared to more than three-quarters of comparable-age men. A similar disparity could be found among politicians in the United States in the 1960s, when twice as many men as women obtained college degrees (Jennings and Thomas 1968:477).

Educational levels are crucial because no single institution is more re-sponsible for bringing future politicians together than Mexican universi-ties. The political mentoring process is often initiated in higher education by college teachers who are already well placed within the public sector. The fact that one out of two women never had the opportunity to be in a college classroom deprived them of contact with these mentors and with student peers who later became successful politicians in their own right.

General data on the educational patterns of Mexicans by gender demonstrate that future women politicians have a much stronger oppor-tunity to make use of educational recruitment. Women now account for 40 percent of all students enrolled and graduating from college. The most in-teresting educational statistic is that larger percentages of women com-pared to men are attending private universities—20 to 16 percent, respec-tively.

This statistic is potentially significant because since the 1980s, private institutions, which account for a small percentage of all college graduates, are increasingly important as campuses producing future politicians and a place where such politicians teach. This has been particularly true in the field of economics, and the most influential institutions have been the Ins-tituto Tecnológico Autónomo de México (Autonomous Technological In-stitute of Mexico, ITAM) in Mexico City, the Universidad Iberoamericana (Ibero-American University) in Mexico City, and the Instituto Tecnológico y de Estudios Superiores de Monterrey (Monterrey Institute of Technol-ogy and Higher Studies, ITESM) in Monterrey, Nuevo León. For the first time in Mexican political history, women's opportunities in the educa-tional recruitment locus, which accounts for approximately one-half to three-quarters of significant contacts in upwardly mobile recruitment to national political office, are equal to and potentially exceed that of men.[7]

Institutional type and location are two of three important variables in the role education plays in Mexican political recruitment. The third con-sideration is the major discipline in which students choose to major. At the beginning of the 1980s, women accounted for only 40 percent of those college students enrolled in the social sciences and administrative fields (including law and economics). Women have been seriously underrepre-sented in engineering, which has traditionally served as a small but con-sistent source of national political figures. But since new disciplines such as political science, communications, and economics are surpassing law, women's representation in the social science fields is essential. Only a decade later, in 1990, women equaled men, numbering half of all majors in that broad field. Specifically, women accounted for 50 percent of stu-dents in accounting, 49 percent in business administration, 66 percent in communications, 37 percent in economics, 55 percent in engineering, and 39 percent in law. Compare these figures to those for 1969 (Table 11.1), the

TABLE 11.1   Distribution of Women Graduates Representing the Salinas-
Zedillo Political Generation in Higher Education

Field	Percentage of All Mexican Women	Percentage of All National Politicians[a]
Accounting	18	NA[b]
Business administration	11	NA
Communications	33	NA
Economics	13	23
Engineering	3	19
Law	14	23
Medicine	21	6
Sciences	60	NA

[a]This column refers to graduates in the Salinas administration only.
[b]NA—not available.

Source: Adapted from data in David E. Lorey, "The Rise of the Professions in Twen-
tieth-Century Mexico, University Graduates and Occupational Change Since
1929," *Statistical Abstract of Latin America Supplement Series,* 2d ed., Vol. 12 (Los Angeles: University of California at Los Angeles, 1994), and Roderic Ai Camp, *Political Recruitment Across Two Centuries: Mexico, 1884–1991* (Austin: University of
Texas Press, 1995).

mid-point year for the political generation (born 1940–1959) producing
Carlos Salinas de Gortari and Ernesto Zedillo.

The data in Table 11.1 suggest that young women were at a distinct disadvantage compared to men when it came to using education as a recruitment tool. In economics and law, only about half as many women were enrolled in those disciplines as were ultimately recruited by the national
administration (1988–1994) that best represented their generation. In engineering, they were woefully underrepresented. Only in medicine, of these
four major fields, did women have more than their fair share of graduates,
a figure that is not very helpful to their cause, given its insignificant rank
among college degrees for all politicians (6 percent) in the Salinas era.

A fundamental experience associated with the recruitment process in
higher education is teaching. Unlike most politicians in the United States,
Mexican public figures teach, often for many years, in leading institutions,
particularly in Mexico City. Not surprisingly, the same institutions that
are influential in their educational backgrounds are those that are important to teaching careers. Politicians as teachers are central to the mentoring role in Mexican politics, selecting their most promising students and
recruiting them to public life. Women must be involved in this teaching
process in order to create a political group of their own and to serve as
crucial role models and mentors to other women. Moreover, teachers
themselves make contacts significant to their own future political oppor-

TABLE 11.2   Teaching Experiences of Female Politicians

Institution	Female Percentages	Male Percentages
Universidad Nacional Autónoma de México	43	59
Escuela Nacional Preparatoria	0	5
Instituto Politécnico Nacional	3	4
Colegio de México	2	3
Private universities	21	10
Other universities	43	30

Source: Adapted from Roderic Ai Camp, *Political Recruitment Across Two Centuries, Mexico, 1884–1991* (Austin: University of Texas, 1995).

tunities, true of an important group of politicians in the Salinas-Zedillo administrations from the Colegio de México and ITAM. As the data in Table 11.2 illustrate, women were at a disadvantage compared to men in that fewer of them taught at the UNAM, the leading place of recruitment, and none taught at the National Preparatory School, for many years a significant institution among earlier generations of politicians. Although women teach significantly more than men at private institutions, just as is true of their attendance at such universities, they are not necessarily teaching at those institutions where political recruitment takes place.

Other than place, level, and type of education, a woman's family background can also function as a critical recruitment tool, extending beyond the role it plays in a woman's formative years in establishing higher levels of interest in public service. Kinship in Mexico, as is the case elsewhere in Latin America, is a crucial variable in the determination of political linkages and success in public life.[8] When the father or mother of successful female politicians is compared to those of men, women compare favorably in the percentages whose parent or parents were themselves active in political life, typically one out of ten. (The figures would likely be higher for both sexes if data were complete.) But when men and women are measured according to the percentage who are known to have a relative active in public life, twice as many men (28 percent) as women (15 percent) claim such linkages.

These kinship ties are important for two reasons. First, it is often a relative, and not a parent, who serves as a role model among young Mexicans in their career choices. This is true among cultural, religious, military, and economic as well as political leaders. Second, all other variables being equal, prospective politicians of either gender will enhance their opportunities in attaching themselves to an influential mentor if an extended family member opens the door or personally serves in that capacity. Women, therefore, are at a distinct disadvantage because of the relative infrequency of those linkages.

The Potential of Women Politicians
Beyond the 1990s

Are the characteristics of female political leaders changing rapidly enough so as to enhance their continued upward mobility within Mexico's system? It is misleading to look at all women because they come disproportionately from the legislative, and to a lesser degree, the judicial branch. Politicians in both of these branches rarely have had success in the executive branch, both for structural reasons involving the distribution of power and because they do not share in the appropriate characteristics enhancing their recruitment opportunities. If we examine only those few women who have achieved the highest levels of national prominence in the executive branch since 1994 (Table 11.4), all of whom are part of the 1940–1959 political generation, what does it tell us?

In the first place, in terms of the kinship variable, two of the women were formed in influential political families. Beatriz Paredes is the daughter of Higinio Paredes Ramos, a rancher and former senator. Her mother was also a public official. Silvia Hernández, whose father was a surgeon, counts a brother who became a PRI official and a senator from her home state, Querétaro. Interestingly, three of the six women were the daughters of physicians.

In terms of careers, these women collectively have followed a pattern differing from that found among the current generation of male political technocrats. The most important feature of their careers is their long-time involvement in party affairs, an overriding characteristic of two of these women, Paredes and Hernández. In fact, Silvia Hernández joined the PRI in high school, at the age of fourteen. As is true of those women who follow paths through affiliated women's organizations, she founded the Insurgencia Nacional de Mujeres. Paredes pursued a similar career, but entrenched much more deeply within the peasant movement incorporated into the PRI corporatist, sectoral organizations. Her first leadership role was that of secretary of indigenous action of the national executive committee of the National Revolutionary Youth Movement of PRI, the party's leading youth organization.

Both Paredes and Hernández also are distinguished from men in the executive branch in that they held local or state appointive or elective posts; early in their careers, they were selected by the PRI as congressional candidates. Hernández became the first Mexican woman to obtain a position on the national executive committee of the PRI (1981). Paredes became the first woman to serve as the party's secretary general, the second-ranked position (1992). Also, Paredes is one of the three female governors Mexico has had, having served as governor of Tlaxcala from 1986 to 1992. Interestingly, both women went on to become heads of the party's sectors: Sil-

TABLE 11.3   Prominent Female Figures in the Executive Branch, 1994–1998

Person	Position Held
María de los Angeles Moreno	President of the CEN of PRI
Silvia Hernández	Secretary of Tourism
Norma Samaniego	Controller General
Beatriz Paredes	Subsecretary of Government
Julia Carabias	Secretary of the Environment
Rosario Green	Secretary of Foreign Relations

via Hernández of the CNOP and Beatriz Paredes of the CNC. María de los Angeles Moreno, although pursuing a career track typical of the younger generation of male technocrats, also served as a congresswoman, as president of the Comité Ejecutivo Nacional (National Executive Committee, CEN) of the PRI (the number one position in the party), and as majority leader of the Chamber of Deputies. Thus three out of six leading women have been elected to congress, an experience which is rare among their male peers. In fact, among all prominent politicians in the executive branch after 1935, only 6 percent held any legislative office.

Norma Samaniego and María de los Angeles Moreno, as far as their early careers are concerned, followed a pattern typical of younger male politicians. Not only have their careers been confined almost exclusively to the federal executive branch, but they started out in agencies typical of those that have produced a disproportionate percentage of top leaders since 1988. Those agencies have been the secretariat of the treasury and the now defunct programming and budgeting (incorporated into treasury). Samaniego began her career in programming and budgeting in 1967, as an analyst, and Moreno spent eight years in treasury and programming and budgeting combined.

Finally, what educational patterns do these women represent? On the surface, these women might appear to represent the technocratic educational characteristics. Two of the women graduated in economics, the favored discipline among the technocratic leadership educated in the 1970s and 1980s. These women, as was true of President Salinas, graduated from the National School of Economics at the National University. That would have placed them at the locus of recruitment for the older generation, but an economics education has shifted away from the National University to selected private universities. The most important of these is ITAM, where a generation of students and teachers surrounding Pedro Aspe, Salinas's influential treasury secretary, can be found. This alone suggests that even though women are choosing the right disciplines emphasized by contemporary decisionmakers in public life, they are a half-step behind in the specific schools they have chosen.

Although we have stressed the importance of higher education and specific disciplines, we have not mentioned the extraordinary importance of graduate education, a phenomenon that took off since the administration of Miguel de la Madrid, the first president with such credentials. Graduate education is significant for two reasons. First, it has raised the educational credentials of Mexican leadership and reduced the size of the pool of prospective politicians. Second, graduate education itself has taken on many of the same recruitment characteristics as undergraduate higher education. Thus, once again, location and discipline become critical. Of the six women in Table 11.3, most have graduate degrees, comparable to what would be found among recent male executive branch leaders. Moreover, women are obtaining advanced work in disciplines similar to those of men: economics and administration. The difference is that none of these women obtained degrees beyond an M.A. level, and perhaps more important, none of them graduated from the "right" university. Of the six women, three attended European universities. Samaniego and Moreno both went to the Netherlands, where they pursued programs at the Institute for Social Studies (though not quite overlapping in their studies abroad). This is not an institution that men have attended. Silvia Hernández, who took a more traditional approach, pursued her work at the Sorbonne in Paris and graduated from the London School of Economics (LSE) in public administration. Although the LSE educated some politicians and influential intellectuals in the past, European and English universities have been passé among politicians since the 1960s.

For graduate education to be of some relevance to upward political mobility and recruitment, given the current pattern in Mexican politics, it must occur in the United States and at half a dozen universities, the most important of which have been Yale, Harvard, Chicago, and Stanford. Of those politicians who have completed graduate work, only 23 percent of women studied in the United States compared to 38 percent for men. In other words, women need to attend these institutions, typically their economics programs, in order to make contact with other future politicians of both genders. The Salinas and Zedillo administrations are replete with examples of major figures whose contacts were cemented in these universities. None of them, however, involve prominent female politicians.

Women, on the other hand, may be better positioned than other leading figures from the governing executive leadership, as distinct from opposition party members, given the important transitions occurring within the Mexican political process. If Mexico continues to increase the pace of political liberalization, reflected in the 1996 agreement among the major parties on electoral reforms and voting rights, this may bode well for women as well as for particular types of male politicians. Why is this the case?

As suggested above, a substantial proportion of Mexico's top female politicians, in figures much greater than men (even when they achieve prominent positions in the executive branch), have backgrounds in interest groups, party bureaucracies, local politics, and elective offices. If President Zedillo continues to strengthen the two weaker branches of government, giving them a larger voice in the decisionmaking process (an intent in which he has already made some headway, given specific reforms to the Supreme Court, reforms affecting a legislative minority's ability to question the constitutionality of recently passed legislation, and the electoral reforms' impact on the competitiveness of congressional elections), all politicians with strong bargaining skills, including those of PRI women, will become highly valued. Thus women such as Silvia Hernández and Beatriz Paredes, whose experience is in the types of careers that enhance those skills, will be favored in a more pluralistic system.

In retrospect, it can be said that women have engineered their career choices in such a way as to become generalists rather than specialists. These qualities characterized Mexican political leadership during the 1950s and 1960s, during the heyday of the PRI's dominance. Although that type of hybrid politician, with one foot in party and elective careers and the other in the federal bureaucracy, has not for several administrations acquired the most influential decisionmaking posts, it is apparent that politicians with such skills are making something of a comeback, suggested by the cabinet shuffles in the Zedillo administration.[9]

If women were to emulate men as a means of strengthening their abilities to obtain influential offices, they might increase their presence among present leadership but do so at a certain price. Although it is unknown to what degree women's values differ, if at all, from their male peers on social, economic, and political matters—if one assumes such values would differ, as value surveys suggest among the general Mexican population—then the short-term achievement of greater numbers might sacrifice a level of diversity that female politicians, with a different set of experiences, might bring to that same leadership.

Strictly from the point of view of major consequences for political recruitment patterns, it can be argued that female politicians may be far more valuable in the immediate future as representatives of qualities (both career [experiential] and educational [ideological]) lacking among the majority of their male peers. Homogeneity among political leadership is a potential danger to a system's stability in that it narrows the pool of potential candidates from which future politicians are most likely to be recruited.

Such politicians, when faced with a rapidly changing political situation, are often the least capable of anticipating and coping with crises. The experiences of Zedillo's collaborators may be a case in point. The nature of one's familial formation and background, type, place, and level of education, as well as breadth of political experience, is very much a reflection of a narrow slice of Mexican society. Women have the potential for replicating the weaknesses already apparent among male leadership or for expanding and strengthening their present qualities.

Notes

1. One of the most massive collections of data, which deserves to be carefully mined for differences between Mexican men and women as well as men and women worldwide, is provided in the comprehensive and detailed data set presented by Basáñez, Inglehart, and Moreno (1996).

2. The volumes of data that make up the World Values Survey, although not published, can be obtained from the Institute of Social Research at the University of Michigan–Ann Arbor and from other data bank libraries.

3. This relationship appears to be true among all types of leaders, regardless of their career choice. For example, important differences exist in the familial formations of Mexican politicians and higher Catholic clergy. See Camp (1997).

4. Women were given the right to vote locally long before it was guaranteed by the Constitution in 1953. The first state to grant the vote to women was Yucatán in 1922, followed by San Luis Potosí in 1923. Women first voted in national elections in 1955.

5. Tourism did not become a full-fledged cabinet secretariat until 1976. Rosa Luz Alegría Escamilla, who took office in 1980, was the second person appointed after the reorganization.

6. Established in 1983 by President de la Madrid, the first two secretaries were men. President Salinas appointed María Elena Vázquez Nava. Zedillo's initial appointee, Norma Samaniego, was removed December 30, 1995.

7. Unfortunately we do not have the breakdown for gender by institution, since the institutions themselves are an even more significant factor. Thus, location is as important as type of education.

8. Prior to 1964, evidence suggests that kinship was a significant variable in the background of female congressional officeholders in the United States. See Werner (1966:20).

9. For example, Emilio Chuayffet became Zedillo's secretary of government in 1995. Chuayffet is a politician with a long career in state party and administrative positions, who left the governorship of the State of México to join the cabinet.

❀ 12 ❀

Feminist Policies in Contemporary Mexico: Strategies and Viability

Alicia Martínez and Teresa Incháustegui

The Mexican feminist movement is currently going through a phase that could be called the third period of its institutionalization. In the first period, during the 1970s, the "first generation" organizations were closely identified with the left. Overwhelmingly, they were of a militant character and focused their activities on denouncing oppression, consciousness raising, and analyzing patriarchy. Also, during this period, the demands on abortion and sexual freedom were imperative.

In the 1980s, the shift toward NGOs and other organizations that provided counseling, support, and services gave way to a "second generation" of institutions. These organizations tended to be more professional, offering services in specific areas to grassroots organizations formed by women peasants, workers, homemakers, neighborhood activists, and the like.

This second generation developed a rationale and a new structure of formal and informal relationships that linked each feminist NGO with a clientele (the women's grassroots organizations they served), as well as with the agencies providing financial support, through specific social practices and policies. Their main demand was to participate in the design of public policies (and sometimes of laws and regulations) dealing with women, such as violence, sexual crimes, technical training, and reproductive health.

In this second period, the 1980s, some feminists began to participate in the electoral arena, but it was not until the 1990s, fueled by the increasing electoral activity in the country, that the feminist movement came into a new phase. This new phase denotes a shift back to politics, but this time with a new perspective: the struggle of women to occupy positions of political representation and to be included in decisionmaking circles of party leadership, based upon their participation, experience, and leadership in popular organizations within the parties themselves or in electoral contests. Campaigns such as Ganando Espacios (Gaining Spaces) and other affirmative action strategies began to be promoted.

The results of these efforts have been limited. Hence, the internal debate of these feminist organizations has turned increasingly toward assessing the efficacy of the different forms of organization the movement has adopted and toward a search for solutions to problems such as political representation, delegation of authority, and differentiation of organizations. These subjects touch upon very sensitive aspects of the political culture developed by Mexican feminist organizations.

Stepping aside from this debate, it seems to us that there are two reasons that explain the limited success of the efforts to achieve a greater political inclusion of women in the 1990s. First, the Mexican political system is currently in a transition stage characterized by an intense dispute for power, an uncertain institutional framework caused by the absence of a clear set of rules of the game, and very high volatility. These features are typical of regimes in the process of democratic transition, as is the case of Mexico, even though in the Mexican case it is not the transition from an authoritarian regime to a democratic one but rather the change from a hegemonic party regime closely tied to the state to a multiparty regime with a pluralist state. Undeniably, this political situation focuses the attention and energies of the political parties on traditionally "male" issues, such as party and campaign financing, the rules of the electoral system, the distribution of positions, and so on, while displacing from their political agenda any and all feminist demands. Even though women's concerns had been only partially adopted by the parties, their incorporation added some luster to the parties during the 1970s and 1980s.

Second, within the context of the country's current political situation, the institutional characteristics and strategic plans of the feminist organizations of this "third generation" implicitly limit their political strength and efficacy. Even though these "third-generation" organizations have been the most successful with respect to substantive demands (such as sexual violence, technical training, and so on) and have supported some proposals regarding women's political participation,[1] they have not been able to remove the many contextual and institutional obstacles that still weigh heavily upon the possibilities of a greater political integration of women.

The topics that are dealt with in this chapter are only a few brush strokes of the issues currently confronted by the Mexican feminist movement, which we hope to expand later. In this chapter, however, we offer our participant observations and reflections as a new set of issues has developed for Mexican women in the political arena.

Some Hypotheses

Our statements above are based on the accepted argument that in contemporary Mexico there are certain contextual and institutional barriers that restrict the political activity of women but that there are also inconsistencies in the behavior of women in public life (Tarrés 1996) that reduce the feminist movement's political efficacy as well as the potential impact of affirmative action policies on the transformation of the gender composition of Mexican politics. This inconsistency can be attributed not only to the individual choice of women in politics but also to the organizational web and the rationale of women's political organizations, which have not been able to generate the public opinion or the social presence capable of removing contextual and institutional obstacles.

This statement is based on two hypotheses. The first one maintains that throughout more than forty years of citizen rights and twenty-five of feminist struggle in Mexico, it cannot be said that there has been a historical threshold of institutional integration of women and their agenda. As demonstrated by various researchers (see Hierro, Parada, and Careaga 1995; Fernández Poncela 1995; Martínez 1993), the political inclusion of women at both the electoral level and in decisionmaking arenas shows considerable fluctuations depending on specific *coyunturas*, especially since the political reform of 1977. In the six congresses between 1979 and 1997, the participation percentages of women in the Chamber of Deputies were respectively 9.0, 11.5, 10.5, 12.0, 9.2, and 13.9. In the Senate, they went from 7.8 percent to 13.3 percent (see Hierro, Parada, and Careaga 1995; INEGI/PRONAM 1997).

In any case, if we consider as a floor the most stable level of women's incorporation that the data present, our threshold would be extremely low, which means that the accomplishments of women even in the most favorable *coyunturas* have not been consolidated.

The second hypothesis is that these fluctuations cannot be completely resolved through affirmative action policies, since the basic problem is to establish relationships among women's organizations, political parties, institutions of political representation (the electoral system, Congress), and policy decisionmaking circles. Doing so would provide a dynamic of change that would allow for the removal of discriminatory practices. In other words, the objective is to incorporate into the system a political actor (woman) with the capacity to eliminate decisively the various discriminatory obstacles and to integrate the feminist demand into existing institutions, and with the capacity to handle strategies at different times (during *coyunturas* and in the short and long terms) and in different arenas (society, politics, and culture).

As the analysis of the process of political integration of women in Mexico demonstrates, the contextual and institutional obstacles that inhibit their incorporation have not been transformed structurally, owing partly to the nature of the political regime and partly to the political rationale of their organizations. Thus, a broad description of this process is relevant.

From the moment the political rights of women were recognized (1953) to the present, two phases can be observed. The first was a period of integration from 1940 to 1979, derived from the pre- and postrevolutionary suffrage activism and later from the growth of the feminist movement, during which the political incorporation of women, although restricted, kept growing. In the last part of this period (from the 1960s to the 1970s), a female political elite began to take shape (mostly *priísta*, but not entirely). Although this elite had a certain mobility within the system, it did not engage in much generational or personal exchange with other women.[2]

The second phase of growth in the inclusion of women into the political elite began in the 1980s as a result of the social advancement of women and of the acceptance of certain feminist values, even in the most conservative circles. Its political gains wore out rapidly, however, because of the changes in the political system that began during those years.

This phase, which can be traced back to the International Year of the Woman (1975), constituted a very favorable *coyuntura* for the political incorporation of women, since important spaces were gained in Congress and in the executive branch. Toward the end of the 1980s, however, the incorporation of women and their upward mobility confronted a deeper sociocultural and institutional resistance not easily removable by virtue of an individual's rise on the political ladder, utilized by many women during the earlier period. It now seems that this resistance to women was in some ways an outcome of the already existing tensions caused by a more intense competition among political parties, as well as of the increasingly fierce battle for power during the mid-1980s, which overwhelmingly favored men with political opportunities within the parties and positions in the executive branch.

In this second phase the female political elite was more plural and diversified and less entrenched, that is, broader, more mobile, and with its own bases of support and its own fields of action. And unlike the first elite, this one (both in the PRI and in opposition parties) did not originate exclusively from the top down. In other words, it did not flow from the positions of power at the top of the social pyramid toward the bottom as occurred in the 1950s and 1970s; rather, this elite had its own channels of recruitment and ascent.

The presence of this female political elite was widely felt and its capability for mobilization and political influence was real, but it lacked the appropriate mechanisms of collective action necessary to attain more effective results in electoral contests and in decisionmaking arenas. For this reason, the fact that women constituted the support base of numerous organizations, parties, and movements that originated in this period was not reflected in the political opportunities within women's reach, which is why they remained mostly in secondary positions (Hierro et al. 1995).

The political reform of 1977 increased the political mobility of women and produced a change in the profile of the female personnel entering the government and administrative elites.[3] More women, with a sociocultural profile different from the earlier period, went into the legislative and executive branches than at any other time.

In addition, since the 1990s the three main political parties (PRI, PAN, PRD) have had different blueprints for the integration and participation of women in politics. Generally speaking, however, there has been a consistent lack of consolidation of the spaces won by women in all three parties. In the most competitive electoral period (1986 to 1997), the leadership of the parties has modified (increasing or reducing), according to the specific *coyunturas*, the proportion of women in the higher positions within the party or in the candidates lists for elected positions.

Thus, as a result of electoral *coyunturas* and with the internal and external competition among the political parties intensifying, women have generally lost ground. Up to the time this chapter was written, the PRI had not officially established a quota for women, and the PAN did not have one; however, there seems to be solid interest in instituting a quota system in both parties. In preparation for the 1997 midterm election, the PRI adopted a quota of 30 percent for women and the PAN, albeit informally, had 24 percent women in its electoral lists. As discussed in the next section, only the PRD has officially established a quota, of 30 percent, but it has yet to be reached.

Quota Systems in the Political Parties

In the PRI, an earlier quota system made possible the participation of women in electoral positions and party leadership posts in the CEN. This participation averaged 12.5 percent between 1980 and 1993.

The fourteenth assembly of the PRI (August 1991) formally eliminated the system of quotas for the selection of candidates in all of its sectors.[4] With the elimination of quotas and despite the fact that two organizations of women are under the party's realm—the Consejo para la Integración de la Mujer (Council for the Inclusion of Women, CIM) and the Congreso de Mujeres por el Cambio (Congress of Women for Change, CMC)—the inclusion of women in the PRI's leadership positions and in elected positions has been very weak.

The crisis over any sort of agreement within the PRI and the instability of party rules, especially since 1994, has been more harmful to women than men, owing to the fact that very few women are part of the political cliques that have survived the *salinismo* crisis. Also, the top-down political dynamics of this party (the so-called party-line culture) have not allowed the women of the various sectors and party organizations to mobilize on their own without paying a price. In this manner, when quotas disappeared, a fluctuating pattern of women's political participation emerged.

Between 1980 and 1990, women of the PRI had an average presence of 10.4 percent in the CEN, and even though in some years the proportion was zero, from 1990 to 1993 there was an increase to 12 percent (Hierro et al. 1995). The fluctuations are more noticeable in positions on the party's state committees and in elected positions at the local level, indicating that the lower the political position, the greater the fluctuation in incorporation.

In the PAN, even though its internal struggles seem somewhat calmer, women's demand for political inclusion and advancement is not as strong as in other parties. The electoral successes of this party since 1983 have opened ample opportunities for integrating local leaderships, in which there are many women. This is especially the case in places where the PAN has lacked a strong support base and in order to compete electorally has needed to co-opt local leaders. As this is something the PRD has also done, this strategy has increased the numbers of women involved at the local level.

Compared to the PRI, the fluctuations in the incorporation of women in the PAN are greater, and the average is smaller (9.7 percent). Between 1980 and 1990 women held 8.3 percent of the positions in the CEN, and from 1991 to 1993 their participation rose to 12.5 percent. A 55 percent increase in female representation in the CEN occurred in the PAN in 1987 (15.1 percent representation compared to the 9.7 percent average in the period), reflecting very clearly the boom in the growth of the party's social bases of support (including women) that occurred after Francisco Barrio's defeat in the elections for the governorship of Chihuahua in 1986.

The PAN has steadily maintained its policy of including a certain number of women in both party leadership positions and elected positions, which appears to reveal a behavior that is less sensitive to sociopolitical *coyunturas* and more entrenched in its own party culture and in the growth of its support bases. The overall growth of its membership and the timing of such growth, which started at the beginning of the 1990s and was accompanied by the mobilization of civil movements in defense of the vote (Navismo in San Luis Potosí in 1989; Resistencia Pacífica in Chihuahua in 1986), have brought into the PAN's ranks numerous groups of women. Many of these groups come from circles different from those of traditional families of *panista* dynasties, which were the main providers of women for party activism from 1939 to 1982.

The PRD is the only party that has a statutory commitment for the inclusion of women. Its 1993 congress assigned a representation quota for women of 30 percent. This quota, to date, has never been reached. Between 1990 and 1993, the PRD placed an average of 21.5 percent women in positions in its National Political Council (Consejo Político Nacional), and 24.6 percent of the PRD seats in Congress in 1997 were held by women. Currently, after the 1997 election, 23 percent of the PRD seats in Congress are held by women. The presence of women in both party leadership positions and elected positions has suffered because it is very clear that PRD leaders have given higher priority to other issues of conflict and negotiation than to the incorporation of women, thereby making it most difficult for women to promote a gender agenda within the party.

Since the 1997 midterm elections, the PAN appears to be the only party to have increased its female representation in Congress. The proportion of women deputies from the PAN grew from 8.5 percent in 1994 to 10.7 percent in 1997. The PRD maintained its female representation almost unchanged, with 24 percent in 1994 and 23 percent in 1997, and so did the PRI, with 14 percent in both 1994 and 1997. This is especially discouraging in the case of the *priístas*, since for the 1997 elections they were already under the 30 percent quota system.

Thus, a general overview of the presence of women in the three political parties as a result of quotas and affirmative action policies favoring greater inclusion and promotion of women shows mixed results. Although there was an increase in women's participation in the legislative branch to 10.4 percent of its positions from 1980 to 1993, most of these (15.3 percent) were for *suplencias* (alternates) (Hierro et al. 1995). From 1994 to 1998, the data show an average of 15 percent. In the top leadership positions of the three parties, the presence of women between 1980 and 1993 was between 9 percent and 20 percent, depending on the party (in the PRD it was 21.5 percent of its National Political Council, in the PAN's CEN 9.7 percent, and in the PRI's CEN 12.5 percent) (Hierro et al. 1995).

Therefore, the presence of women in elected, party leadership and decisionmaking positions, whether within the parties or in government, continues to be very small, especially when compared with the size of the female electorate (58 percent). Even though quotas guarantee a certain percentage of female presence in party positions and in electoral contests, they do not solve the problem of strategic consistency between theory and practice. In the absence of an established political presence of women, the filling of quotas has been subject to the political practices and traditions of the parties, such as the PRI's corporatism. A key factor restricting the relative efficacy of affirmative action policies in the Mexican political regime is the nature of the highly discretional rules of the political game, following the traditions of *presidencialismo*. In spite of many changes, these traditions are still a key element in the appointments for public positions and in the selection of candidates to elected positions. Certainly this remains a critical issue for the women of the PRI.[5]

Thus, our assessment of the position of women in the parties and affirmative action efforts does not provide an optimistic picture, especially when considering the absence of better-structured strategies.

Alternative Strategies

Affirmative action policies constitute a resource for removing certain sociocultural and institutional discriminatory barriers, but their impact can only be solid and long lasting if they create and establish a political actor capable of being politically efficacious at different times and in different areas. In this case what is crucial is to develop organizational mechanisms that will link the feminist movement with women politicians, with the purpose of building a political majority that will promote the structural transformation of the various contextual and institutional restrictions that preclude the integration of the women's cultural and political movement.

The relevant point is that the current relationships between women's organizations and women politicians have assumed a rather restrictive character that does not allow and is not conducive to societal change. The result of this lack of coordination is that the demonstration effect of more women in elected positions and in decisionmaking circles is limited and has not led to any effective change in the popular perception of women in politics.

In some cases this rather precarious relationship is the product of a lack of understanding, underlined by ignorance or disinterest, of women politicians in appointed or elected positions toward the demands of feminist or women's organizations. In other instances the relationships are based on personal connections, which are useful in certain *coyunturas* but tend to be sporadic and politically ineffective, and are certainly not useful for achieving a unity that will lead to a true transformation of women's political efficacy in the long term.

It is also noteworthy that as a result of the advising and consulting relationships of women and feminist NGOs with various government institutions, women have been able to exert some influence in public policies. This influence has been limited, however, because it has not been institutionalized and has remained at the mercy of the political fluctuations caused by the changes in the governing elite every *sexenio*.

All this adds up to a real disincentive for the female electorate, women's organizations, and the feminist movement in general to stimulate and promote the political careers of women. The result has been an inability to form an indispensable critical mass that can remove institutional and societal restrictions and make gender issues a matter of general interest and concern.

The strategies adopted by "third-generation" feminist organizations seem to offer great promise and have come to play a critical role, taking advantage, as they have, of the country's political *coyuntura*. It is important to observe, however, that these strategies are still far from being recognized by all organizations of the feminist movement, partly because feminism's self-image or constructed identity is based on the idea that feminist forms of internal organization and activity are not institutionalized but on the contrary are "open," "flexible," and "creative."

Moving beyond the degree of formalized strategies of these organizations, new institutionalism studies have found that organizations that do not have a strongly formalized internal organization structure and activity agenda, even the most simple ones, tend to be incomplete concoctions of rules, norms, operational procedures, routines, and mechanized standards that define and defend values, interests, identities, and beliefs and that not only define the responsibilities of their actors and their areas of activity but also choose the timing and development alternatives that are considered "appropriate" to their structure. In other words, they restrict and bias the attention of their members to certain issues instead of others, and they affect the distribution of resources, the selection of policies and priorities, and even the types of self-transformations that are permissible. All this occurs regardless of the degree of formality and structure of the rules and values that regulate their operation (March and Olsen 1989; Offe 1987).

Our assessment thus leads us to believe that it is necessary to abandon the naive vision of feminist movement organizations and to analyze in greater detail the effect that the structure of disincentives and restrictions is having on them as well as on the direction and impact of their political efficacy. The current model of institutionalization of feminist and women's organizations (thematic NGOs and other broad groups) has provided several opportunities for the growth of the movement and possesses certain advantages for benefiting from specific *coyunturas*, but at the same time it restricts a more structured action. Although some contextual obstacles have been removed, the structure of disincentives and restrictions that precludes a larger incorporation of women in politics and has stalled the progress of the feminist agenda remains.

Actually, the flexibility of rules and the preference for building strength through broad clienteles and alliances have made possible a greater capacity to react and act defensively in the short term, as well as to take advantage of *coyunturas* initiated by other actors. However, this does not lead to building opportunities and to creating the women's' own *coyunturas* nor to selecting the most appropriate time-managed strategies.

The accumulation of power and influence based on broadly spread support groups and loosely structured mechanisms has prevented the formation of strong support bases and of intermediary leadership, leading to a certain personalization and very limited leadership. The incentive of building leadership from the accumulation of strength built on unity limits the development of leadership in the women's movement because the ability to influence and to relate to the government or other political actors has become a zero-sum game in which what one woman leader accomplishes another woman leader loses. In this manner, the political competition generated is inefficient and unproductive.

This blueprint has also stimulated a centralist bias, a product of the structure of the Mexican political system. It is an undesirable ill from which political movements in Mexico suffer, in detriment of a broader strategy for most movements (including women's) of development and growth.

The idea of unified action, both internally and toward other social organizations and movements, has allowed women to have a strong presence among the actors of the current *coyuntura* who are searching for deep transformations in the Mexican political regime. However, the loose coordination and the few key agreements that are reached have a very short impact with respect to the long-term agenda of institutional and contextual transformations that a democratic project of gender seeks.

Thus, the current forms of institutionalization of women's organizations are useful but not sufficient for establishing a feminist politics in Mexico and indeed may even have diminishing political returns in the long run. For this reason, it is worthwhile to reflect upon the movement's political efficacy.

The Political Efficacy of Mexico's Feminist Movement

In today's Mexican feminist movement, the issue of political efficacy has a central place. In a variety of documents, forums, and other formal and informal meetings, the question of how to design an internal organizational strategy that will lead to greater external political efficacy is often present. The question is frequently approached from the perspective of what type of mechanisms would be the most appropriate to ensure the presence of the political and social agenda of women in the changing political climate that has swept through Mexico in recent years. As is recognized in several of these forums, political efficacy for the feminist movement cannot be equated with placing women in elected and decisionmaking positions, that is, it is not a question of affirmative action strategies. The complexity of the feminist demand goes far beyond the issue of quotas.

Two concepts are particularly useful in our analysis. The first, from Claus Offe (1992), relates to the meaning of political efficacy in the new social movements. The second, from Alicia Martínez (1997b), concerns the specificity of the feminist demand.

According to Offe, a social actor has political efficacy when this actor's basic demands and methods of action are recognized as legitimate by the wider community. This is because the new social movements demand not only the inclusion of their substantive demands but also the incorporation of their values and culture into the institutional and normative order.

The degree of political efficacy attained by these actors is dependent upon the integration of the three levels at which their demands are formulated. The first level, the substantive, is when the governing elites incorporate into their policy decisions the demands of the new actors. The second level is the procedural, when the incorporation of an actor's demands into the official agenda includes the decisionmaking procedures by which that actor arrived at the formulation of the group's basic demands. And the third level, the political, is reached when the proposals to change the social or political order made by the new actor are incorporated into the normative functions of government institutions.

Jean Cohen (see Riechmann and Fernández Buey 1994:48) adds a strategic component to new cultural movements that, like feminism, aspire to change the existing order. This is the concept of self-contained radicalism, which refers to the capacity of effecting partial but dramatic transformations in social institutions. In Cohen's conception, reform and radicalism are not opposing terms, as in the Marxist-Leninist paradigm.

From these perspectives, Mexican feminism as a cultural movement searching to change the existing order requires that it reconstruct itself as a political actor capable of recognizing its internal differentiation and of working in different political arenas and levels. This inevitably means that feminism will become more institutionally complex.

In Mexico today, the feminist demand (Martínez 1997b) is integrated by a diversity of actors with different rationales for political activity. First, there are the grassroots (base) organizations. By and large, these tend to be sectoral (workers, peasants, Indians, homemakers, and so on), are organized according to a variety of criteria (region, ideology, party, ethnic background, and so on), and are mobilized by their struggle to obtain basic conditions for the development of women as human beings. Their demand is substantiated in material goods or in key issues that affect their living conditions.

Second, there are those organizations that add to the material demands of grassroots organizations a symbolic demand, that is, those that struggle to incorporate the values that have arisen from the women's movement. Following a rationale of citizen mobilization and firmly recognizing that there is equality in difference, they demand the removal of restrictions and barriers to women's social, economic, and political participation.

Finally, there is the faction of gender, of identity per se, where all the preceding demands come together in a struggle to transform the institutional rules that determine the allocation of power and resources. Their aspiration is the recognition of the female symbolic universe (deconstructed and reconstructed) in the economy, politics, technology, knowledge, and culture. In other words, they search to transform the codes of Western culture and society. This is the utopian and radical project of feminism.

In this framework, the Mexican feminist movement has only begun its struggle for political efficacy and institutional and societal change. It is a struggle for the political presence of women to materialize, a struggle that will ensure the removal of barriers and restrictions and give way to the incorporation of the feminist demand in institutional agendas.

The Prospects for Mexico's Political Feminism

It is not easy to define with any degree of certainty the medium- and long-term prospects for Mexico's political feminism at a time when the institutions and rules of the game of the political system are undergoing such a profound process of change. The political parties are rapidly changing in order to adapt and adjust to the changes in the electoral landscape, especially since 1997, when the two-party trajectory dominating since 1983 gave way to a more competitive pluralism. For women, this current environment of electoral competitiveness and pluralism may be seen as representing a major opportunity for women in all parties to promote their interests and to further a gender agenda. In our view, however, political women seem to have failed to recognize this opportunity, or if they have, they have not shown sufficient organizational strength or willingness to use it to their advantage.

In the current political environment and with a view to the year 2000, a presidential election year in which it is likely that interparty coalitions will dominate, women should begin working on building a gender alliance that could be used strategically to strengthen their interests and increase their political efficacy. But to take advantage of the current situation, both feminists and politicians must speedily initiate a long overdue discussion about the efficacy of the current organizations of the feminist movement and the existing mechanisms for forging alliances.

One of the most pressing issues that must be formally incorporated into the discussion and dealt with immediately (it has been pending since 1993) is the demand for increasing and stabilizing the political leadership of Mexican women through the use of quotas and other affirmative action strategies. Up until now, quotas are not part of a normative element in the political system but rather are the product of a negotiation that is repeated and renewed in virtually every election. Even though two parties (PRD and PRI) have established in their party statutes a quota system and the Federal Electoral Code in 1993 incorporated a "recommendation" to promote the candidacy of more women to compete for electoral positions, there is still a long way to go before a quota system can count on the full support of party members and an even longer way before any affirmative action effort is firmly incorporated into the country's political culture.

The consolidation of a quota system would require, additionally, that an increased number of female candidates be perceived as beneficial to the political parties. Altogether, the uncertainty of electoral success is considerably higher for women than for men. Although many factors explain this, the one we wish to highlight here is that in Mexico women are still undervalued as political figures in the eyes of the electorate. Clearly this constitutes a major disincentive for consolidating a quota system in the parties, especially in light of the increased electoral competitiveness.

The feminist organizations and their allies in the political parties have yet to establish a clear strategy to deal with the issue of quotas. An effective strategy would require that the quota system be consolidated in constitutional norms and that its effective implementation be overseen closely. It also requires that political women be willing to tackle discrimination head on by communicating more closely with the general electorate, and with the female electorate in particular, to persuade them of the advantages of voting for a woman when casting their vote.

A final point we wish to consider relates to the alliances built between women in the feminist movement and political women. Over time we have observed that this alliance was originally built, and is increasingly strengthened, by the close personal ties and ideological respect that exists among these women. Such a solid relationship has yielded concrete results, such as the passage of legislation regarding rape, domestic violence, and sexual harassment in the workplace. But such an alliance is also limited; in the long run, it cannot serve as a stable and long-term mechanism for an effective representation of gender interests or for the consolidation of female leadership.

A strategy for meeting these objectives would necessarily have to create mechanisms for strengthening the alliance between the women in the feminist organizations and the political parties and giving it a long-term perspective. Such mechanisms would have to offer some guarantee for a capacity to formulate strategic legislative and public policy proposals that could potentially lead to more equity as well as open avenues for building consensus and enlarging the gender agenda. And more important, the strategy would have to meet the need to generate among society in general, but especially in the provinces, an increased sensitivity to women's issues.

Notes

1. Among these was their influence in obtaining presidential approval for an Advisory Council of the National Women's Program 1994–2000 (Consejo Consultivo del Programa Nacional de la Mujer 1994-2000), including women from nongovernmental organizations.

2. For instance, from 1955 to 1986, 276 positions in the executive, legislative, and judicial branches were occupied by women. However, these 276 positions were filled by the same 228 women, that is, each woman filled an average of 1.2 positions (see Hierro et al. 1995).

3. This political reform, initiated by President José López Portillo (1976–1982), recognized for the first time political parties of the left. It also guaranteed representation to minority parties in Congress, based on direct election and proportional representation.

4. Since 1943, the PRI has been integrated by three sectors: the peasant sector, conformed in the CNC and others; the workers' sector, or Confederación de Trabajadores Mexicanos (CTM, Confederation of Mexican Workers); and the popular sector, formed by the CNOP, which covers numerous groups. The CNOP has been subsequently reorganized, most notably by the addition of the Movimiento Territorial in 1993, which originated under PRONASOL.

5. At least 700 positions in the federal executive branch are appointed by the president.

❀ 13 ❀

Women in the Local Arena and Municipal Power

Alejandra Massolo

Throughout time and into the present, a universal pattern persists that shows that the presence and actions of women in the local arena are associated with everyday family life and with domestic tasks. The social divisions and inequalities between male and female have led women to the neighborhood, the vicinal community, and the locality as the places of social life where they have been better able to evolve and project their roles, interests, abilities, and struggles. This is the public world with which they are most familiar.

Paradoxically, the social and cultural baggage embedded in the roles of mother, wife, and housewife has turned out to be as permissive as it is restrictive. The control and the limitation inherent in their immediate space have facilitated women's training and participation in everyday public affairs. The higher levels of formal politics and political power, however, remain as male prerogatives and domain.

Various studies have analyzed the diverse aspects of the interconnection of gender, community, and local government. It is worth mentioning that gender as an analytical category (even though subjected to different approaches and debates within the theoretical currents of feminism) designates a social relation between men and women that is unequal and hierarchical, prescribing a gendered division of labor and the appropriate roles that correspond to men and women in society. Gender is a historical and cultural product. Consequently, it implies a rejection of biological explanations and determinisms and leads to various manifestations of inequality and subordination among women.

Numerous studies conducted in several countries have proven that "typically" women are interested in issues that are relevant at the local and community levels. Women become actively involved in neighborhood associations in order to obtain public services, and they create groups and networks of solidarity, find in the municipal realm a greater sense of political efficacy that allows them to exercise influence and leadership, and take problems that are considered "nonpolitical" to the political arena. Finally, they are predominantly housewives who combine self-help with pressures and protests aimed at local authorities (Randall 1987).

The inclination and preference of women for the politics that Randall refers to as "community" and "protest" are understandable, since it responds to the issues and demands that most concern and preoccupy women in their roles as housewives and mothers. However, although various studies have emphasized the fact that the public participation of women is facilitated at the municipal level and in community politics, given the spatial proximity and the possibility of greater time flexibility, these studies have also provided acute criticisms. For example, in the field of urban research, the concept of community and the ideology of domestic life that equates "the place of women" with the local sphere, merging home and community and therefore concealing situations of gender oppression and exploitation, have been criticized and rejected. In addition, neoliberal policies serve to cover up the feminization of poverty, the transfer of state responsibilities to women in the form of domestic tasks, and community self-help (Massolo 1994b).

Of course, one must take care to avoid idealizing the community and the local level because injustices may become rationalized (Probyn 1990) and the differences between individuals denied. Iris Young (1990) questioned the "community ideal," arguing that it privileges unity over difference, attempts to be all inclusive and socially homogeneous, overestimates the genuineness of one-to-one relationships, and presupposes that women can best achieve this ideal because they are less individualistic than men and more oriented toward care-giving and cooperation. Young's feminist critique highlights the relation between two opposites: individualism/community and masculinity/femininity. Masculinity is identified by values associated with individualism, self-sufficiency, competition, and formal equality of rights, whereas femininity is associated with community values, affective relationships, care-giving, and mutual help. Consequently, this idealized link between women and community excludes any understanding of gender differences, the contradictions of social life, the violence of one-to-one relationships, and feminist principles of heterogeneity (Young 1990).

Another aspect of the female pattern found in the local arena has to do with the small number of women who occupy positions of representation and leadership in municipal governments, which is a reflection of a double restriction: on the one hand, the so-called male chauvinism of politics, which views women as "intruders" (Randall 1987); on the other, the lack of motivation and determination among women to battle for those positions and participate in formal politics. Since the 1970s, however, female participation in local government has increased in many countries, even though a two-sided phenomenon prevails: the unequal access of women to rural municipalities, as female representation is inversely related to the political importance of a municipality, and the specialization-concentration of women in certain areas of municipal governance, such as social welfare, health, and education.

In our Hispanic world, Spain provides a good example for assessing the link between gender and municipality by observing the strategic importance of citizen movements for democratic municipal governments and of national public policies favoring women. Very early in the transition to democracy, local governments pioneered the inclusion in their agendas of a preoccupation with equality and the promotion of women. In 1977, they proposed three objectives: information on women's rights and legal assistance; attention to health, family planning, and sexual education; and sociocultural promotion. The creation of the Woman's Institute in 1983, the approval of the First National Plan for Equal Opportunity for Women in 1988, and the second plan in 1993 have provided the framework and the institutional drive for the design and implementation of policies for municipal administrations and autonomous regions. They moved from traditional assistance practices and paternalistic actions to challenging inequality of opportunities and seeking ways to prevent this inequality (Sampedro 1993). The following proposal clearly expresses this new perspective, which we should adopt in Latin America:

> It is necessary to vie, in a definitive manner, for a comprehensive policy in the local arena aimed at all female citizens, one that will involve all areas of municipal administration and will contemplate the prevention of inequality and the social promotion of women as basic acting criteria. It is necessary to prioritize the decentralization of resources and services, bring both male and female citizens closer to the administration of social welfare, and recognize the local context as the most appropriate for practicing equality of opportunity. (Sampedro 1993:105)

In Latin America:
Among Crisis, Survival and Democracy

The devastating economic crisis of the 1980s (which continues to have a profound effect in the 1990s), the structural adjustment policies, the neoliberal reforms, the transition to democracy in some countries, and the policies of decentralization and municipal reform all fostered a boom in the interest in municipal government and in all forms of political activity at the local level. An uncommon stream of interest in linking the themes of gender and local government ensued, based above all upon the crucial role played by women of urban popular sectors as agents of social welfare who also undertook the overwhelming struggle for their families' subsistence and a unified collectivization of survival while suffering the "invisible adjustment" denounced by the United Nations International Culture and Education Fund (UNICEF).

However, the narrow social relationship between women and their local space does not refer exclusively to the urgency to satisfy the needs for basic goods and services for the family and improvement of their habitat. The relationship also refers to a desire for new social experiences and participation in the public sphere and an aspiration to acquire and build self-esteem and to come out of the enclosure and domestic routine of the home. The formidable female presence among Latin America's poor has had serious physical, emotional, and moral risks and costs, but it is not one of crushed victims; rather, it is the presence of an active social force that influences and transforms the conditions of individual and collective everyday life.

Women's access to municipal power in Latin America is also unequal compared to men, with some exceptional cases of female mayors elected to head municipalities that are important demographically, politically, and economically. For example, in 1988, Luiza Erundina (PT) won the municipal elections in São Paulo, the most important metropolis in Brazil and the second largest in Latin America after Mexico City. Another woman of the PT won the municipality of Natal, Brazil, the most important port of the Atlantic coast in South America. Brazilian female mayors (*prefeitas*) represented 2.4 percent of the total of 4,425 municipalities in 1988. In Ecuador, a woman was elected mayor for the first time in 1988, winning Guayaquil, the largest city in the country. In Colombia, female mayors won 5.6 percent of the total of 1,006 municipalities in the elections of 1992. In Venezuela, 8.6 percent of the total of 246 municipalities were won by women in the elections of 1989, and in Chile 18 female mayors were elected out of 334 municipalities in 1992 (see Arboleda 1993; IULA/CEL-CADEL 1991b).

In the studies that have been conducted on female mayors in Latin America, some common characteristics can be observed: Their age is between forty and fifty; several are professionals in the field of education; and some of them have the background and reputation of community participation and of leadership of popular organizations and civic movements.

Female presence in local government, even though it is growing, is still a minority. Table 13.1 provides a glimpse of just how low the numbers of women at the local level are; even though the data in this table are from

TABLE 13.1   Female Mayors in Latin America (percentages)

Country	Year	Percent
Argentina	1992	3.6
Bolivia	1993	10.0
Brazil	1991	2.4
Chile	1994	7.2
Colombia	1992	5.6
Costa Rica	1994	0.0
Cuba	1993	5.3
Ecuador	1992	3.1
El Salvador	1994	11.1
Guatemala	1994	1.2
Honduras	1994	12.7
Mexico	1992	2.9
Nicaragua	1994	9.8
Panama	1994	9.0
Paraguay	1993	4.9
Peru	1993	6.2
Dominican Republic	1990	4.9
Uruguay	1992	15.8
Venezuela	1992	6.3

Source: Mujeres Latinoamericanas en Cifras, Tomo Comparativo (Santiago de Chile: FLACSO, 1995).

the early 1990s, the numbers have not improved in the second part of the decade. Significantly, a demand for an increased female presence has begun to appear in proposals and discussions about democratic reconstruction in municipal governments. The processes of democratic opening, as well as new feminist perspectives and strategies with regard to participation in elections and public office, have favored the gradual inclusion of gender issues and women's demands. The question and the challenge are whether female participation strengthens and invigorates local democracy, promotes gender equality, and influences the transformation in the exercise of municipal power (Arboleda 1993).

Women in Mexican *Ayuntamientos*

The municipality was the territorial entity where Mexican women first accomplished their political citizenship. In February 1947, a constitutional reform gave women the right to vote and to be voted for but only in municipal elections (they did not get universal suffrage until 1953). The municipality was viewed as the "natural" place to allow women to participate in political public life and to contribute their "feminine virtues" gained through the traditional roles of mother, wife, and housewife in the spheres of family and private life. The expectation was that such roles would transfer to municipal administration and to the exercise of political rights. Thus, from the very beginning the relationship between women and the municipality was legitimized and limited by their condition as domestic citizens (Massolo 1995).

Article 115 of the Mexican Constitution consecrates the *municipio libre* (free municipality) and establishes the authorities and duties of the *ayuntamiento* (local government), conceived as a collective and deliberating government integrated by a mayor, several aldermen (*regidores*) selected by direct election and proportional representation, and one or more trustees (*síndicos*).[1] They are the local authorities elected directly by the citizenry every three years and cannot be reelected for consecutive terms.

If municipalities in Mexico have never been really free, autonomous, efficacious, or a "school of democracy," they have served much less as the institution supposedly receptive to the needs and interests of familial everyday life, attentive and open to women's participation, and followers of any principle of political equality among men and women. It is also important to underscore the fact that heterogeneity and inequality are distinctive attributes of Mexican municipalities. Thus, the opportunities, forms, and accomplishments of women's participation in public local life must be placed within such heterogeneous local and regional contexts.

The *Alcaldesas*

Between 1984 and 1986, in the aftermath of the municipal reform of 1983 decreed by then President Miguel de la Madrid, a total of sixty-nine women were elected mayors in Mexico, representing 3 percent of the 2,378 municipalities that existed at that time. These figures are not only dramatically small but, even more important, also show a clear pattern of segregating female authority to rural municipalities or to urban centers of lesser importance. Of the 51 *alcaldesas*, or female mayors, elected in 1991 (2 percent of the total), 39 governed municipalities with a population of fewer than 30,000 and 12 headed municipalities with a population between 5,000 and 10,000 (Martínez 1993). However, there were some significant exceptions (which have not been repeated up to now) in which women presided over *ayuntamientos* in state capitals: Aguascalientes (PRI), Mérida (PAN), and Toluca (PRI).

In the first half of 1994, prior to the federal elections of August of the same year, there were eighty-six *alcaldesas*, which slightly raised the proportion to 3.5 percent of the total 2,392 municipalities.[2] These women were in charge of governing municipalities that are predominantly rural and have a high or very high marginality index according to the National Population Council criteria (Consejo Nacional de Población 1993). Altogether, seventy-seven of these eighty-six women were elected to govern municipalities of less than 50,000. A total of eight women were elected to municipalities with a population between 50,000 and 100,000 and only one to a municipality of more than 100,000.

In early 1996, there were 85 *alcaldesas*. Even though this number remained almost unchanged from the previous election, the number of municipalities increased to 2,412, and therefore female representation actually decreased. Of those 85 women governing at the local level in early 1996, 30 governed municipalities with populations of 30,000 and fewer, 11 were elected in municipalities with a population between 50,000 and 100,000, and only 2 in municipalities with a population of more than 200,000, which do not happen to be great cities: Nuevo Laredo, Tamaulipas (PRI), and Uruapan, Michoacán (PAN). Women presided over *ayuntamientos* in twenty states, with Veracruz having the most (a total of fifteen women). No woman has become *alcaldesa* in any of the state capitals the PAN has won.

All these data are evidence of the fact that women are grossly underrepresented in the governments of the more developed and urban municipalities. Men dominate larger and urban municipalities, whereas women are clearly relegated to rural and smaller ones. There is also a clear regional distribution pattern: Half of the eighty-six female mayors governing in early 1996 were in the southern region, the poorest region in Mexico; 15 percent governed in the central area, and 35 percent in the north.

Thus, municipal power in Mexico (at all levels of the *ayuntamiento*) is chiefly dominated and exercised by men. Even though a gradual increase of women being elected *alcaldesas* (and alderwomen) can be observed, gender plurality is still minimal. And the political plurality of *alcaldesas* is even worse. In fact, political plurality in the composition of the *ayuntamientos*, even with its gradual growth, is reduced by the hegemony of the PRI, the party that for more than sixty years has controlled the federal government, other institutions, and public resources. In the first half of 1994, 90 percent of the municipalities were governed by the PRI. Of the main opposition parties, the PAN (center right) had won 103 *ayuntamientos*, or 4.3 percent of the total, and the PRD (center left), 85, or 3.5 percent of the total.[3] In 1996, the percentage of Mexican municipalities governed by parties other than the PRI rose to 19, and at the beginning of 1998 to 43. This relative progress in political pluralism is important and is one of the fundamental changes that must be encouraged and consolidated, but it is a process that bears gender inequality and therefore limits political pluralism.

Of the 85 *alcaldesas* governing in 1996, 70 were from the PRI (less than 1 percent of the 1,542 municipalities governed by the PRI), and only 15 belonged to the opposition: PAN 7, out of 221; PRD 4, out of 180; and others 4 (PFCRN 2, PT 1, PPS 1). Altogether, these women governed a total pop ulation of 2,316,833, according to the 1990 census. PAN was the opposition party that achieved greater advances in the municipal elections of 1995, winning 52 *ayuntamientos* in Jalisco, 19 in Veracruz, and 13 in Yucatán. The PRD won 180 municipalities. But women were the *alcaldesas* in only 11 of all of these municipalities, showing that opposition parties, who are so adept at preaching and demanding political pluralism and the alternation of power, nonetheless make little effort to widen and encourage a plurality of gender in their municipal offices. Even worse, most women in those parties do not seem too eager to vindicate their rights or to fight for attaining a larger slice of municipal power. The inequity of gender has persisted in spite of the political plurality of local governments since the mid-1990s. As shown in Table 13.2, only eighty-two municipalities were governed by women in early 1998, in spite of the dramatic advances made by the opposition at the state and local levels.

Alderwomen and Trustees

The *cabildo* (city council) is the formal institution in which, in theory at least, local representative democracy is exercised through elected municipal authorities. However, the democratic performance of *cabildos* is generally very deficient owing to several obstacles and vices that continue to seriously damage the role of local governments. Even though things are now beginning to change, some of the most serious obstacles are the concentration of power and authoritarianism *(presidencialismo local)* in the mayor, the lack of public responsibility of elected authorities toward the citizenry, the failure to respect and follow municipal laws, electoral fraud and conflicts, and the limited authority assigned to *regidores*.

Regidores lack any executive power. The only authority they have is to attend and vote at *cabildo* meetings, take charge of assigned commissions depending on the services and activities of the municipality, and propose initiatives and promote activities to meet the needs and demands of the community. The restricted authority of *regidores* has traditionally been felt more severely by those members who are from political parties other than the PRI and have gained a seat on the *cabildo* through proportional representation. Apparently, it seems that it is still not a political habit of the *ayuntamientos* presided over by the PRI (with some exceptions) to recognize that the role of *regidores* of proportional representation should be carried out with dignity and responsibility. This is not to say, of course, that by definition all the men and women who represent the political plurality of a municipality try to fulfill their roles in a positive and dignified manner.

Notwithstanding the obstacles and limitations, the position of *regidor* is potentially valuable and challenging as well as useful to the community and to the democratic development of municipalities. For many women it represents the first link to representative democracy and the first step in

TABLE 13.2   Municipal Governments, by Party and State, Governed by Women, 1998

State	Total Number of Municipalities	Number Governed by Women			
		PRI	PAN	PRD	PFCRN
Aguascalientes	11				
Baja California	5				
Baja California Sur	5				
Campeche	9				
Chiapas	111				
Chihuahua	67	1			
Coahuila	38	1			
Colima	10		1		
Durango	39	2	1		
Guanajuato	46		1		
Guerrero	76	3		1	
Hidalgo	84	5			
Jalisco	124	1	1		
México	122	6	1	1	
Michoacán	113	2	1		
Morelos	22				
Nayarit	20				
Nuevo León	51	3	1		
Oaxaca	570	4		2	
Puebla	217	8			
Querétaro	18	2			
Quintana Roo	8				
San Luis Potosí	58	1	1		
Sinaloa	18				
Sonora	70	2		1	
Tabasco	17	2			
Tamaulipas	43	4	1		1
Tlaxcala	60	3	1		
Veracruz	207	7	1	1	
Yucatán	106	6			
Zacatecas	56	1			
Total	2,412	64	11	6	1

Source: Data compiled from Centro de Desarrollo Municipal (CEDEMUN), Secretaría de Gobernación, Mexico City.

learning and experiencing formal participation in the exercise of government. However, *regidoras* (alderwomen) are a small minority, whether they win the position through direct election or proportional representation. The general ratio is one or two women for every seven or ten men, depending on the size of the *ayuntamientos*. Table 13.3 illustrates this; it shows the distribution of *regidor* positions by gender in some of the metropolitan municipalities and important cities won by the PAN in the elections of 1995.

TABLE 13.3   *Regidor* Positions by Gender in Five Large *Panista* Cities, 1995

	Direct Election		Proportional Representation	
City	Women	Men	Women	Men
Guadalajara, Jalisco	3	6	1	3
Monterrey, Nuevo León[a]	3	13	2	5
Mérida, Yucatán	2	11	1	3
Córdoba, Veracruz	2	2	3	0
Naucalpan, Estado de México[b]	2	9	2	3
Total	12	41	9	14

[a]Information provided by PAN *regidora* Marina Guzmán.
[b]Information provided by Carola Conde, El Colegio Mexiquense.

Source: Centro Nacional de Desarrollo Municipal (CEDEMUN), Sistema Nacional de Información Municipal.

A significant change that is occurring in Mexico, particularly since the dramatic presidential election of 1988 (a change that is also duplicated in other countries in Latin America), is the transfer of women activists in urban popular movements and community organizations to the electoral arena, especially for *regidor* positions in local government. This process has been referred to as "the municipalization of the neighborhood" and in Mexico is observed in several cases of alderwomen of the PRD, for example.

The role of trustee is also potentially useful and challenging if it is undertaken with determination and responsibility. Generally speaking, a trustee's duties include overlooking the collection and use of financial resources, coordinating the municipal public finance commission, participating in the meetings of the *cabildo*, leading the legal activities of the *ayuntamiento*, and exercising legal representation for it in conjunction with the mayor. For a woman, it represents a position of public visibility that puts her honesty and carefulness to a test. Like alderwomen, women trustees are a minority in Mexico. As an example, after the 1995 municipal elections, in the state of Nuevo León there were nine women trustees in the state's 51 *ayuntamientos*, and in Jalisco thirteen out of 124.

Closing Comments

In Mexico, there is still little knowledge and analysis on the presence and participation of women in municipal government and local power structures. A line of research that ties studies on women with studies on local government has yet to be developed. This lack of knowledge precludes us from having an informed discussion about the trajectories, characteristics, and experiences of that participation as well as the influence of gender in local government and democracy. However, interest in this field has awakened and is growing, particularly in light of the political developments of the last few years, the changes in civil society, the interest in municipalities (notably from the left), the tendency toward political pluralism in the local political arena, changes in the perspective of some sectors of the feminist movement, and the support to research projects on gender issues in the local arena offered by institutions such as the Ford Foundation and the Programa Interdisciplinario de Estudios de la Mujer (Interdisciplinary Program for Women's Studies, PIEM) at El Colegio de México.

This changing scenario and the challenges it poses inevitably raise some negative issues for debate. Why do we want women in municipal power if they act as *cacicas* (political bosses), or represent corporate leaderships, or are decorative puppets who reproduce the worst vices that are typical of local authorities, such as authoritarianism, clientelism, corruption, irresponsibility, and subordination, in addition to not assuming the rights and demands of women? This line of questioning, however, has to be addressed to men as well. And it must be emphasized that women, under the laws of political equality, have the right to be candidates, to be voted for, and to govern municipalities. The ultimate aspiration, of course, is that women bring prestige to local government and to their gender.

In Mexico, today, the exclusion of women from the new agenda of municipal government in the process of democratic transition is unacceptable. A gender perspective in this new agenda must be comprehensive, not relegating gender issues to a secondary place by incorporating them into the needs and demands of social welfare. Gender issues must not be isolated. The local level of government is a wide arena for opening and developing more opportunities for women and for the feminist movement. But in order for this arena to become a reality, women must be willing and prepared to explore it and conquer it.

Notes

This chapter is dedicated to María de la Luz Nuñez, mayor of Atoyac de Alvarez, Guerrero (1993–1996). I wish to thank Victoria Rodríguez for compiling the data in Table 13.2.

1. In some states, such as Chihuahua, Sinaloa, and Yucatán, the role of trustee does not exist; in others, such as Baja California and Jalisco, trustees are not elected but are appointed by the mayor.

2. The data on the *alcaldesas* and other female municipal officials are from the Centro de Desarrollo Municipal (Center for Municipal Development, CEDEMUN), Sistema Nacional de Información Municipal, Secretaría de Gobernación, Mexico City.

3. Data were provided by CEDEMUN.

❀ 14 ❀

Women in the Border:
The *Panista* Militants of Tijuana
and Ciudad Juárez

Lilia Venegas

As a result of one of the most distinctive traits of contemporary Mexico—its growing politicization—political participation seems to be extending rapidly into the diverse regions of the country, even though in rather dissimilar patterns and very unequal rhythms. In this chapter I explore some of the social aspects that condition the entrance and activism of women in politics as militants of the PAN in two cities in the northern border of Mexico: Tijuana, Baja California, and Ciudad Juárez, Chihuahua.

The Border Cities

Tijuana is a place that deserves special attention in matters of political analysis. In a nutshell, the peculiar electoral behavior of its citizens is worthy of special notice. In the presidential elections of 1988, the majority voted for the center-leftist Frente Democrático Nacional (National Democratic Front, FDN), the precursor to the PRD, led by Cuauhtémoc Cárdenas. Only a year later the majority vote went to the rightist PAN; the *panista* candidate, Ernesto Ruffo, won the governorship of Baja California, thereby becoming the first opposition governor in the country. In 1995, once again, the electoral results for the state governorship favored the *panista* Héctor Terán, who will govern until 2001. During three consecutive trienniums (1989–1992, 1992–1995, 1995–1998), Tijuana's city government was in *panista* hands while the state's capital, Mexicali, remained steadfastly in *priísta* hands—it was not until 1995 that the PAN won, for the first time, the mayorship of Mexicali.

In addition, and independently of the party they vote for, Tijuanans (and Baja Californians in general) have one of the lowest indexes of electoral abstention in the country: Between 1974 and 1989 the abstention average percentage in the state was 43.86 percent in elections of local deputies (Rodríguez Araujo and Arreola Ayala 1993).

The profile of the Tijuanan electorate has been drawn in differing ways: Salas Porras (1989) argued that the progress of the *neocardenista* movement in 1988 was an outcome of the traditional influence of Lázaro Cárdenas in the peninsula and of the historical memory of its citizens as well as a consequence of the accumulated balance of popular struggles. Nolasco (1991), in a study on electoral results in deputies' campaigns, pointed out that the electorate's behavior is erratic and more concerned with the personalities of the candidates in question than with party preferences and loyalties. Guillén (1992) remarked that one of the main characteristics of the Tijuanan population is a high degree of citizen participation with an inclination toward the opposition and that the electoral preferences (from center-left [FDN/PRD] to right [PAN]) are only that, electoral, and not political. This electorate's profile is one that is politically modern, democratic, concerned with the citizen-government relationship and almost lacking institutional bonds with parties.

A survey conducted among the population of Tijuana in 1995 showed that 98.3 percent obtained information through television, radio, the press, and other media; 63.1 percent read the newspaper; 44.5 percent stated that they were very interested in politics; and 86.3 percent thought that political parties were important for democracy.[1] These data tell us that this population is notably more informed and interested in politics than the national average. Certainly a high index of registered voters and voting itself stand out in Tijuana. Moreover, citizens participate actively in the media (radio, television, and the press) and particularly in activities in which they get involved for addressing neighborhood, ecology, and labor problems.

Ciudad Juárez has also shown an interesting political development in the rocky course of Mexico's transition to democracy. In 1983 the PAN and its candidate, Francisco Barrio, won the election for the mayorship of the city, a pioneering event that preceded the forthcoming advance of the *panista* opposition at the national level. In 1986 the city found itself embroiled in one of the decade's most important postelectoral conflicts, confronted with a questionable electoral process that "re-conquered" Chihuahua for the PRI. Since 1992 the governorship of the state has been in the hands of the PAN (with the return of Francisco Barrio), as well as the mayorship of Ciudad Juárez, which has also been governed by members of that party for two trienniums, 1992–1995 and 1995–1998.

The average percentage of abstention in elections for local deputies for 1974–1989 shows that the state of Chihuahua, at 51.2 percent, is slightly more abstentionist than Baja California (Rodríguez Araujo and Arreola Ayala 1993). Over all, however, Chihuahua is one of the more participative and dynamic states at the national level in electoral terms.

The political electoral behavior of *Juarenses*, particularly in the three elections mentioned above (1983, 1986, 1992), has led to various studies and interpretations clustered under the general theme of the border's political culture. Some of these studies have focused especially on Ciudad Juárez; others have adopted a comparative focus with other cities in the northern border or with other inland cities.[2] Among the authors who have approached this matter we find points of view such as the following: First, *Juarenses* show a low index of belonging to and participating in social institutions, especially political ones, that is, they tend to keep at a distance and to be critical of political parties and of government (Béjar Navarro and Capello 1988). Second, the right, identified with a neoliberal and anti-state discourse and as a gradual promoter of "democratic transformations leading to capitalist modernity," has permeated several layers of the population and especially the population of the northern border (Baca Olamendi and Cisneros Ramírez 1988). Third, among specific cultural features, those that stand out are an anticentralist and liberal tradition, a modernization that is incompatible with traditional practices and policies (corporatism, clientelism, one-party rule, fraud), and the influence of U.S. culture (Palma Cabrera 1988). And fourth, Alvarado Mendoza (1992) pointed out the coexistence of "modern" traits (e.g., high electoral competitiveness, autonomous and critical organizations of civil society) with elements of a more "traditional" nature (e.g., the Messiah-like, enterprising, and religious leadership represented by Francisco Barrio). In Alvarado's view, the unpredictable nature of the northern electorate could very well be the result of a culture that emphasizes this type of leadership, based almost exclusively on personal charisma. We now turn to the role played by women in the border's political culture.

Border Women in the PAN

Women have played a key role in the *panista* opposition in both Tijuana and Ciudad Juárez. Even though electoral results do not reveal the proportion of votes cast by women, one can unequivocally state that the female vote has been decisive for the PAN's victories. Francisco Barrio, the present governor of Chihuahua, remarked:

> In 1993 we were looking at a very difficult scenario as the PRI had never before lost the elections. Mid-way through the campaign, opinion polls did not favor us. We then observed that women, especially housewives, were the least compromised: most were undecided. We recognized that they were

going to decide the outcome of the election. We thought of a strategy that was not very difficult: the PRI candidate led a messy and dissipated life, with a rather dysfunctional family. Without mentioning this, we gave more room to my wife, who always accompanied me. We began to emphasize family values, and those of couples . . . and that worked out just swell.[3]

However, the role of women in the advances of the PAN is not limited to casting votes. Their presence and participation in the party has been a determining force in several areas and instances of political party activity, such as in electoral campaigns, in everyday political work in the *colonias*, and in mobilizations in defense of the vote. An understanding of what makes women join and become militants of this party is, as pointed out earlier, the main preoccupation of the research presented in this chapter. This subject is interesting for the following reasons, among others: First, the PAN has been commonly cataloged as a party of the middle class, and this research explores the *panista* militancy of women of the popular sector. Second, the PAN has achieved substantial success in the national political panorama; in 1996 it governed 30 percent of the country's population, and since the 1997 election it holds the governorship of six states (Chihuahua, Baja California, Jalisco, Guanajuato, Nuevo León, and Querétaro). And third, the cities analyzed here, Ciudad Juárez and Tijuana, are located in two of those states governed by the PAN.

The first phase of the research was conducted among *panista* militant women in Ciudad Juárez (Venegas 1994). The rationale for continuing the project in Tijuana was to gather enough material to allow us to explain the relationship of women to political life and their *panista* militancy. The comparison between the two cities is possible not only because of their shared characteristics of being border cities with specific social, demographic, and geopolitical conditions but also because both have experienced *panista* governments at the state and local levels.

The following section discusses the character of the political linkages of women to the PAN in Tijuana, highlighting some of the principal differences and similarities with the results of the project in Ciudad Juárez.

Old and New Party Militants

In both Tijuana and Ciudad Juárez two clearly differentiated militant groups can be identified, depending on the length of time they have belonged to the party. The first one is composed of "lifelong *panistas*"; the second one is made up of militants who joined the party as a result of its electoral advances in both cities. It is also common for senior *panistas* who had distanced themselves from political life to return to the party as a result of the PAN's victories in their communities.

Senior Militants

It is interesting to observe that in both Ciudad Juárez and Tijuana the party has a relatively long history. In Tijuana, the interviews conducted for this research offer proof of the important participation of women in the *panista* opposition since the mid-1950s. We identified three routes that brought people—women in particular—closer to the PAN in those years: first, through the defense of land for the construction of housing; second, through popular movements in defense of the vote; and third, through the migration of *panista* families from the central region of the country.

The first route offers the opportunity to analyze the process through which social and political organizations are joined together and, from the viewpoint of the PAN and the women of the popular sector, how collective action around a specific issue led to formal participation within a political party. Rafaela Martínez Cantú, formerly a member of the state congress, tells how she joined the PAN around 1957, when she struggled with other *colonia* residents to defend some plots in the Zona del Río.[4] From that time date the strength and influence of Salvador Rosas Magallón—a senior member of the PAN in Baja California who engaged in serious disputes with other factions of the party and who was also the political mentor of Martínez Cantú—who is recognized, "in spite of it all," for his political work among popular sectors during more than thirty years.

The second route to joining the PAN revolves around the electoral conflicts that, in both Baja California and Chihuahua, have become historic. The following account is from Cecilia Barone de Castellanos, a high-level collaborator in Baja California's state government:

> My husband was president of the party, it was 1968, and they [the PRI] sent us a ballot of procurers, of traffickers [for the elections]. We then started to look for candidates who would represent the party, truly Tijuanan candidates, with roots, truly representative, honest, that loved Tijuana. A very good ballot was put together, we undertook an incredible campaign, we won, we triumphed, the whole town awakened to political participation. We defended the vote and proved that the PAN won. [But given that the PAN victory was not officially recognized, that] was really the greatest fraud in history. . . . We as women organized, and 43 of us went on a bus all over the nation to defend the case of Baja California.

The bus went all the way to Mexico City, where the women intended to meet with President Gustavo Díaz Ordaz, but he did not receive them. Instead, the women exchanged fliers and chatted with the strike committee of the student movement.

The third route to joining the PAN in those times was through migration, that permanent border phenomenon. María de Sánchez Hidalgo, widow of an outstanding *panista*, narrates how her family, like many others, came to Tijuana from zones of *sinarquista* influence (states in the Bajío region, Jalisco, and Querétaro). She tells us that upon arriving in Tijuana, she and her husband looked for a political party that would at least be similar to the Unión Nacional Sinarquista, with a view to joining it. This party turned out to be the PAN, but the couple always maintained a certain critical distance from it "because of its abandonment of their religious beliefs" and what she considers as "civil excesses."

The New Militancy

The new militants of Tijuana, unlike the senior militants, have followed patterns similar to those observed earlier in Ciudad Juárez, at least in two types of cases. First, as in Ciudad Juárez, *panista* administrations in Tijuana have promoted the Comités de Vecinos (Neighborhood Committees) as the privileged path for negotiation of public services provision and problem solving, especially in the *colonias populares*. Even though the committee members act in their capacity as citizens, regardless of their party affiliation (if they have one), it is a fact that *panista* militants are among the main female promoters of these organizations, who tell of incidents such as the following: "We don't mention politics in the meetings of the neighborhood committees . . . but one time some folks came up to me and said, 'ma'am, we'd like to go to one of those meetings of the PAN, how do we go about it?' 'That's simple,' I told them, 'just go.' Then I led them to the party offices close to their homes."

When Francisco Barrio was mayor of Ciudad Juárez (1983–1986), he was criticized even inside the party for what was considered an excessive politicization of the Neighborhood Committees (or the political usage of these organizations, in harsher words). Ernesto Ruffo and the *panista* mayors of Tijuana practiced special caution in dealing with these committees, which is perhaps why they had less impact there than in Ciudad Juárez in terms of attracting new party members. In this regard it is also important to consider the striking difference between the range and influence of social organizations in the *colonias populares* of both cities; by and large, it appears that these are more numerous and powerful in Tijuana than in Ciudad Juárez.

In spite of the differences between the land defense struggles of the 1950s and those aimed at improving the quality of neighborhood public services in recent times, the presence of the party and its politicization efforts within the *colonias* are clear. In the same vein, it seems clear that one of the routes for individuals joining the party is and has been their prior linkage with urban popular movements and organizations.

In the second type of case, new militant women seeking to join the PAN seem to follow the same route of defending the vote as did the women pioneers of 1968 in Baja California. The bitter electoral contests in which the opposition has felt it had a real possibility of winning power are, undoubtedly, key moments in which the population has been politicized and mobilized. The electoral processes of the late 1980s and early 1990s in Ciudad Juárez, as was the case in Tijuana, attracted many women (and men) who had never before thought of belonging to and participating in a political organization. In Tijuana, the 1989 elections managed to involve 10,000 persons in defense of the vote. Such a collective frame of mind perhaps fed upon the memory of the fraud of 1968 or maybe upon a fresher one, the one of 1988.

The threat of fraudulent elections can potentially be counterproductive to participation and defense of the vote, but if such a threat is deactivated publicly before it occurs, it can lead to very active citizen participation and more votes for the opposition. It seems this is what happened (among other things) in the 1989 elections in Tijuana. The female militants of the PAN at the front of Ernesto Ruffo's electoral campaign believe that the discovery and public disclosure of the fraud that was planned in the huge neighborhood of Camino Verde (which was going to be carried out through the use of 21,000 counterfeit voter identification cards) worked in favor of the *panista* vote and also increased the number of active female militants. Cecilia Barone de Castellanos, then coordinator for Ruffo's campaign, remarks:

> When we detected irregularities in the number of registered voters, we decided to check names and addresses in Camino Verde. When the PAN delegation arrived in the *colonia*, we were received by Roxana Soto (a leader of the Grupo México, of *priísta* affiliation) and her gang of *cholos*; rocks were thrown at us, we were threatened with blades, they slit the tires of the cars . . . everything appeared in the press the following day and a scandal ensued, but something awakened inside the people of Camino Verde: "Why did they beat them? Why did they throw rocks at them? Something's going on here!"

The incident of Camino Verde was a key factor for increasing the number of women joining the PAN, but the attack on the *panista*s was not the only reason. Susana Ayala and a group of women residents of Camino Verde had initiated, some time before, a series of battles against the *priísta* leadership and its reputed corruption, impunity, clientelism, and plundering. With the victory of the PAN for the governorship of the state and the mayorship of Tijuana, this group promptly affiliated itself with the PAN, leading the entrance of Ruffo and the PAN into the *colonia*, which precipitated the downfall of Roxana Soto and Alejandro Herrera (the latter died in jail shortly thereafter). As this case illustrates, the increase in *panista* militancy has also fed upon the mistakes and excesses of the traditional exercise of power.

The Family and Social Class in the PAN

For both old and new women militants, the family plays an important role in their decision to join the PAN. In both Tijuana and Ciudad Juárez, militancy within the party appears to be, in good measure, a tradition that is transmitted from one generation to the next. This tradition can be readily observed in the composition of *panismo* at the national level, where it is common to identify *panista* militants by their surnames. Although this applies to all *panistas*, for women it appears that their family name (indicative of party affiliation for several generations) functions as a "legitimate" access channel to a privileged male world. It is not the same thing to join the party of one's father or mother—or husband, in many cases—as it is to do it on one's own. Indeed, men actually encourage the participation of women in the PAN when their family is identified as *panista*.

Panista militants are distinguished from those of other parties, among other things, by a political style that stresses the centrality of the family not only in their discourse but also in the characteristic style of their political activities, such as charity bazaars, picnics in parks and public gardens, family get-togethers for a political purpose, and so on. This family orientation is present in all socioeconomic levels.

A larger number of women of the popular sector exist among *panista* militants in Ciudad Juárez than in Tijuana, where the middle class seems to predominate. However, beyond the differences in numbers between both cities, the social class women belong to seems to play an important role in both cases. Among the women interviewed in Ciudad Juárez (all from the popular sector), their dealing with wealthy people that "treat you as an equal, without making any differences" appears to be one of the attractions of the PAN. A woman interviewed commented that the social class mix that the PAN encourages allowed them, for example, to obtain a letter of recommendation for employment or for helping one of their children to be admitted into high school.

The success of the PAN among the popular sectors in Ciudad Juárez could be explained, thus, because of its approach to civil society as a whole. It does not appeal to any sector in particular (as does the PT, the Labor Party, for example), which is why it seems to be very appropriate for the political culture attributed by some authors to the border population—a situation that could be replicated in Tijuana. However, some of the interviews conducted in both cities clearly indicate that the relationship between the militants of popular sectors and those of middle and upper class are definitely not idyllic. In fact, some of the women who carried out social work projects in the *colonias* through the PAN and through another organization independent from the party (the Unión de Usuarios y Servicios Públicos, a group of users of public services) explained that they had left the party's women's sector (Promoción Política de la Mujer, or Political Promotion of Women) in order to avoid being in contact with the wealthier women who, according to one interviewee, do not like to leave their neighborhoods and their comfort. In Tijuana, the frequent internal conflicts within the PAN, whether due to candidate nominations or to internal confrontations between groups, are often accompanied by accusations with class overtones. The group supported by Ruffo, for instance, was accused of being elitist and of referring to the popular sectors as *chusma* (riff-raff).

From Party Militancy to Government

In contrast with the high number of women who participate in the party's electoral activities, the number of women who occupy political office in *panista* governments is very low. As a matter of fact, the number of women occupying public office, instead of growing, has decreased. In Tijuana, the number of women in the city's government went down from the 1989–1992 triennium to the most recent one, 1995–1998. In the first triennium, 6 out of 9 *regidores* were women; currently there is only 1 *regidora*. The same decline in the number of women from one administration to the next can be observed at the state level. In the governorship of Ernesto Ruffo (1989–1995), 4 women occupied cabinet positions; in the current one of Héctor Terán Terán, there are only 2. The state legislature has fared even worse: In the previous state congress (1989–1992) there was only 1 woman; in the current one there is none.

The few *panista* women who have occupied public office have rarely done so at the highest levels. In Tijuana, only the director of Desarrollo Integral de la Familia (Integrated Family Development, DIF) holds a top position, and only one woman is department head. And when women do occupy top positions, these are overwhelmingly in areas traditionally associated with women: DIF (which is always headed by the wife of the head of the executive branch at all levels of government), social welfare, child protection, cultural programs, civil registry, and so on. Both the chiefs of staff (*oficial mayor*) in the city of Tijuana and in the state government are women, and although these are indeed senior positions, it is noteworthy that their tasks are somewhat similar to those of family and home management.

However, the most active women militants within the PAN who do not occupy government positions continue their party activism. Some of them, indeed, occupy positions within the party, albeit all of them of secondary rank or in a clerical category. Yet others continue preparing for public life; of these, for example, some have even joined Toastmasters International.

Without wishing to be overly pessimistic, the picture that emerges from Tijuana regarding the participation of women in government is not very promising. And this does not relate exclusively to the number of positions occupied. Rather, the lack of pressure exerted by women, and even the low enthusiasm among them to conquer a broader space for themselves, can be attributed to a variety of factors. The most relevant of these appear to be the following.

The personal history of the women who come to occupy government positions is, without question, one of the principal factors explaining the behavior and attitudes of women toward government. As mentioned earlier, women who belong to *panista* family dynasties have a different perspective of party activism, and this perspective extends to government. An elementary knowledge of the principal *panista* families in the state of Baja California shows where the leading women stand: Cecilia Barone, secretary general for Ernesto Ruffo (among other top positions), is married to Héctor Castellanos, who belongs to a family with strong *panista* traditions; Ruth Hernández, chief of staff in Tijuana, is daughter of Rafaela Martínez Cantú, a former congresswoman; and so on down the line. Examples such as these are abundant.

When Ruth Hernández speaks about this issue she is rather defensive, explaining how these are not cases of nepotism. It is just a part of their personal histories. When she was only thirteen, Ruth gave her first political speech. Because they are "the daughter of" or "the wife of" means they have been exposed to politics by virtue of belonging to a family where (*panista*) politics are important. Gaby Chumacera recalls that since her childhood, "in our house we always had PAN for breakfast" (*pan* being bread, hence the play of words) while her father read the newspaper and pointed out the injustices and the need for change. Even though many of these women have prepared and trained for leadership positions and gained considerable experience through party activism, there is no doubt that family lineage and traditions grant them a considerable advantage for their political self-esteem and desire to climb the political ladder.

The personal history of these women affects their political careers and aspirations in other ways. For many of these women, the decision to become politically active or to decline to do so is affected by the time and effort involved. The age of their children is one of the principal problems. Ruth Hernández declined to be *regidora* several years ago because she had an eighteen-month-old child, and her husband said the child would be left unattended. However, in 1993, she occupied that very same post, even though she had another eighteen-month-old in addition to two other young children. Gaby Chumacera declined a candidacy "because my son was fourteen years old—the age of 'don't look at me, don't touch me.' I asked myself, is it worth spending three years [as *diputada*], away from my son? And I said no! Perhaps later, when there is more time. . . . " Estela Varela, department head in the municipal government in 1996, is an accomplished politician who could easily and happily occupy a top cabinet position but also held back on this point:

> But I haven't gone crazy! I know that my family comes first. My only limitation to how far I wish to advance politically is my family. For instance, I will not run for congress because I would have to live in Mexicali. The age of my children is also a consideration. But it doesn't matter; I'm going to live a long life, and when I am 50 I will still be in politics.

Thus, the discourse on family as an obstacle is somewhat mixed. It is not clear, for instance, at what age of children it would be most convenient for their mother to become politically active. What determines whether at a certain point an eighteen-month-old is an impediment but at another point is not—is it whether or not it is the first child? Adolescence is another difficult period. Does a woman have to wait until she is fifty? Cecilia Barone de Castellanos described her bus trip to Mexico City in 1968, when she had been married for ten years and had six children: "I don't know how I could have left them, I have always been so attached to them! Perhaps even a little too much. But I did it for them. If I had done nothing, I would be ashamed for them to ask me, why didn't you do something?"

Among the *panista* women interviewed in Tijuana, as was the case with their counterparts interviewed earlier in Ciudad Juárez (Venegas 1994), the family appears as one of the main reasons—if not the main reason—for becoming politically active: "to leave my children a better Mexico"; "to set for them a good example"; "so they won't challenge me later for doing nothing." And in some cases, women do not even hesitate to put themselves at risk personally, as is the case during hunger strikes or in an action such as that on July 20, 1986, when women blocked the international bridge between Ciudad Juárez and El Paso, Texas, in protest over the electoral results earlier that month. Husbands and children appear to be tolerant of almost everything (staying out late at night, beds unmade, no fresh hot meals) for the sake of the family. At the opposite end of the spectrum, the family also serves as a reason for declining to become politically involved. Thus, it seems that the family has become for the PAN an all-encompassing reason for explaining women's political participation—or lack of it.

Because of the strong family orientation within the PAN and its extension of this familial character to many of the party's activities, as described earlier, the transition from party to government for *panista* women is almost the equivalent of entering the political space for the first time. Party activities are considered family, not political, activities. Thus, when entering government, the first shock for women is to be surrounded by the realities of political life; and the first shock, by and large, is the lack of prestige associated with politics: "We owe it to the PRI," says Estela Varela, "that people think that every politician is dishonest and that no woman could climb the political ladder if it were not in exchange for sexual favors."

As far as external obstacles to the greater involvement of women in government are concerned, such as the lack of trust of male militants, the women interviewed all agreed on one point: *Panista* men, especially the older ones, do not trust women to occupy top positions—women are fickle and like to gossip. Blanca Hernández, delegate for the Tijuana government in the Mesa de Otay in 1996 and former president of the party's municipal committee in Tijuana, commented how the 1995 elections meant a special challenge to herself and her team because they were all women. There were many reasons for winning, but above anything else these women wanted to demonstrate to their *compañeros* that they were capable of working as well as the men.

In addition to the general lack of trust in women's abilities, the women interviewed commented that *panista* men also distrust women to govern because they break down easily emotionally and are prone to burst into tears when confronted with an especially difficult or conflictive situation. But the problem is somewhat deeper. "The real issue is that men don't like to receive orders from a woman," says Cecilia Barone de Castellanos. And she adds, "You have to learn to modulate your voice. It works very well, for instance, to speak in a motherly tone: come on, be a good boy."

The criticism of this male attitude, however, is filtered and somewhat justified by the women. These men are *machistas* because they are Mexican, not because they are *panistas*. It is a national cultural problem, not a party problem, and therefore almost impossible to resolve. Although this does not entirely justify the men's attitude, in the view of the women, it does soften somewhat the criticism. Thus, an ambiguity among *panista* women surfaces clearly; even though they recognize that in the party there is a clear division of labor along gender lines—"*ellos toman decisiones; ellas hacen las tortas*" (men make decisions; women make sandwiches)—and there is clear dissatisfaction and restlessness among the women about this (especially now that the party has had a string of electoral victories), when it comes to making demands to advance themselves as women, they hesitate: "The men have to understand that we do not wish to compete, that we do not wish to displace and overthrow them . . . we are not going to turn into feminists."

Finally, there is consensus among the women interviewed that if there are not more women in government, it is because women have chosen so. In addition to the obstacles mentioned above, which preclude or make difficult the participation of women, most women simply choose not to aim for high government positions. And those who do, should attain positions on the basis of personal merit, not simply because they are women. The *panista* women interviewed in Tijuana made very clear that they did not favor any special treatment, such as quotas.

Conclusion

The decision to participate politically or to join a particular party cannot be attributed in a conclusive manner to the presence of certain geographical, socioeconomic, and cultural conditions. Nonetheless, such elements undoubtedly play an important role in the decision, however personal and subjective, to join a political party, another one, or none at all. The accounts and life stories of the women interviewed for this project, both in Ciudad Juárez and in Tijuana, indicate that certain phenomena peculiar to the border have had something to do with their decision to become politically involved. The similarities between militants of both cities suggest the same idea. These findings also coincide with those of some of the authors who analyze the border's political culture, referred to at the beginning of this chapter. Among such phenomena it is worthwhile to point out the following:

First, the physical distance of these cities from the economic and political center of the country stimulates the formation of autonomous local and regional groups, which soon come into conflict with the traditional structures of government and political organization. Indeed, the profile of the opposition drawn by Tonatiuh Guillén (1992) seems to be based, at least in part, on this type of perceptions that associates the PRI with the geographic and power center. In this regard it is worthy to recall the emphasis Cecilia Barone de Castellanos put to the characteristics of the candidates of the PRI: "a ballot of procurers, of traffickers" as compared to those of the PAN: "truly Tijuanan candidates, with roots." The emphasis on roots is immensely important in a city of immigrants, such as Tijuana, and therefore it is imperative to prove that one has roots in the city.

Second, the nearness to and the cultural exchange with the United States also affects the configuration of a political culture that is participative, democratic, and willing to accept (and even demand) that different political parties alternate in occupying public office. The concepts of democracy referred to by the women interviewed often draw examples from the other side of the border. The same occurs with their collective imagination: The first world is within their reach, and for some of them life in the United States is part of their own daily life experience. Perhaps the frequent reference and self-reference as "citizens" comes from this nearness to the United States (in more southern regions the terms more often used are "people" or "Christians"). Susana Ayala, a resident of the *colonia* Camino Verde, negotiated with the leaders of the PRI to "buy" a hill. Her intention, so she tells us, was to "fill it up with fruit trees . . . so when the people climb it on the day of Santa Cruz they can be in the shade. . . . You can see how bald the hills are here. . . . I was on the other side, where everything is pretty, and I wanted this hill to be pretty too."

Third, as pointed out earlier, one of the routes for joining the party is a previous linkage with urban popular organizations. As is well known, this phenomenon occurs in various regions and with other political parties. What seems to be especially distinctive in border cities is the combination of the following elements: a constant formation of new *colonias* in which urban services are permanently lagging, inhabited by a population with relatively high levels of education and income. The decision to join the opposition, therefore, does not appear to depend on economic development and democratic imperatives but is an answer to the righting of wrongs.

Fourth, the massive incorporation of women into the formal labor sector via the *maquiladora* industry in the border region has contributed to a change in the more traditional and conservative cultural patterns, in such a way that the strict division of space and activities by gender has become more flexible. In the last thirty years, since the first *maquiladoras* were established, a certain social atmosphere has been generated that today perceives as natural the fact that women in these cities participate in political activities and join political parties.

And finally, one of the most important features of the border's political culture refers to migration. New residents arrive in Tijuana and in Ciudad Juárez carrying a baggage of very diverse political influences and traditions. When Baja California gave its majority vote to Cuauhtémoc Cárdenas and the National Democratic Front in the presidential election of 1988, one of the hypotheses explaining this outcome was the high number of migrants from the state of Michoacán. As for the advances and strength of the PAN, we find that the main migratory currents that come to these border cities are from the most politically conservative states of the country, places where not only the *panista* presence has been strong but also the rightist Unión Nacional Sinarquista, a political offspring of the *cristero* movement of the 1920s.

As for the women, there is no question that historically they have played a key role in the political developments of Mexico's northern border. Given their strong political activism, it is surprising and disappointing that this activism has not led them to seek more involvement in government. This is especially unsettling in the case of Tijuana, which boasts one of the more developed and sophisticated political cultures in the nation.

Notes

1. Gabinete de Estudios de Opinión, "Preferencias Electorales en Baja California," *El Nacional*, June 24 and 25, 1992. For a wider version of this summary, see Venegas (1995).

2. For a more detailed discussion of these studies and their findings, see Venegas (1995).

3. Speech delivered to the Association of Women Writers, Mexico City, June 8, 1993.

4. The testimonials that are quoted here are based on interviews I conducted in Tijuana in 1992, 1993, and 1996. I am grateful for the information provided by Rafaela Martínez Cantú, Cecilia Barone de Castellanos, María de Sánchez Hidalgo, Susana Ayala, Hortencia Guerrero, Gaby Chumacera, Ruth Hernández, and Estela Varela.

✦ 15 ✦

Conclusion: *Haciendo Política*— The Mexican Case in Perspective

Jane S. Jaquette

The chapters in this book are impressive on several grounds. They show how deep, complex, and sophisticated women's engagements in Mexican politics have become. At a time when Mexico is in the throes of a severe political and institutional crisis, women's movements seem strong and effective, women leaders are visible in parties and government positions, and the linkages between women's movements and the political system appear to be evolving in directions consistent with Robert Putnam's thesis that the state and civil society can, indeed must, develop apace (Putnam 1993).

In addition to reflecting the varieties of women's political participation, the chapters also reveal that a range of approaches can be useful to study and understand them. They further show that to ignore women in Mexican politics would be to miss an important part of the picture, one that will surely have a major impact on the shape of Mexico's political future. At the same time, the tone of these chapters is refreshingly realistic, recognizing that women's participation and women's constructions of politics have been idealized in the past, to the detriment of self-criticism and more lasting political impact.

These are significant accomplishments. But these chapters also provoke further thought. What are the emerging relations between gender and the state that can be discerned from the study of the Mexican "transition" in comparative contexts? How are women's NGOs (professional, politicized, and middle class, as Tarrés's chapter shows) and women's popular and grassroots organizations connected in Mexico and with what implications for women's representation and for the political agenda? How democratic are women's political practices and how transparent? Do the political experiences of women in Mexico and in the wider region contribute to a more complex understanding of "women and politics" and to the construction of a world that is more secure and just than the worlds we have thus far been able to create?

The Mexican Case in Brief

Mexico is undergoing a historic transition, and the chapters in this book show that women are visible and active in this process. As Victoria Rodríguez notes, women occupy 17 percent of the seats in the Mexican Congress, higher than the percentage in the United States and in Latin America and the Caribbean as a whole. Although important, this is only one measure of women's political participation. Women have built a political infrastructure of NGOs in a variety of sectors, and although women have long been present in party politics, their activism is becoming more sustained and pervasive. In all three major parties, and even in the important symbolic opposition represented by the Chiapas uprising, women have played key roles and have the expectation, which is not unrealistic, that they will continue to expand their influence in the future.

Part of women's growing political clout can be attributed to their increasing participation in the economy, from wage workers to women managers and entrepreneurs. And part is surely due to cultural changes that now make it possible for women to be perceived, and to see themselves, as legitimate political actors. What these preceding chapters also show is that women are becoming politically more experienced and effective, building on their roles in popular organizing or party work and channeling their professional expertise into NGO activism.

In Mexico, as elsewhere in the region, women are increasingly running for office and winning. In office, they are breaking many of the long-held stereotypes of women politicians as reactive and sidelined. Perhaps as significantly, women are increasingly appointed to portfolios traditionally reserved for men. Two obvious examples are María de los Angeles Moreno's rise to head the PRI and President Zedillo's appointment of Rosario Green as foreign minister. On the negative side, especially troublesome given accounts of high levels of grassroots activism, women's representation at the local level is still low—municipal representation is 4.2 percent compared to 6.0 percent for the region as a whole, and the region itself is low in global terms. However, this is consistent with the evidence that women's organizations are more "explicitly and implicitly" influenced by the feminist movement in urban centers (Tarrés, this volume). Much of local politics is still rural and lags behind or is resistant to trends at the center.

In Mexico, women's new-found power has been reflected in a series of legislative victories (Rodríguez, this volume), as women learn to blend their concerns for "women's" issues into larger programs and wider alliances and to work across party lines without distancing themselves from party identifications (Lamas, this volume). In the new world of political pluralism in Mexico, women come from the gamut of parties and political positions, but they have been able to unite on key issues, recognizing that such cooperation is neither inevitable (due to "natural" agreement among women) nor doomed (by the return to, or in Mexico's case the emergence of, competitive party politics).

Finally, although Alicia Martínez and Teresa Incháustegui (this volume) judge Mexico's experiment with nomination quotas for women a "failure," the effort to represent women more effectively has been articulated as a goal, one that continues to motivate party leaderships to recruit and promote women. In Mexico, as elsewhere, it remains to be seen whether women's group representation is consistent with feminist claims to "universal citizenship" that, as Foweraker (this volume) characterizes them, are "an automatic challenge to the particularism of clientelist and patrimonial power relations." Instead, group representation may produce a more modernized and gender-inclusive form of clientelism, as some would argue of Mujeres en Solidaridad, the women's program within the National Solidarity Program promoted by President Salinas.

The sea change in attitudes about women's political participation and representation has several causes that have been addressed in the literature over the last twenty years. They include the establishment of democratic forms of governance; the ways in which women's groups inserted themselves into the transition process, emphasizing new issues and new ways of doing politics; and the hegemony of neoliberal economic policies, which have kept women organized to confront "practical" gender issues while challenging patriarchal attitudes in the concrete arrangements of everyday life. The steady consolidation of a role for women in politics, in Mexico and elsewhere in the region, suggests that research on women in politics must go beyond asking Where are the women? and What are they doing? to address the institutionalization of women's participation and the changing ideologies of women's movements and to assess the broader effects of women's representation.

The material in this book about Mexico, like the analysis developed in Elisabeth Friedman's work on Venezuela (1996), moves us beyond the very specific form of transition politics to anticipate future trends. Mexico, though arguably in the throes of a transition, is undergoing a process that, in contrast to those in the Southern Cone and Central America, does not privilege social movements over political parties nor unite disparate groups to reach an overriding goal on which all can agree: the end of military rule. Mexico's pluralist political arena, the increasing vulnerability of a growth strategy that deepens inequalities, the rising wave of violence, the lack of transparency, and the weakness of the rule of law are characteristics that are shared to a greater or lesser degree in the existing democracies of the region. Thus the Mexican case can offer useful insights into the emerging roles for women in a political environment that is far from the civil utopia both democrats and feminists had hoped for and that is complicated by the unforseeable consequences of intense globalization. It challenges researchers to new thinking.

Looking Backward: Changing Perceptions of the "Woman Question" in Latin American Politics

It is commonplace to argue that feminist approaches to the study of any discipline, politics included, have gone through three identifiable stages: the call to include women "as a variable" in research projects, the intense focus on and revaluation of women's experiences, and the "strategic" stage that challenges both the practices of the discipline and the male norms of social and political behavior.

The early work on women's political participation in the region was motivated by feminist empiricist concerns—that is, stage one, efforts to put women in the picture. At the same time, such work engaged in stage two, revaluations of women's political activity, and stage three, challenges to disciplinary practices. Morris Blachman's (1973) work is an early example. Data on women's political participation showed that women voted less and were less active in political parties and other political organizations (as per Blough 1972; Morton 1962; Lewis 1971). The dominant "pluralist" approach attributed lack of participation in a "gender-neutral" way to apathy or satisfaction with political outcomes (see Bachrach 1967); thus women, like nonparticipant men, had no one but themselves to blame if they were poorly represented. Blachman argued both that the lack of women's representation and participation was indeed a serious issue and that its cause was structural, not individual. Women were neither satisfied nor apathetic but alienated from male-dominated politics, an interpretation consistent with surveys that showed women declaring politics a "man's world" or, as in the Mattelarts's study of Chile (1968), a "waste of time."

First stage research reflected an egalitarian feminist position that accepted male citizenship as the norm for appropriate and/or effective political behavior. Elsa Chaney's very sympathetic study of women politicians in Chile and Peru (which was first summarized in a chapter in a 1973 anthology but not published in book form until 1979—a sign of the resistance of the discipline to studies of women in politics outside the United States) was concerned that the tendency of women to extend their roles as wives and mothers into the political arena—as *supermadres*—

would limit their political reach and impact. On the other hand, Ximena Bunster's characterization of the female politician as a *"mamá* who approves, sanctions, [and] corrects" (quoted in Chaney 1973), has a distinct "second stage" or what we might now call "difference" feminism ring: Because the woman views herself and is viewed in the role of *mamá*, she can avoid the direct competition that females experience in the United States. Second-stage analysis revalues women's experience on the grounds that it is more authentic to women, that it represents higher values (as in the case of the Madres of the Plaza de Mayo, for example), or that it is more successful for women than imitating male behavior.[1]

Third-stage research is more ambitious and highly prescriptive, arguing that women's behavior is not only valid but superior and should become the norm for both men and women. Third-stage feminist research attacks not only the canon but also the methods of the discipline, though in political science as in economics and philosophy, the feminist critique has had little impact on mainstream research (see Staudt and Weaver 1997; Jaquette 1995).

Today the mobilization of Latin American women into politics as mothers is taken as an empirical given and as desirable (Chuchryk 1989a, 1989b; Schirmer 1993), in contrast to the selfish individualism of the male model of universal citizenship and, directly or by implication, to the individualist norm represented by mainstream "liberal egalitarian" feminism in the North. More broadly, studies of women in movement politics emphasize their distinct qualities: the quest to maintain autonomy, opposition to hierarchies, and the congruence between women's practical gender interests and the needs of the community as a whole. By contrast, "male" politics is seen as power driven and self-serving, repressively reinforcing race and class hierarchies and tolerating all forms of corruption. This discourse has permeated treatments of the Madres of the Plaza de Mayo, women's human rights groups in Central America, and women's grassroots survival organizations throughout the region. In their representations of women's political activity in Latin America, critics of democracy-as-interest-group-pluralism find some basis to hope that "democracy" can have a Latin American future that is more communitarian and egalitarian than its history to date would suggest.

A few researchers have voiced some dissent. María de Carmen Feijoó expressed some skepticism of the liberatory possibilities of politicized motherhood (1989) but was strongly challenged and conceded the effectiveness of motherhood as a practical identity (1994); and Maruja Barrig and Teresa Caldeira cautiously reassert the value of individualism for feminists in their essays in a collection comparing women's roles in Latin America and in Central and Eastern Europe (Jaquette and Wolchik 1998). Carina Perelli (1994) criticized the adoption of the discourse of the Madres by interest groups as both ingenuous and undemocratic in her essay on Uruguay. I take Marta Lamas's critique of the feminist myths in Chapter 7 in this book ("feminists are not interested in power"; "the consensus is democracy") to be offered in part in this same spirit.[2]

Less analyzed is why the choices between "egalitarian" and "difference" feminism, which have deeply divided the U.S. women's movement (Tobias 1997), seem less relevant to the political experiences of Latin American women and thus less a barrier to political action and thought. Temma Kaplan (1982) almost squared the circle in her analysis of women activists in early-twentieth-century Barcelona:

> Female consciousness centers upon the rights of gender, on social concerns, on survival. Those with female consciousness accept the gender system of their society; indeed, such consciousness emerges from the division of labor by sex, which assigns women the responsibility for preserving life. But accepting this task *women with female consciousness demand the rights that their obligations entail.* (Quoted in Alvarez 1990a:49; italics mine)

Perhaps we are now seeing the development of a fourth (but undoubtedly not the last) stage of feminist research practices: the experimentation with post-structural or post-modern approaches to the study of gender politics in Latin America. Insofar as these have been interpreted as "taking race and class into account," a possibility that is in keeping with, but falls well short of, the "post-" critiques, of course there have been such efforts. Latin American and Anglo researchers have long focused on class. But the Marxist perspectives they share are similar to empiricist approaches in that Marxism sees itself as empirically based and "scientific"; Marx was as suspicious of playing with meaning ("ideology") as Hobbes was of the abuses of language ("rhetoric"). This helps explain why Marxist class analysis has been more consistent with "vanguardism" than with the recognition of the "other."

Post-modernism has had a major impact on the study of Latin American literature, and this could potentially spill over to the study of women in Latin American politics, illuminating the continuing impact of U.S. dominance, the meanings of borders and identity, and the continuing dynamics of gender, race, and class within and across national cultures and political systems. Sarah Radcliffe and Sallie Westwood attempt to move in this direction in their introduction to *Viva: Women and Popular Protest in Latin America* (1993), but the essays (though quite valuable in their own right) are a tentative beginning to what could be a much wider shift in perspective and understanding. One interesting place to start is to look at the influences shaping the Latin American study of Latin American women (including the influence of Italian feminists visible in Chapter 7 of this book), identifying different approaches and deconstructing the assumptions of U.S. and British research.

Women and Democratization

Looking at women in Latin American politics from a methodological perspective obscures the most important fact of the last twenty years: the turn to democracy. In retrospect, it is striking to recall how narrow the empirical base was to study women's democratic participation in the mid-1970s. One of the issues scholars who studied women were debating was how to formulate researchable questions on women's participation in "corporatist" regimes (see Tabak 1983). The global standard for women's participation was set by the highly visible leadership roles and radical agendas by and for women in revolutionary regimes and guerrilla movements. Democracy was notable by its absence.

Yet it is not clear that the issues raised in these earlier debates should now be ignored. From a feminist standpoint, women's participation in capitalist markets is always problematic, as women continue to be expected to take virtually full responsibility for creating the conditions of family life while competing with men for limited resources. The economic stabilization programs of the 1980s reduced social services and incomes, and the globalization of the 1990s appears to increase inequality and to have gendered effects on women's employment. These conditions create the very real possibility that women can be mobilized to support promising economic policies that go beyond the neoliberal consensus and may help to strengthen the capacity of the state. And if, as some researchers would argue, contemporary democracy in the region continues to reflect and to adapt corporatist and clientelist features of the region's political past, then the implications of these continuities for women deserve attention. Quotas for electing women can be assessed from several perspectives, but one would surely be the degree to which this is a form of corporatist representation. And, if that is the case, what are the likely consequences in terms of sustainability of quotas and the kinds of policy changes such representation is likely to produce?[3]

The "fall" of communism appears to have made democracy the preferred form of governance in the region. Yet it is not yet clear except in the formal sense what democracy is, what kinds of political cultures will be able to support it or coexist with it, or whether particular patterns of representation or policy outputs will come to be associated with it. As I have argued elsewhere, the transitions to democracy offered particular advantages to social movements and especially to women (Jaquette 1989, 1994), favoring symbolic politics and capitalizing on the commitment to serious social and political change that characterized the political debates at the time. Women's movements, and social movements in general, gave concrete substance to a more progressive image of democracy (León 1994:11–12), which had been attacked throughout much of the twentieth century by both the left (for being unrepresentative and incrementalist) and the right (for being ineffective and prone to violence). Women's movements, first visible in the Southern Cone and Peru, became active in Central America in the 1980s, reinforcing the transitions away from military rule in the region and participating in the party-competitive politics that emerged from the peace process in Nicaragua.

The period of transitions in Latin America coincided with a wave of political mobilization of women worldwide, in large part a result of the Decade for Women that was launched in Mexico City in 1975. Latin American women's movements provided inspiration to others in their fight for human rights and resistance to torture and to women's groups seeking institutional mechanisms to promote women's agendas, from women's councils and police precincts to address violence against women to strategies to promote women's issues within political parties and across party lines.

Democracy as an everyday reality, and no longer an idealized goal, presented new challenges. The strengths of women's movements—their lack of hierarchy, spontaneity, and intensity, were often weaknesses in democratic politics as usual, which responds less to the political drama of mass demonstrations and women's *reivindicaciones* (vindication) and more to persistent organization and strong institutional connections across class, race, and rural-urban lines. As in the North, "strategic" gender demands produced backlash and divided women themselves, although the casting of women's mobilization in terms of motherhood and family needs softened the confrontation.

But it is increasingly difficult to justify a set of policies as "for women" or to maintain strong institutionalized voices for women within the state, although global trends may make women's needs more urgent, and women still need the space to become subjects, not objects, of state policy. In the democratic environment, it is critical to track and critique the changing patterns of state-gender relations and to read constructively the changing linkages between NGOs, particularly those that define themselves as feminist, and grassroots women's organizations. Both kinds of research will strengthen women's representation and action while addressing important issues in the comparative study of gender-state relations and how they are mediated by legislative representation, by bureaucratic politics, and by NGOs and grass-roots movements.

One final observation. It has proven very difficult to insert the study of gender and politics into mainstream research in the discipline. The current scholarship on democratic transitions and consolidations is clear evidence that gender is simply absent from researchers' minds, despite the obvious fact that women make up more than half of most electorates and that their votes are critical to the sustainability of the legitimacy of democracy as a form of government and to the future evolution of state/market relations, basic to the success of democracy's "third wave."

As researchers, we need to make clearer the linkages between women's participation and the future of global politics. The current willingness to expand definitions of security from the traditionally narrow focus on missile counts and sovereignty toward issues such as population, the environment, and the sustainability of democracy itself offers considerable scope for making new connections between women's participation and the prospects for social justice and nonviolent change (Jaquette 1997b). These are issues in which we all—men and women alike—have a profound stake.

Notes

1. Second-stage political science was strongly influenced by the work of Carole Gilligan (1982) and Jean Bethke Elshtain. For a discussion, see Jaquette (1991) and Staudt and Weaver (1997).

2. For a provocative critique of the micropolitics and macronarrative of "good motherhood," see Jane Flax (1997). In a section entitled "God Is Dead/Long Live Mother," Flax noted that we are in danger of installing a "Holy Mother [to] protect/preserve the possibility of innocence" (320) and commented that "certain fantasies about mothers ward off profound anxieties and discontents from which contemporary Westerners often suffer" (321).

3. Philippe Schmitter, in his chapter in Jaquette and Wolchik (1998), speculates on the positive possibilities for women of combining pluralism and corporatism.

References

Aguayo, Sergio, and María Luisa Tarrés. 1995. "Las organizaciones no gubernamentales y la democracia en México." El Colegio de México, Mexico City. Mimeographed.

Aguirre, Irma Estela, Gloria Carmona de Alva, and Pilar Alberti. 1995. *De la práctica a la teoría del feminismo rural*. Mexico, Red Nacional de Promotoras y Asesoras Rurales, Documento Mujer Rural no.3.

Alvarado Mendoza, Arturo. 1992. "Unidad y diversidad en la frontera norte." *Boletín Editorial* (El Colegio de México) no. 42:3–8.

Alvarez, Sonia. 1989a. "Politicizing Gender and Engendering Democracy." In Alfred Stepan, ed., *Democratizing Brazil: Problems of Transition and Consolidation*, 205–251. Oxford and New York: Oxford University Press.

_____. 1989b. "Women's Movements and Gender Politics in the Brazilian Transition." In Jane Jaquette, ed., *The Women's Movement in Latin America: Feminism and the Transition to Democracy*, 18–71. Winchester, MA.: Unwin Hyman.

_____. 1990a. *Engendering Democracy in Brazil: Women's Movements in Transition Politics*. Princeton: Princeton University Press.

_____. 1990b. "Contradictions of a Women's Space in a Male-Dominant State: The Political Role of the Commissions on the Status of Women in a Postauthoritarian Brazil." In Kathleen Staudt, ed., *Women, International Development and Politics: The Bureaucratic Mire*, 37–78. Philadelphia: Temple University Press.

Alvarez, Sonia, and Arturo Escobar, eds. 1992. *The Making of Social Movements in Latin America: Identity, Strategy, and Democracy*. Boulder: Westview Press.

Alvarez, Sonia, Evelina Dagnino, and Arturo Escobar. 1997. *Cultures of Politics, Politics of Cultures: Re-Visioning Latin American Social Movements*. Boulder: Westview Press.

Amorós, Celia. 1987. "Espacio de los iguales, espacio de las idénticas. Notas sobre poder y principio de individuación." *Arbor* (December) Madrid.

ANFER [Asociación Nacional Femenina Revolucionaria]. 1984. *Participación política de la mujer en México, siglo XX*. Mexico City: ANFER.

Arboleda, María. 1993. "Mujeres en el poder local." In María Arboleda, Regina Rodríguez, and María Antonieta Saa, eds., *El espacio posible. Mujeres en el poder local*, 20–42. Santiago de Chile: ISIS Internacional Ediciones de las Mujeres.

Archenti, Nélida, and Patricia Gómez. 1994. "Las legisladoras argentinas: Su quehacer en la transición democrática 1983–1991." In *América Latina Hoy*, bulletin 9, 61–69. SEPLA Universidad Complutense de Madrid/Instituto de Estudios Iberoamericanos, Universidad de Salamanca.

Ardaya Salinas, Gloria. 1986. "The Barzolas and the Housewives Committee." In June Nash and Helen Safa, eds., *Women and Change in Latin America*, 326–343. South Hadley, MA: Bergin and Garvey.

Arizpe, Lourdes. 1990. "Foreword: Democracy for a Small Two-Gender Planet." In Elizabeth Jelin, ed., *Women and Social Change in Latin America*, xiv–xx. London: Zed Books; Geneva: UNRISD.

Arizpe, Lourdes, and Margarita Velázquez. 1994. "La participación de las mujeres en el sector público: Hacia una nueva cultura política." In Patricia Galeana, comp., *La mujer del México de la transición*, 73–77. Mexico City: Federación Mexicana de Universitarias, Universidad Nacional Autónoma de México.

Baca Olamendi, Laura, and Isidro Cisneros Ramírez. 1988. "La cultura política de la derecha social mexicana." *Revista A* 9 (23–24):107–119.

Bachrach, Peter. 1967. *The Theory of Democratic Elitism*. Boston: Little, Brown.

Barreda, Horacio. 1909. "Estudio sobre el feminismo." *Revista Positiva* 103.

Bartra, Eli. 1994. "The Struggle for Life, or Pulling Off the Mask of Infamy." In Barbara Nelson and Najma Chowdhury, eds., *Women and Politics Worldwide*, 448–460. New Haven: Yale University Press.

Basáñez, Miguel, Ronald Inglehart, and Alejandro Moreno. 1996. "Human Values and Beliefs: A Cross-Cultural Sourcebook." Mimeographed.

Béjar Navarro, Raúl, and Héctor Cappello M. 1988. *La conciencia nacional en la frontera norte mexicana*. Mexico City: UNAM-CRIM.

Benería, Lourdes, and Martha Roldán. 1987. *The Crossroads of Class and Gender: Industrial Homework, Subcontracting, and Household Dynamics in Mexico City*. Chicago: University of Chicago Press.

Bennett, Vivienne. 1992. "The Evolution of Urban Popular Movements in Mexico Between 1968 and 1988." In Arturo Escobar and Sonia Alvarez, eds., *The Making of Social Movements in Latin America: Identity, Strategy, and Democracy*, 240–259. Boulder: Westview Press.

———. 1995a. *The Politics of Water: Urban Protest, Gender, and Power in Monterrey, Mexico*. Pittsburgh: University of Pittsburgh Press.

———. 1995b. "Gender, Class, and Water: Women and the Politics of Water Service in Monterrey, Mexico." *Latin American Perspectives* 22 (2):76–99.

Blachman, Morris. 1973. *Eve in an Adamocracy: Women and Politics in Brazil*. New York: Ibero-American Language and Area Center, New York University. Occasional Paper no. 5.

———. 1980. "Selective Omission and Theoretical Distortion in Studying the Political Activity of Women." In June Nash and Helen Safa, eds., *Sex and Class in Latin America*, 245–264. New York: Praeger.

Blondet, Cecilia. 1990. "Establishing an Identity: Women Settlers in a Poor Lima Neighbourhood." In Elizabeth Jelin, ed., *Women and Social Change in Latin America*, 12–46. London: Zed Books; Geneva: UNRISD.

Blough, William. 1972. "Political Attitudes of Mexican Women." *Journal of Inter-American Studies and World Affairs* 14 (2):201–224.

Bocchetti, Alessandra. 1990. "Para mí, para sí." *debate feminista* 2 (September): 221–225.

Boschi, Renato. 1987. "Social Movements and the New Political Order in Brazil." In John D. Wirth, Edson de Oliveira Nunes, and Thomas E. Bogenschild, eds., *State and Society in Brazil*, 179–212. Boulder: Westview Press.

Bourque, Susan C. 1985. "Urban Activists: Paths to Political Consciousness in Peru." In Susan C. Bourque and Donna Divine, eds., *Women Living Change,* 25–56. Philadelphia: Temple University Press.

_____. 1989. "Gender and the State: Perspectives from Latin America." In Sue Ellen Charlton, Jana Everett, and Kathleen Staudt, eds., *Women, the State and Development,* 114–129. Albany: State University of New York Press.

Boyle, Catherine. 1993. "Touching the Air: The Cultural Force of Women in Chile." In Sarah A. Radcliffe and Sallie Westwood, eds., *Viva: Women and Popular Protest in Latin America,* 156–172. London: Routledge.

Bruera, Silvana, and Mariana González. 1993. "Uruguay: Participación municipal de la mujeres." In María Arboleda, Regina Rodríguez, and María Antonieta Saa, eds., *El espacio posible. Mujeres en el poder local,* 133–150. Santiago de Chile: ISIS Internacional Ediciones de las Mujeres.

Bulnes, Francisco. 1916. *The Whole Truth About Mexico: President Wilson's Responsibility.* New York: M. Bulnes Book Co.

Bunster-Burotto, Ximena. 1986. "Surviving Beyond Fear: Women and Torture in Latin America." In June Nash and Helen Safa. eds., *Women and Change in Latin America,* 297–325. South Hadley, MA: Bergin and Garvey.

CAIPORA Women's Group. 1993. *Women in Brazil.* London: Latin America Bureau.

Caldeira, Teresa Pires de Rio. 1990. "Women, Daily Life, and Politics." In Elizabeth Jelin, ed., *Women and Social Change in Latin America,* 47–78. London: Zed Books; Geneva: UNRISD.

Calderón, Fernando, ed. 1985. *Los movimientos sociales ante la crisis.* Buenos Aires: CLACSO.

Calderón, Fernando, and Elizabeth Jelin. 1987. *Clases y movimientos sociales en América Latina.* Buenos Aires: CEDES.

Calderón, Fernando, Alejandro Piscitelli, and José Luis Reyna. 1992. "Social Movements: Actors, Theories, Expectations." In Arturo Escobar and Sonia E. Alvarez, eds., *The Making of Social Movements in Latin America: Identity, Strategy, and Democracy,* 19–36. Boulder: Westview Press.

Camp, Roderic Ai. 1984. *The Making of a Government. Political Leaders in Modern Mexico.* Tucson: University of Arizona Press.

_____. 1995a. *Mexican Political Biographies, 1935–1993.* 3d ed. Austin: University of Texas Press.

_____. 1995b. *Political Recruitment Across Two Centuries: Mexico, 1884–1991.* Austin: University of Texas Press.

_____. 1997. *Crossing Swords: Religion and Politics in Mexico.* New York: Oxford University Press.

Cano, Gabriela. 1988. "El coronel Robles, una combatiente zapatista." *fem* 12 (April):22–24.

_____. 1991. "Las feministas en campaña." *Debate Feminista* 4 (September):269–294.

Cano, Gabriela, and Verena Radkau. 1989. *Ganando espacios.* Mexico City: UAM.

Cardoso, Ruth Corrêa Leite. 1983. "Movimentos Sociais Urbanos: Balanço Critico." In Bernardo Sorj and Maria Herminia Tavares de Almeida, eds., *Sociedade y Política no Brasil Pos–1964,* 215–239. São Paulo:Editora Brasiliense.

_____. 1987. "Movimentos Sociais na America Latina." *Revista Brasileira de Ciencias Sociais* 1 (3):27–37.

_____. 1992. "Popular Movements in the Context of the Consolidation of Democracy in Brazil." In Arturo Escobar and Sonia E. Alvarez, eds., *The Making of Social Movements in Latin America: Identity, Strategy, and Democracy*, 291–302. Boulder: Westview Press.

Carrillo, Teresa. 1990. "Women and Independent Unionism in the Garment Industry." In Joe Foweraker and Ann Craig, eds., *Popular Movements and Political Change in Mexico*, 213–233. Boulder: Lynne Rienner Publishers.

Carroll, Susan J. 1985. "Political Elites and Sex Differences in Political Ambition: A Reconsideration." *Journal of Politics* 47 (4):1231–1243.

Castellanos, Laura. 1994. "Las mujeres de Chiapas, protagonistas invisibles." *Doble Jornada*, February 7, p. 4.

Cernea, Michael. 1988. *Nongovernmental Organizations and Local Development*. World Bank Discussion Papers, no. 40. Washington, DC: World Bank.

Chaney, Elsa M. 1973. "Women in Latin American Politics: The Case of Peru and Chile." In Ann Pescatello, ed., *Female and Male in Latin America*, 103–140. Pittsburgh: University of Pittsburgh Press.

_____. 1979. *Supermadre: Women in Politics in Latin America*. Austin: University of Texas Press.

_____. 1993. *Supermadre: La mujer dentro de la política en América Latina*. 2d ed. Mexico City: Fondo de Cultura Económica.

Chaney, Elsa M., and María García Castro, eds. 1989. *Muchachas No More: Household Workers in Latin America and the Caribbean*. Philadelphia: Temple University Press.

Chant, Sylvia. 1991. *Women and Survival in Mexican Cities: Perspectives on Gender, Labour Markets and Low-income Households*. Manchester: Manchester University Press.

Charlton, Sue Ellen, Jana Everett, and Kathleen Staudt, eds. 1989. *Women, the State and Deveopment*. Albany: State University of New York Press.

Chinchilla, Norma Stoltz. 1992. "Marxism, Feminism, and the Struggle for Democracy in Latin America." In Arturo Escobar and Sonia E. Alvarez, eds., *The Making of Social Movements in Latin America: Identity, Strategy, and Democracy*, 37–51. Boulder: Westview Press.

Chou, Bih-Er, and Janet Clark. 1994. "Electoral Systems and Women's Representation in Taiwan: The Impact of the Reserved-Seat System." In Wilma Rule and Joseph F. Zimmerman, eds., *Electoral Systems in Comparative Perspective. Their Impact on Women and Minorities*, 161–170. Westport, CT: Greenwood Press.

Chuchryk, Patricia. 1989a. "Subversive Mothers: The Women's Opposition to the Military Regime in Chile." In Sue Ellen Charlton, Jana Everett, and Kathleen Staudt, eds., *Women, the State and Development*, 130–151. Albany: State University of New York Press.

_____. 1989b. "Feminist Anti-Authoritarian Politics: The Role of Women's Organizations in the Chilean Transition to Democracy." In Jane Jaquette, ed., *The Women's Movement in Latin America: Feminism and the Transition to Democracy*, 149–184. Winchester, MA.: Unwin Hyman.

Collier, George, with Elizabeth Lowery Quaratiello. 1994. *Basta: Land and the Zapatista Rebellion*. San Francisco: Food First.

Consejo Nacional de Población [CONAPO]. 1993. *Indicadores socioeconómicos e índice de marginación municipal*. Mexico City: CONAPO.

Convención Estatal de Mujeres Chiapanecas. 1994. *Escribiendo nuestra historia*. San Cristóbal de las Casas. Mimeographed.

Convención Nacional de Mujeres. 1995. "Manifiesto. Sólo habrá patria para las mujeres cuando juntas luchemos por ella." Querétaro. Mimeographed.

Corcoran-Nantes, Yvonne. 1990. "Women and Popular Urban Social Movements in São Paulo, Brazil" *Bulletin of Latin American Studies* 9 (2):249–264.

———. 1993. "Female Consciousness or Feminist Consciousness? Women's Consciousness Raising in Community-Based Struggles in Brazil." In Sarah A. Radcliffe and Sallie Westwood, eds., *Viva: Women and Popular Protest in Latin America*, 136–155. London: Routledge.

Córdova, Arnaldo. 1979. *La política de masas del cardenismo*. Mexico City: ERA.

———. 1995. *La Revolución en Curso: La aventura del Maximato*. Mexico City: Cal y Arena.

Cornelius, Wayne. 1996. *Mexican Politics in Transition: The Breakdown of a One-Party-Dominant Regime*. La Jolla: Center for U.S.-Mexican Studies, University of California at San Diego. Monograph Series, no. 41.

Cornelius, Wayne, Ann Craig, and Jonathan Fox, eds. 1994. *Transforming State-Society Relations in Mexico: The National Solidarity Strategy*. La Jolla: Center for U.S.-Mexican Studies, University of California at San Diego.

Costain, Anne N. 1992. *Inviting Women's Rebellion: A Political Process Interpretation of the Women's Movement*. Baltimore: Johns Hopkins University Press.

Costantini, Edmond, and Kenneth Craik. 1972. "Women as Politicians: The Social Background, Personality, and Political Careers of Female Party Leaders." *Journal of Social Issues* 28:217–380.

Craske, Nikki. 1993a. "Women's Political Participation in Colonias Populares in Guadalajara, Mexico." In Sarah A. Radcliffe and Sallie Westwood, eds., *Viva: Women and Popular Protest in Latin America*, 112–135. London: Routledge.

———. 1993b. "Women's Participation in Mexican Urban Politics: The Case of Guadalajara." Ph.D. diss., Department of Government, University of Essex.

———. 1994. "Corporatism Revisited: Salinas and the Reform of the Popular Sector 1988–1992." Institute of Latin American Studies, London. Mimeographed.

Cubitt, Tessa, and Helen Greenslade. 1997. "The End of Dichotomy: Empowerment or Reinforced Subordination?" In Elizabeth Dore, ed. *Gender and Power in Latin America: Theory and Practice*, 52–65. New York: Monthly Review Press.

De la A a la Z. 1993. Documento de presentación. Mexico City. Mimeographed.

"Del amor a la necesidad." 1987. *fem* 11 (60):15–17.

del Castillo, Adelaida R. 1993. "Covert Cultural Norms and Sex/Gender Meaning: A Mexico City Case." *Urban Anthropology* 22 (3–4):237–258.

Dietz, Mary. 1992. "Context Is All: Feminism and Theories of Citizenship." In Chantal Mouffe, ed., *Dimensions of Radical Democracy*, 63–85. London: Verso.

Documentos del Movimiento Campesino. 1984. "Acuerdos y resoluciones del II congreso nacional ordinario de la CNPA." *Textual* 5 (17):115–127.

Dresser, Denise. 1994. "La promoción de la democracia en México." *Este País*, no. 40 (July).

Eber, Christine. 1995. *Women and Alcohol in a Highland Town*. Austin: University of Texas Press.

Eder, Klaus. 1993. *The New Politics of Class Social Movements and Cultural Dynamics in Advanced Societies*. London: Sage.

Escobar, Arturo, and Sonia E. Alvarez, eds. 1992. *The Making of Social Movements in Latin America: Identity, Strategy, and Democracy*. Boulder: Westview Press.

Feijoó, María del Carmen. 1989. "The Challenge of Constructing Civilian Peace: Women and Democracy in Argentina." In Jane Jaquette, ed., *The Women's Movement in Latin America: Feminism and the Transition to Democracy*, 72–94. Winchester, MA.: Unwin Hyman.

Feijoó, María del Carmen, with Marcela María Alejandra Nari. 1994. "Women and Democracy in Argentina." In Jane Jaquette, ed., *The Women's Movement in Latin America: Participation and Democracy*, 109–129. 2d ed. Boulder: Westview Press.

FEMAP [Mexican Federation of Private Associations]. 1995. *Seeds Across the Border: Proceedings of a Women and Development Conference*. October 30. Ciudad Juárez: FEMAP.

Fernández-Kelly, María Patricia. 1983. *For We Are Sold, I and My People*. Albany: SUNY Albany Press.

Fernández Poncela, Anna M. 1995. *Participación política. Las mujeres en México al final del milenio*. Mexico City: El Colegio de México, PIEM.

Fisher, Jo. 1993. *Out of the Shadows: Women, Resistance and Politics in South America*. London: Latin American Bureau.

FLACSO [Facultad Latinoamericana de Ciencias Sociales]. 1993. *Mujeres latinoamericanas en cifras*. Santiago: FLACSO.

Flax, Jane. 1997. "Forgotten Forms of Close Combat: Mothers and Daughters Revisited." In Mary M. Gergen and Sara N. Davis, eds., *Toward a New Psychology of Gender*, 311–324. New York: Routledge.

Foweraker, Joe. 1988. "Transformism Transformed. The Nature of Mexico's Political Crisis." *Essex Papers in Politics and Government*. Colchester: University of Essex.

_____. 1989a. *Making Democracy in Spain: Grass-roots Struggle in the South, 1955–1975*. New York: Cambridge University Press.

_____. 1989b. "Popular Movements and the Transformation of the System." In Wayne Cornelius, Judith Gentleman, and Peter Smith, eds., *Mexico's Alternative Political Futures*, 109–129. La Jolla: Center for U.S.-Mexican Studies, University of California at San Diego.

_____. 1993. *Popular Mobilization in Mexico: The Teachers' Movement 1977–1987*. New York: Cambridge University Press.

_____. 1995a. *Theorizing Social Movements: Critical Studies in Latin America*. London: Pluto Press.

_____. 1995b. "Measuring Citizenship in Mexico." In Victor Bulmer-Thomas and Mónica Serrano, eds., *Rebuilding the State: Mexico After Salinas*, 79–98. London: Institute of Latin American Studies.

Foweraker, Joe, and Ann Craig, eds. 1990. *Popular Movements and Political Change in Mexico*. Boulder: Lynne Rienner Publishers.

Fox, Jonathan, and Luis Hernández. 1992. "Mexico, Difficult Democracy: Grassroots Movements, NGOs and Local Government." *Alternatives* 17:165–208.

Franco, Jean. 1992. "Gender, Death and Resistance: Facing the Ethical Vacuum." In Juan E. Corradi, Patricia Weiss Fagen, and Manuel Antonio Garretón, eds., *Fear at the Edge,* 104–118. Berkeley: University of California Press.

Friedman, Elisabeth. 1996. "Paradoxes of Party Politics: The Impact of Gendered Institutions on Women's Incorporation in Latin American Politics." Paper presented at the Annual Meeting of the American Political Science Association, San Francisco.

Fuentes, Marta, and Andre Gunder Frank. 1989. "Ten Theses on Social Movements." *World Development* 17 (2):179–191.

Ganando Espacios. 1992. *Documento de trabajo.* Acapulco: Mimeographed.

García, Brígida, and Orlandina de Oliveira. 1997. "Motherhood and Extradomestic Work in Urban Mexico." *Bulletin of Latin American Research* 16 (3):367–384.

García de León, Antonio. 1994. "La Vuelta del Katun (Chiapas: a 20 años del Primer Congreso Indígena)." *Perfil de la Jornada,* Mexico City, October 12.

Gertzog, Irwin. 1984. "Changing Patterns of Recruitment." In *Congressional Women, Their Recruitment, Treatment, and Behavior,* 34–47. New York: Praeger.

Gilbert, Alan, ed. 1989. *Housing and Land in Urban Mexico.* La Jolla: Center for U.S.-Mexican Studies, University of California at San Diego. Monograph Series, no. 31.

Gilligan, Carole. 1982. *In a Different Voice.* Cambridge: Harvard University Press.

González Ascencio, Gerardo. 1993. "Las organizaciones no gubernamentales de alta rentabilidad social." Paper presented to the Asociación mexicana contra la violencia, Covac, April.

González de la Rocha, Mercedes, and Agustín Escobar Latapí, eds. 1991. *Social Responses to Mexico's Economic Crisis of the 1980s.* La Jolla: Center for U.S.-Mexican Studies, University of California at San Diego.

Guillén, Tonatiuh. 1992. "Baja California, una década de cambio político." In Tonatiuh Guillén, ed., *Frontera norte: Una década de política electoral,* 139–185. Mexico City: El Colegio de México.

Guillermoprieto, Alma. 1995. "Marcos and Mexico." *The New York Review of Books,* March 2, 42 (4):34–43.

Haber, Paul. 1992. "Collective Dissent in Mexico: The Politics of Contemporary Urban Popular Movements." Ph.D. diss., Columbia University.

Habermas, Jurgen. 1973. *Legitimation Crisis.* London: Heinemann.

_____. 1987. *The Philosophical Discourse of Modernity.* Cambridge: MIT Press.

Harvey, Neil. 1994. "Rebellion in Chiapas: Rural Reforms, Campesino Radicalism, and the Limits to Salinismo." In *The Transformation of Rural Mexico.* La Jolla: Center for U.S.-Mexican Studies, University of California at San Diego. Ejido Research Project, no. 5.

Hellman, Judith A. 1983. *Mexico in Crisis.* 2d ed. New York: Holmes and Meier Publishers.

_____. 1994. *Mexican Lives.* New York: New Press.

Hernández, Eduardo, and Julio Boltvinik. 1995. *Informe sobre la pobreza en México.* Mexico City: Universidad Nacional Autónoma de México and El Colegio de México.

Hernández Castillo, Rosalva Aída. 1989. "Del Tzolkin a la Atalaya: Cambios en la religiosidad en una comunidad Chuj-K'anhobal de Chiapas." In Andrés Fáregas et al., eds., *Religión y sociedad en el sureste de México*. Cuadernos de la Casa Chata 162, vol. 2, 123–124. México City: Centro de Investigaciones y Estudios Superiores en Antropología Social.

———. 1994. "La 'fuerza extraña' es mujer." *Ojarasca* 30:36–37.

Hernández Chávez, Alicia. 1980. *La mecánica cardenista*. Mexico City: El Colegio de México.

Hernández Navarro, Luis. 1995. "En el país de Gulliver. ONG, democracia y desarrollo." *Revista Enfoque*, diario *Reforma*, June 25.

Hidalgo, Berta. 1980. *El movimiento femenino en México*. Mexico City: Editores Asociados Mexicanos.

Hierro, Graciela, Lorenia Parada, and Gloria Careaga. 1995. *La participación de mujeres en cargos públicos, de 1970 a 1993*. Mexico City: Centro de Estudios de Género, UNAM.

Hierro, Graciela, Lorenia Parada, Lina Pérez, and Gloria Careaga. 1995. *Participación en la vida pública y acceso a la toma de decisiones*. Mexico City: Ediciones CONAPO.

Hirschman, Albert O. 1982. *Shifting Involvements: Private Interest and Public Action*. Princeton: Princeton University Press.

———. 1986. *Interés privado y acción pública*. Mexico City: Fondo de Cultura Económica.

———. 1991. *Retóricas de la intransigencia*. Mexico City: Fondo de Cultura Económica.

Hofstede, Geert. 1984. *Culture's Consequences*. Newbury Park, CA: Sage.

Incháustegui, Teresa, and Alicia I. Martínez. 1996. "Política social y cambios a final de siglo: Contexto y valores en relación a los nuevos actores." In Alicia Ziccardi, ed., *Las políticas sociales en México en los años noventa*, 61–74. Mexico City: Plaza y Valdés.

INEGI [Instituto Nacional de Estadística, Geografía e Informática]. 1990. *Perfil sociodemográfico. XI Censo general de población y vivienda*. Mexico: INEGI.

———. 1993. *La mujer en México*. Mexico: INEGI.

INEGI/PRONAM [Programa Nacional de la Mujer]. 1997. *Mujeres y hombres en México*. Mexico: INEGI/PRONAM.

Inter-American Development Bank. 1995. *Women in the Americas: Bridging the Gender Gap*. Washington, DC: Inter-American Development Bank.

Inter-Parliamentary Union. 1991. *Distribution of Seats Between Men and Women in National Parliaments: Statistical Data from 1945 to 10 June, 1991*. Geneva: Inter-Parliamentary Union. Rapports et Document no.18, plus appenda for 1993 and 1994.

IULA [Unión Internacional de Municipios y Autoridades Locales]/CELCADEL [Centro Latinoamericano de Capacitación y Desarrollo de los Gobiernos Locales]. 1991a. *Métodos de investigación de género y formulación de políticas municipales dirigidas a mujeres*. Quito: IULA/CELCADEL. Programa Mujer y Desarrollo Local, Cuaderno no. 9.

———. 1991b. *Mujer y municipio: Una nueva presencia comunitaria en el desarrollo local de América Latina*. Quito: IULA/CELCADEL. Programa Mujer y Desarrollo Local, Cuaderno no.7.

Jaquette, Jane S. 1980. "Female Political Participation in Latin America." In June Nash and Helen Safa, eds., *Sex and Class in Latin America*, 221–244. South Hadley, MA: J. F. Bergin.

_____. 1992. "Political Science: Whose Common Good?" In Dale Spender and Cheris Spender, eds., *The Knowledge Explosion: Generations of Feminist Scholarship*, 141–152. New York: Athene Series.

_____. 1993. "Women's Movements and Democracy in Latin America: Some Unresolved Tensions." In *Women and the Transition to Democracy: The Impact of Political and Economic Reform in Latin America.* Washington, DC: Woodrow Wilson International Center for Scholars.

_____. 1995. "Rewriting the Scripts: Gender in the Comparative Study of Latin American Politics." In Peter H. Smith, ed., *Latin America in Comparative Perspective: New Approaches to Methods and Analysis*, 111–134. Boulder: Westview Press.

_____. 1997a. "Women in Power: From Tokenism to Critical Mass." *Foreign Policy* 108 (Fall):23–37.

_____. 1997b. "Women's Political Participation: Implications for International Security." Rethinking Security Seminar, Paper 13, University of California's Center for International Studies.

Jaquette, Jane S., ed. 1989. *The Women's Movement in Latin America: Feminism and the Transition to Democracy.* London and Winchester, MA.: Unwin Hyman.

_____. 1994. *The Women's Movement in Latin America: Participation and Democracy.* 2d ed. Boulder: Westview Press.

Jaquette, Jane S., and Sharon L. Wolchik, eds. 1998. *Women and Democratization in Latin America and Central and Eastern Europe.* Baltimore: Johns Hopkins University Press.

Jelin, Elizabeth. 1987. *Ciudadanía e identidad: Las mujeres en los movimientos sociales latino-americanos.* Geneva: UNRISD.

Jelin, Elizabeth, ed., 1985. *Los nuevos movimientos sociales.* 2 vols. Buenos Aires: Centro Editor de América Latina.

_____. 1990a. *Women and Social Change in Latin America.* London: Zed Books; Geneva: UNRISD.

_____. 1990b. "Citizenship and Identity: Final Reflections." In Elizabeth Jelin, ed., *Women and Social Change in Latin America*, 184–207. London: Zed Books; Geneva: UNRISD.

Jennings, Kent M., and Norman Thomas. 1968. "Men and Women in Party Elites: Social Roles and Political Resources." *Midwest Journal of Political Science.* 12 (November):469–492.

Jonas, Susanne, and Nancy Stein, eds. 1990. *Democracy in Latin America: Visions and Realities.* New York: Bergin and Garvey.

Jones, Mark. 1996. "Increasing Women's Representation via Gender Quotas: The Argentine Ley de Cupos" *Women and Politics* 16 (4):75–98.

Kanter, Rosabeth. 1993. *Men and Women of the Corporation.* 2d ed. New York: Basic Books.

Kaplan, Temma. 1982. "Female Consciousness and Collective Action: The Case of Barcelona, 1910–1918." *Signs* 7 (3):545–566.

Kirkwood, Julieta. 1983. "Women and Politics in Chile." *International Social Science Journal* 35:625–637.

_____. 1990. *Ser política en Chile. Nudos de sabiduría feminista.* Chile: Editorial Cuarto Propio.

Knight, Alan. 1990. *The Mexican Revolution.* Vol. 2. Lincoln: Nebraska University Press.

Küppers, Gaby, ed. 1994. *Compañeras: Voices from the Latin American Women's Movement.* London: Latin American Bureau.

"La ley revolucionaria de mujeres." 1994. *Doble Jornada,* February 7, p. 8.

Lamas, Marta. 1994. "Algunas características del movimiento feminista en Ciudad de México." In Magdalena León, comp., *Mujeres y participación política: Avances y desafíos en América Latina,* 143–165. Bogotá: T/M Editores.

Lamas, Marta, Alicia Martínez, María Luisa Tarrés, and Esperanza Tuñón. 1995a. "Building Bridges: The Growth of Popular Feminism in Mexico." In Amrita Basu, ed., *The Challenge of Local Feminisms: Women's Movements in Global Perspective,* 324–351. Boulder: Westview Press.

_____. 1995b. "Encuentros y desencuentros: El Movimiento Amplio de Mujeres en México, 1970–1993." Mexico City. Ford Foundation working paper.

Lau, Ana, and Carmen Ramos. 1993. *Mujeres y revolución.* Mexico City: INEHRM.

Lavrin, Asunción. 1993. "Women in 20th Century Latin American Society." In Leslie Bethell, ed., *The Cambridge History of Latin America,* Vol. 6, pt. 2, 483–544. Cambridge: Cambridge University Press.

Lehmann, David. 1990. *Democracy and Development in Latin America: Economics, Politics and Religion in the Post-War Period.* Philadelphia: Temple University Press.

León, Magdalena, comp. 1994. *Mujeres y participación política: Avances y desafíos en América Latina.* Bogotá: Tercer Mundo Editores.

Lewis, Paul. 1971. "The Female Vote in Argentina, 1958–1965." *Comparative Political Studies* 3 (4): 425–441.

Librería de Mujeres de Milán. 1991. *No creas tener derechos.* Madrid: Editorial Horas y Horas.

Llamada de atención a la conciencia nacional. 1940. Mexico City: N.p.

Loaeza, Soledad. 1989. "Cambios en la cultura política mexicana: el surgimiento de una derecha moderna (1970–1988)." *Revista Mexicana de Sociología* 51 (3):221–235.

Logan, Kathleen. 1990. "Women's Participation in Urban Protest." In Joe Foweraker and Ann Craig, eds., *Popular Movements and Political Change in Mexico,* 150–159. Boulder: Lynne Rienner Publishers.

Lomnitz, Larissa, and Ana Melnick. 1991. *Chile's Middle Class: A Struggle for Survival in the Face of Neoliberalism.* Boulder: Lynne Rienner Publishers.

Lópezllera, Luis. 1988. *Sociedad civil y pueblos emergentes.* México: Promoción del desarrollo popular.

Lovera, Sara. 1994a. "Militares violan a tres mujeres tzeltales." In Rosa Rojas, ed., *Chiapas: Y las mujeres qué?,* 103–113. Mexico City: Ediciones La Correa Feminista.

_____. 1994b. "Tzeltales violadas: Cronología de otra impunidad." In Rosa Rojas, ed., *Chiapas: Y las mujeres qué?,* 113–118. Mexico City: Ediciones La Correa Feminista.

Lovera, Sara, and Gaspar Morquecho. 1994. "Día contra la violencia hacia las mujeres; exigen que civilies juzguen a los violadores de las 3 tzeltales." In Rosa Rojas, ed., *Chiapas: Y las mujeres qué?,* 121–124. Mexico City: Ediciones La Correa Feminista.

Macías, Anna. 1974. "The Mexican Revolution Was No Revolution for Women." In Lewis Hanke, ed., *Latin America: A Historical Reader,* 591–601. Boston: Little, Brown.

_____. 1979. "Antecedentes del feminismo en México en los años veinte." *fem* 11 (November-December):5–32.

_____. 1980. "Women and the Mexican Revolution, 1910–1920." *The Americas* 37 (1):53–82.

Mainwaring, Scott, and Eduardo Viola. 1984. "New Social Movements, Political Culture and Democracy: Brazil and Argentina in the 1980s." *Telos* 61 (Fall):17–52.

Mainwaring, Scott, and Timothy Scully, eds. 1995. *Building Democratic Institutions: Party Systems in Latin America.* Stanford: Stanford University Press.

March, James, and Johan Olsen. 1989. *Rediscovering Institutions: The Organizational Basis of Politics.* New York: The Free Press.

Martin, Janet M. 1989. "The Recruitment of Women to Cabinet and Subcabinet Posts." *Western Political Quarterly* 42 (March):161–172.

Martínez, Alicia I. 1993. *Mujeres latinoamericanas en cifras: México.* Mexico City: FLACSO.

_____. 1997a. "Política en cuerpo de mujer." In Rosalía Winocur, ed., *Culturas políticas a fin de siglo,* 221–241. Mexico City: Miguel Angel Porrúa/FLACSO.

_____. 1997b. "Identidad y estilos de vida: Estructura de las demandas feministas." FLACSO, Mexico City. Mimeographed.

Marx Ferree, Myra. 1992. "The Political Context of Rationality: Rational Choice Theory and Resource Mobilization." In Aldon D. Morris and Carol McClurg Mueller, eds., *Frontiers in Social Movement Theory,* 29–52. New Haven: Yale University Press.

Massolo, Alejandra. 1988. *Memoria del Pedregal, memoria de mujer. Testimonio de una colona.* México: Mujeres para el Diálogo.

_____. 1992. "Políticas urbanas y mujer: Una aproximación." In María Luisa Tarrés, ed., *La voluntad de ser. Mujeres en los noventa,* 291–309. Mexico City: El Colegio de México.

_____. 1994a. "Minoría de mujeres en los ayuntamientos." *Artículo 115,* 7 (April).

_____. 1994b. "La dimensión de género en la agenda de la investigación urbana." *Revista Interamericana de Planificación* 27 (107–108):139–148.

_____. 1994c. "La marca del género: Mujeres protagonistas de la ciudad." In Augusto Bolívar, René Coulomb, and Carmen Muñoz, eds., *Gestión metropolitana y política,* 419–444. Mexico City: Universidad Autónoma Metropolitana-Azcapotzalco.

_____, ed. 1994d. *Los medios y los modos: Participación política y acción colectiva de las mujeres.* Mexico City: El Colegio de México.

_____. 1995. "Participación femenina en el gobierno municipal." In Anna M. Fernández Poncela, ed., *Participación política. Las mujeres en México al final del milenio,* 137–146. México City: El Colegio de México, PIEM.

Massolo, Alejandra, and Lucila Díaz Ronner. 1983. "La participación de las mujeres en los movimientos sociales urbanos." Programa Integrado de Estudios sobre la Mujer, El Colegio de México. Mimeographed.

Mattelart, Armand, and Michelle Mattelart. 1968. *La mujer chilena en una nueva sociedad.* Santiago: Editorial del Pacífico.

McAdam, Doug, John McCarthy, and Mayer Zald. 1988. "Social Movements." In Neil Smelser, ed., *Handbook of Sociology,* 695–738. Newbury Park, CA: Sage.

Miller, Francesca. 1991. *Latin American Women and the Search for Social Justice.* Hanover, NH: University of New England Press.

Mogrovejo Aquise, Norma. 1990. "Feminismo popular en México: Análisis del surgimiento, desarrollo y conflictos en la relación entre la tendencia feminista y la Regional de Mujeres de la CONAMUP." Master's thesis, Facultad Latinoamericana de Ciencias Sociales (FLACSO, Mexico City) .

Moisés, José Alvaro. 1982. "O Estado, as Contradições Urbanas e os Movimentos Sociais." In José Alvaro Moisés et al., eds., *Cidade, Povo e Poder*, 14–29. Rio de Janeiro: Paz e Terra.

Molyneux, Maxine. 1985. "Mobilization Without Emancipation? Women's Interests, the State and Revolution in Nicaragua." *Feminist Studies* 11 (2):227–254.

_____. 1990. "The 'Women Question' in the Age of Perestroika." *New Left Review* 183:23–49.

Moreno, Daniel. 1995. "ONG. Los nuevos protagonistas" and "ONG. Hay que poner orden." *Revista Enfoque*, diario *Reforma*, June 25.

Morris, Aldon D., and Carol McClurg Mueller, eds. 1992. *Frontiers in Social Movement Theory*. New Haven: Yale University Press.

Morton, Ward M. 1962. *Woman Suffrage in Mexico*. Gainesville: University of Florida Press.

Moser, Caroline. 1987. "The Experiences of Poor Women in Guayaquil." In Eduardo P. Archetti, ed., *Sociology of "Developing" Societies: Latin America*, 305–320. New York: Monthly Review Press.

Mouffe, Chantal. 1988. "Hegemony and New Political Subjects: Toward a New Concept of Democracy." In Cary Nelson and Lawrence Grossberg, eds., *Marxism and the Interpretation of Culture*, 89–104. Chicago: University of Illinois Press.

Munck, Gerardo. 1990. "Identity and Ambiguity in Democratic Struggles." In Joe Foweraker and Ann Craig, eds., *Popular Movements and Political Change in Mexico*, 23–42. Boulder: Lynne Rienner Publishers.

Nash, June. 1986. *Women and Change in Latin America*. South Hadley, MA: Bergin and Garvey.

Nash, June, and Helen I. Safa, eds. 1980. *Sex and Class in Latin America: Women's Perspectives on Politics, Economics and the Family in the Third World*. South Hadley, MA: J. F. Bergin.

Nava de Ruiz Sánchez, Julia. 1922. "Informe que rinde la secretaria de la delegación mexicana al Consejo de Baltimore ante el centro feminista mexicano sobre la comisión que le confirmó la Liga Nacional de Mujeres Votantes." Mexico City. Mimeographed.

Nelson, Barbara, and Najma Chowdhury, eds. 1994. *Women and Politics Worldwide*. New Haven: Yale University Press.

Nolasco, Margarita. 1991. *Cambios políticos en las fronteras nacionales*. La Jolla: Center for U.S.-Mexican Studies, University of California at San Diego.

Norderval Means, Ingunn. 1972. "Political Recruitment of Women in Norway." *Western Political Quarterly* 25 (September):491–521.

Norris, Pippa. 1985. "Women's Legislative Participation in Western Europe." In Sylvia Bashevkin, ed., *Women and Politics in Western Europe*, 90–101. London: Frank Cass.

O'Donnell, Guillermo. 1984. "Democracia en la Argentina micro y macro." In Oscar Oszlak, ed., *"Proceso," crisis y transición democrática*, 13–30. Buenos Aires: Centro Editor de América Latina.

Offe, Claus. 1987. "Challenging the Boundaries of Institutional Politics: Social Movements Since the 1960s." In Charles S. Maier, ed., *Changing Boundaries of the Political*, 63–105. Cambridge: Cambridge University Press.

———. 1992. *Movimientos sociales y partidos políticos.* 2d ed. Madrid: Editorial Sistema.

Olivé, León, and Fernando Salmerón, eds. 1994. *La identidad personal y la colectiva.* Mexico City: UNAM. Cuadernos del Instituto de Investigaciones Filosóficas.

Oszlak, Oscar. 1987. "Privatización autoritaria y recreación de la escena pública." In Oscar Oszlak, ed., *"Proceso," crisis y transición democrática*, 31–48. Buenos Aires: Centro Editor de América Latina.

Palma Cabrera, Esperanza. 1988. "Notas sobre el neopanismo y la cultura política norteña." *Revista A* 9 (23–24):93–105.

Paré, Luisa. 1990. "The Challenge of Rural Democratization in Mexico." *Journal of Development Studies* 26 (July):79–96.

Pateman, Carole. 1988. *The Sexual Contract.* Cambridge: Polity Press.

Perelli, Carina. 1994. "The Uses of Conservatism: Women's Democratic Politics in Uruguay." In Jane Jaquette, ed., *The Women's Movement in Latin America: Participation and Democracy*, 131–149. 2d ed. Boulder: Westview Press.

Pérez Arce, Francisco. 1990. "The Enduring Union Struggle for Legality and Democracy." In Joe Foweraker and Ann Craig, eds., *Popular Movements and Political Change in Mexico*, 105–120. Boulder: Lynne Rienner Publishers.

Pérez Duarte, Alicia Elena. 1994. "El papel de la mujer en la actualidad pública." In Patricia Galeana, comp. *La mujer del México de la transición*, 85–92. Mexico City: UNAM.

Pérez Güemes, Efraín, and Alma Rosa Garza del Toro. 1984. "El movimiento de posesionarios en Monterrey, 1970–1985." Monterrey, Mexico. Mimeographed.

Perón, Eva. 1951. *La razón de mi vida.* Buenos Aires: Ediciones Peuser.

PIEM [Programa Interdisciplinario de Estudios de la Mujer]. 1993. *Directorio de organizaciones no gubernamentales que trabajan en beneficio de la mujer.* 2d ed. Mexico City: El Colegio de México.

Pinto, Mara D. Biasis Ferrari. 1993. "Brasil: Ejecutivo local en femenino." In María Arboleda, Regina Rodríguez, and María Antonieta Saa, eds. *El espacio posible. Mujeres en el poder local*, 67–96. Santiago de Chile: ISIS Internacional Ediciones de las Mujeres.

Pozas Garza, María. 1990. "Los marginados y la ciudad." In Víctor Zuñiga and Manuel Ribeiro, eds., *La marginación urbana en Monterrey*, 15–58. Monterrey: Facultad de Filosofía y Letras, Universidad Autónoma de Nuevo León.

Primer informe anual que rinde el CEN del PNR a todos los sectores sociales del país. 1936. Mexico City: N.p.

Probyn, Elspeth. 1990. "Travels in the Postmodern: Making Sense on the Local." In Linda Nicholson, ed., *Feminism/Postmodernism*, 176–189. New York: Routledge.

PRONAM [Programa Nacional de la Mujer]. 1997. *Más mujeres al congreso.* Mexico City: PRONAM.

PUEG [Programa Universitario de Estudios de Género]. 1995. *Directorio ONGs de mujeres.* Mexico City: Coordinación de Humanidades, UNAM.

Putnam, Robert D. 1993. *Making Democracy Work: Civic Traditions in Modern Italy.* Princeton: Princeton University Press.

Quintana Silveyra, Víctor M. 1991. *Movimientos populares en Chihuahua.* Ciudad Juárez: Universidad Autónoma de Ciudad Juárez. Estudios Regionales 3.

Radcliffe, Sarah A., and Sallie Westwood, eds. 1993. *Viva: Women and Popular Protest in Latin America.* London: Routledge.

Ramírez Saiz, Juan Manuel. 1986. *El movimiento urbano popular en México.* Mexico City: Siglo XXI.

_____. 1987a. *Política urbana y lucha popular.* Mexico City: Universidad Autónoma Metropolitana–Xochimilco.

_____. 1987b. "El movimiento urbano popular en la administración de Miguel de la Madrid." In Germán Pérez and Samuel León, eds., *17 ángulos del sexenio,* 423–470. Mexico City: Plaza y Valdés.

Ramos Escandón, Carmen. 1994. "Women's Movements, Feminism and Mexican Politics." In Jane Jaquette, ed., *The Women's Movement in Latin America: Participation and Democracy,* 199–221. 2d ed. Boulder: Westview Press.

Randall, Vicky. 1987. *Women and Politics: An International Perspective.* 2d ed. London: MacMillan.

Rao, Aruna, Hilary Feldstein, Kathleen Cloud, and Kathleen Staudt. 1991. *Gender Training and Development Planning: Learning from Experience.* New York: Population Council; Bergen, Norway: Chr. Michelsen Institute.

Riechman, Jorge, and Francisco Fernández Buey. 1994. *Redes que dan libertad.* Barcelona: Editorial Paidós.

Ríos Cárdenas, María. 1942. *La mujer mexicana es ciudadana. Novela con fisonomía de una novela de costumbres.* Mexico City: A. del Bosque, Impresor.

Ríos Tobar, Marcela. 1994. "El rol de las organizaciones femeninas de base en la construcción de la ciudadanía en Chile." Master's thesis, Facultad Latinoamericana de Ciencias Sociales (FLACSO).

Roberts, Bryan. 1993. "Enterprise and Labor Markets: The Border and the Metropolitan Areas." *Frontera Norte* 5 (9):33–66.

Robles, Martha, Patricia Ruiz, and Gregorio Ortega. 1994. *Cecilia Soto: El poder de la nueva fuerza política.* Mexico City: Grupo Editorial Planeta.

Robles de Mendoza, Margarita. 1931. *La evolución de la mujer en México.* Mexico City: Imprenta Galas.

Rodríguez, Victoria E. Forthcoming. *Women in Contemporary Mexican Politics.* Austin: University of Texas Press.

Rodríguez, Victoria E., and Peter M. Ward. 1992. *Policymaking, Politics, and Urban Governance in Chihuahua. The Experience of Recent Panista Governments.* Austin: LBJ School of Public Affairs, University of Texas at Austin.

_____. 1994. *Political Change in Baja California: Democracy in the Making?* La Jolla: Center for U.S.-Mexican Studies, University of California at San Diego. Monograph Series, no. 40.

Rodríguez, Victoria E., and Peter M. Ward, eds. 1995. *Opposition Government in Mexico.* Albuquerque: University of New Mexico Press.

Rodríguez, Victoria E., et al. 1995. *Women in Contemporary Mexican Politics. Memoria of the Bi-National Conference.* Austin: The Mexican Center of ILAS, University of Texas at Austin.

_____. 1996. *Women in Contemporary Mexican Politics II: Participation and Affirmative Action. Memoria of the Bi-National Conference.* Austin: The Mexican Center of ILAS, University of Texas at Austin.

Rodríguez Araujo, Octavio, and Alvaro Arreola Ayala. 1993. "Las caras del abstencionismo: Baja California, Chihuahua y Michoacán." In Gustavo Emmerich, ed., *Votos y Mapas,* 267–281. Mexico City: UAEM.

Rodríguez Cabo, Matilde. 1937. "La mujer y la revolución." Lecture delivered at the Frente Socialista de Abogados, Mexico City.

Rosaldo, Michelle. 1980. "The Use and Abuse of Anthropology: Reflections on Cross-Cultural Understanding." *Signs* 5 (3):389–417.

Ross, John. 1994. *Rebellion from the Roots: Indian Uprising in Chiapas.* Monroe, ME: Common Courage Press.

Rovira, Guiomar. 1994. *Zapata Vive! La rebelión indígena de Chiapas contada por sus protagonistas.* Barcelona: Virus Editorial.

_____. 1997. *Mujeres de Maíz.* Mexico City: Ediciones ERA.

Rubin, Jeffrey W. 1990. "Popular Mobilization and the Myth of Corporatism." In Joe Foweraker and Ann Craig, eds., *Popular Movements and Political Change in Mexico,* 247–267. Boulder: Lynne Rienner Publishers.

Rule, Wilma. 1987. "Electoral Systems, Contextual Factors and Women's Opportunity for Election to Parliament in Twenty Three Democracies." *Western Political Quarterly* 40 (3):477–498.

_____. 1994. "Parliaments of, by, and for the People: Except for Women?" In Wilma Rule and Joseph F. Zimmerman, eds., *Electoral Systems in Comparative Perspective. Their Impact on Women and Minorities,* 15–30. Westport, CT: Greenwood Press.

Rus, Jan. 1994. "The 'Comunidad Revolucionaria Institucional': The Subversion of Native Government in Highland Chiapas, 1936–1968." In Gilbert Joseph and Daniel Nugent, eds., *Everyday Forms of State Formation: Revolution and the Negotiation of Rule in Modern Mexico,* 265–300. Durham: Duke University Press.

Saa, María Antonieta. 1993. "Desacralizar el poder." In María Arboleda, Regina Rodríguez, and María Antonieta Saa, eds., *El espacio posible. Mujeres en el poder local* 9–19. Santiago de Chile: ISIS Internacional Ediciones de las Mujeres.

Saez Royo, Artemisa. 1954. *Historia político social cultural del movimiento femenino en México, 1914–1950.* Mexico City: Manuel León Sánchez.

Safa, Helen. 1980. "Class Consciousness Among Working-Class Women in Latin America: Puerto Rico." In June Nash and Helen Safa, eds., *Sex and Class in Latin America,* 69–85. South Hadley, MA: J. F. Bergin.

_____. 1990. "Women's Social Movements in Latin America." *Gender and Society* 4 (3):354–369.

Saint-Germain, Michelle, and Martha I. Morgan. 1991. "Equality: Costa Rican Women Demand the 'Real Thing.'" *Women and Politics* 11 (3):23–75.

Salas Porras, Alejandra. 1989. "La frontera: Una larga lucha por su independencia." In Alejandra Salas Porras et al., eds., *Nuestra frontera norte,* 43–80. Mexico City: Editorial Nuestro Tiempo.

Sampedro, María Rosario. 1993. "Una política dirigida a la mujer." In María Arboleda, Regina Rodríguez, and María Antonieta Saa, eds., *El espacio posible. Mujeres en el poder local,* 97–106. Santiago de Chile: ISIS Internacional de las Mujeres.

Saucedo, Irma. 1991. "El difícil camino a la individuación." *Hilos, nudos y colores.* Mexico City: CICAM.

Scherer-Warren, Ilse, and Paulo Krischke. 1987. *Uma Revolução no Cotidiano? Os Novos Movimentos Sociais na America do Sul.* São Paulo: Brasilense.

Schild, Veronica. 1991. "Disordering Differences: Women and the 'Popular' Movement in Latin America." Paper presented at the 16th Congress of the Latin American Studies Association, Washington, D.C., April 4–6.

Schirmer, Jennifer. 1993. "The Seeking of Truth and the Gendering of Consciousness: The Comadres of El Salvador and the CONAVIGUA Widows of Guatemala." In Sarah Radcliffe and Sallie Westwood, eds., *Viva: Women and Popular Protest in Latin America,* 30–64. London: Routledge.

Schmitter, Phillipe C., and Terry Karl. 1993. "What Democracy Is . . . and Is Not." In Larry Diamond and Marc F. Plattner, eds., *The Global Resurgence of Democracy,* 49–62. Baltimore: Johns Hopkins University Press.

Selby, Henry, et al. 1990. *The Mexican Urban Household: Organizing for Self-Defense.* Austin: University of Texas Press.

Silva, Luz de Lourdes. 1989. "Las mujeres en la élite política de México: 1954–1984." In Orlandina de Oliveira, ed., *Trabajo, poder y sexualidad,* 269–302. Mexico City: El Colegio de México.

Skard, Toild, with Helga Hernes. 1981. "Progress for Women: Increased Female Representation in Political Elites in Norway." In Cynthia Fuchs Epstein and Rose Laub Coser, eds., *Access to Power: Cross National Studies of Women and Elites,* 76–89. London: Allen and Unwin.

Skirius, John. 1978. *José Vasconcelos y la cruzada de 1929.* Mexico City: Siglo XXI.

Sklair, Leslie. 1993. *Assembling for Development: The Maquila Industry in Mexico and the United States.* La Jolla: Center for U.S. Mexican Studies, University of California at San Diego.

Smith, Margot L. 1973. "Domestic Service as a Channel of Upward Mobility for the Lower-Class Woman: The Lima Case." In Ann Pescatello, ed., *Female and Male in Latin America,* 191–208. Pittsburgh: University of Pittsburgh Press.

Snow, David A., and Robert D. Benford. 1992. "Master Frames and Cycles of Protest." In Aldon D. Morris and Carol McClurg Mueller, eds., *Frontiers in Social Movement Theory,* 133–155. New Haven: Yale University Press.

Soto, Sherlene. 1990. *Emergence of the Modern Mexican Woman.* Denver: Arden Press.

Spoerer, Sergio. 1990. "Las ONGs latinoamericanas: Democracia y cooperación internacional." In *Gestión y políticas institucionales en organizaciones no gubernamentales,* 63–75. Lima, Perú: IRED-Desco.

Staudt, Kathleen. 1989. "Women in High-Level Political Decision Making: A Global Analysis." Paper prepared for the Expert Group Meeting on Equality in Political Participation and Decision Making, United Nations/DAW, Vienna, September 18–22.

_____. 1994. "Political Representation: Engendering Democracy." *Background Papers for the 1995 Human Development Report,* 21–70. New York: United Nations.

_____. 1996. "Struggles in Urban Space: Street Vendors in E1 Paso and Ciudad Juarez." *Urban Affairs Review* 31 (4):435–454.

_____. 1998. *Free Trade? Informal Economies at the U.S.-Mexico Border.* Philadelphia: Temple University Press.

Staudt, Kathleen, and Carlota Aguilar. 1992. "Political Parties, Women Activists' Agendas, and Class: Elections on Mexico's Northern Frontier." *Mexican Studies/Estudios Mexicanos* 8:87–106.

Staudt, Kathleen A., and William G. Weaver. 1997. *Political Science and Feminisms: Integration or Transformation?* New York: Twayne/Prentice Hall International.

Stein, Alfredo. 1991. "Las organizaciones no gubernamentales (ONGs) y su rol en el desarrollo social de América Latina." *Pensamiento Iberoamericano*, no. 19. Spain, CEPAL.

Stephen, Lynn. 1989. "Popular Feminism in Mexico: Women in the Urban Popular Movement." *Zeta* (Baja California) 2 (12):102–106.

_____. 1991. *Zapotec Women*. Austin: University of Texas Press.

_____. 1992. "Women in Mexico's Popular Movements: Survival Strategies Against Ecological and Economic Impoverishment." *Latin American Perspectives* 19 (1):73–96.

_____. 1995. "The Zapatista Army of National Liberation and the National Democratic Convention." *Latin American Perspectives* 22 (4):88–100.

_____. 1997. *Women and Social Movements in Latin America: Power from Below*. Austin: University of Texas Press.

Sternbach, Nancy Saporta, Maryssa Navarro Aranguren, Patricia Churchryk, and Sonia Alvarez. 1992. "Feminism in Latin America: From Bogotá to San Bernardo." In Arturo Escobar and Sonia Alvarez, eds., *The Making of Social Movements in Latin America: Identity, Strategy, and Democracy*, 207–239. Boulder: Westview Press.

STPS [Secretaría del Trabajo y Previsión Social]/U.S. Department of Labor. 1992. "The Informal Sector in Mexico." Washington, DC: U.S. Department of Labor; Mexico City: STPS.

Suárez, Enrique, and Octavio Chávez. 1996. *Profile of the United States–Mexico Border*. Ciudad Juárez: Mexican Federation of Private Associations [FEMAP].

Swarup, Hem Lata, et al. 1994. "Women's Political Engagement in India: Some Critical Isues." In Barbara Nelson and Najma Chowdhury, eds., *Women and Politics Worldwide*, 361–379. New Haven: Yale University Press.

Tabak, Fanny. 1983. *Autoritarismo e participação política da mulher*. Rio de Janeiro: Graal.

Tarrés, María Luisa. 1989. "Mas allá de lo público y lo privado. Reflexiones sobre la participación social y política de las mujeres de clase media en Ciudad Satélite." In Orlandina de Oliveira, ed., *Trabajo, poder y sexualidad*, 197–218. Mexico City: El Colegio de México.

_____. 1991. "Campos de acción social y política de la mujer de clase media." In Vania Salles and Elsie McPhail, eds., *Textos y pre-textos. Once estudios sobre la mujer*, 77–115. Mexico City: El Colegio de México, PIEM.

_____. 1993. "Luchadoras urbanas." *debate feminista* 7 (March):373–375.

_____. 1996. "Espacios privados para la participación pública: algunos rasgos de las ONGs dedicadas a la mujer." *Estudios Sociológicos* 14:7–32.

Tarrés, María Luisa, ed. 1992. *La voluntad de ser. Mujeres en los noventa*. Mexico City: El Colegio de México.

_____. 1998. *Género y cultura en América Latina*. Mexico City: El Colegio de México/UNESCO.

Tarrow, Sidney. 1989. "Struggle, Politics and Reform: Collective Action, Social Movements, and Cycles of Protest." Center for International Studies, Cornell University. Western Societies Program, Occasional Paper no. 21.

Taylor, Verta, and Nancy Whittier. 1992. "Collective Identity in Social Movement Communities: Lesbian Feminist Mobilization." In Aldon D. Morris and Carol McClurg Mueller, eds., *Frontiers in Social Movement Theory*, 104-129. New Haven: Yale University Press.

Tiano, Susan. 1993. *Patriarchy on the Line: Labor, Gender, and Ideology in the Mexican Maquiladora Industry*. Philadelphia: Temple University Press.

Tilly, Charles. 1978. *From Mobilization to Revolution*. New York: Random House.

Tirado Jiménez, Ramón. 1990. *Asamblea de barrios: Nuestra batalla*. Mexico City: Editorial Nuestro Tiempo.

Tobias, Sheila. 1997. *Faces of Feminism: An Activist's Reflections on the Women's Movement*. Boulder: Westview Press.

Tuñón, Esperanza. 1992. *Mujeres que se organizan*. Mexico City: Porrúa.

Tuñón Pablos, Enriqueta. 1987. "La lucha política de la mujer mexicana por el derecho al sufragio y sus repercusiones." In Carmen Ramos Escandón, ed., *Presencia y Transparencia*, 181–189. Mexico City: El Colegio de México.

United Nations. 1992. *Women in Politics and Decision-making in the Late Twentieth Century*. Dordrecht: Martinus Nijhoff Publishers.

_____. 1995. "Convention on the Elimination of All Forms of Discrimination Against Women." Available on Internet.

United Nations/CEPAL [Comisión Económica para América Latina] and INEGI [Instituto Nacional de Estadística, Geografía e Informática]. 1993. "Informe sobre la magnitud y evolución de la pobreza en México, 1984–1992." CEPAL and INEGI, Mexico City. Mimeographed.

United Nations Development Programme (UNDP). 1990–1995. *Human Development Report*. New York: Oxford University Press.

Valdes, Teresa, and Enrique Gomariz. 1995. *Latin American Women: Compared Figures*. Santiago: FLACSO.

Valenzuela, M. 1990. "Mujeres y política: Logros y tensiones en el proceso de redemocratización." *Proposiciones* 18:210–232.

Vélez-Ibáñez, Carlos. 1983. *Rituals of Marginality: Politics, Process and Culture Change in Central Urban Mexico, 1969–74*. Berkeley: University of California Press.

Venegas, Lilia. 1994. "Mujeres en la militancia blanquizaul." In Alejandra Massolo, ed., *Los medios y los modos: Participación política y acción colectiva de la mujeres*, 45–80. Mexico City: El Colegio de México.

_____. 1995. "Political Culture and Women of the Popular Sector in Ciudad Juárez, 1983–1986." In Victoria E. Rodríguez and Peter M. Ward, eds., *Opposition Government in Mexico*, 97–112. Albuquerque: University of New Mexico Press.

Walzer, Michael. 1991. "The Idea of Civil Society." *Dissent* (Spring):293–304.

Waylen, Georgina. 1993. "Women's Movements and Democratisation in Latin America." *Third World Quarterly* 14 (3):573–587.

Welch, Susan. 1978. "Recruitment of Women to Public Office: A Discriminant Analysis." *Western Political Quarterly* 31 (September):372–380.

Werner, Emmy. 1966. "Women in Congress, 1917–1964." *Western Political Quarterly* 19 (March): 16–30.

Womack, John. 1969. *Zapata y la revolución mexicana*. Mexico City: Siglo XXI.

Young, Gay, and Lucia Fort. 1994. "Household Responses to Economic Change: Migration and Maquiladora Work in Cd. Juárez, Mexico." *Social Science Quarterly* 75 (3): 675–678.

Young, Iris M. 1990. "The Ideal of Community and the Politics of Difference." In Linda Nicholson, ed., *Feminism/Postmodernism*, 300–323. New York: Routledge.

Zendejas, Adelina. 1975. "El movimiento femenil en México." *El Día*, June 21.

About the Editor
and Contributors

Vivienne Bennett teaches Latin American politics in the Liberal Studies Program at California State University, San Marcos. She received her Ph.D. in Latin American Studies from The University of Texas at Austin. She is the author *of The Politics of Water: Urban Protest, Gender, and Power in Monterrey, Mexico* (1995). She has published extensively on urban popular movements in Mexico and is currently researching the history of clandestine political movements in Mexico during the 1970s and their impact on political change in the 1980s and 1990s.

Roderic Ai Camp received his Ph.D. from the University of Arizona in 1970. He joined the Claremont McKenna College in 1998. He is the author of numerous articles and of twenty books on the Mexican political system. Among his best known works are *Generals in the Palacio. The Military in Modern Mexico* (1992); *Political Recruitment Across Two Centuries, Mexico 1884–1991* (1994); *Mexican Political Biographies, 1935–1993* (1995); *Politics in Mexico* (1992 and 1996); and *The Successor* (a political thriller; 1993). His most recent book is *Crossing Swords: Politics and Religion in Mexico* (1997). He is a frequent consultant to national and international media.

Elsa M. Chaney did her graduate work at the University of Wisconsin in political science. For the past thirty years she has done extensive research and consulting on women in international development as well as research on household workers. She is the author of the classic *Supermadre. Women in Politics in Latin America* (1979). She is also the coeditor, with Mary Garcia Castro, of *Muchachas No More: Household Workers in Latin America and the Caribbean* (1989). Her latest publication is a coedited volume with Mary Garcia Castro: *Muchacha, cachifa, criada, empleada, empregadinha, sirvienta y . . . más nada: Trabajadoras del hogar en América Latina y el Caribe* (1993).

Nikki Craske is lecturer in politics at the Queen's University of Belfast, Northern Ireland. She received her doctorate (with a thesis on women and popular protest in Guadalajara) from the University of Essex and has held positions at the Institute of Latin American Studies, the University of London, and the University of Manchester. She is the author of *Corporatism Revisited: Salinas and the Reform of the Popular Sector* (1994) and is coeditor of *Dismantling the Mexican State?* (1996) and *Mexico and the North American Free Trade Agreement: Who Will Benefit?* (1994). She is currently preparing a book on women and politics in Latin America.

Joe Foweraker is professor of government and head of the Department of Government at the University of Essex, United Kingdom. He studies social movements, citizenship rights, and political and democratic change. He has written books and essays on Brazil, Spain, Mexico, and Latin America. He is coeditor of *Popular Movements and Political Change in Mexico* (1990) and author of *Popular Mobilization in Mexico* (1993). His most recent books are *Theorizing Social Movements* (1995) and *Citizenship Rights and Social Movements* (1997).

Teresa Incháustegui received her B.A. in sociology from the Universidad Nacional Autónoma de México and a doctorate in political science from the Facultad Latinoamericana de Ciencias Sociales (FLACSO)–Mexico in 1997. She is author of numerous articles and book chapters. She has served as adviser to the Secretaría de Comercio y Fomento Industrial (SECOFI) (1983–1985), was editorial coordinator of the supplement "Política Económica" of the magazine *Tiempo* (1985–1988), and was directora de area in the Comisión de Gasto y Financiamiento of the Secretaría de Programación y Presupuesto (SPP) (the Ministry of Programming and Budget). From 1989 to 1991 she was coordinator of social and urban studies in the PRI for the Federal District and adviser to the Dirección de Desarrollo Social in the Departamento del Distrito Federal. She has participated in the feminist movement since 1979 and forms part of the De la A a la Z group.

Jane S. Jaquette is Bertha Harton Orr Professor in the Liberal Arts, professor of politics, and chair of the Department of Diplomacy and World Affairs at Occidental College. She served as president of the Latin American Studies Association from 1995 to 1997. She has written widely in the fields of women in politics and women and development, with a particular focus on women's political roles in Latin America. Her most recent book is on women and the politics of democratization in Latin America and Central and Eastern Europe (coedited with Sharon Wolchik) (1998). Her latest publication is an article, "Women in Power: From Tokenism to Critical Mass," in the Fall 1997 issue of *Foreign Policy*.

Marta Lamas is an anthropologist with a psychoanalytic interest and specialization. She has been at the forefront of the feminist movement in Mexico since 1971 and was founder member and activist in Mujeres Trabajadoras Unidas A.C. (MAS/MUTAC). She is also a journalist and has regular editorials in *La Jornada*. Along with others, she founded the magazine *fem* (1976), the supplement *Doble Jornada* (1987), and the journal *Debate Feminista* (1990), of which she is the director. In 1992 Lamas founded the Grupo de Información en Reproducción Elegida (GIRE), a prochoice NGO that she currently directs. She has taught courses on gender and feminist issues at the Universidad Nacional Autónoma de México, at the Escuela Nacional de Antropología e Historia, and at the Colegio de México.

Alicia Martínez is researcher at FLACSO (Mexico), where she also teaches. Her bachelor's degree is in anthropology from the Escuela Nacional de Antropología e Historia and her master's and doctorate degrees from the Colegio de México. She is the author of numerous chapters and articles on Mexican feminism and women in politics and of two books: *Mujeres latinoamericans en cifras* (1993) and *Gobierno y sociedad. Políticas públicas en México y Centroamérica* (1992).

Alejandra Massolo is researcher in the Department of Sociology at the Universidad Autónoma Metropolitana-Iztapalapa in Mexico City, where she also teaches. She has a master's degree in urban sociology. She has collaborated regularly in the Interdisciplinary Program of Women's Studies (PIEM) at the Colegio de México, which also published her book, *Por amor y coraje. Mujeres en movimientos urbanos de la Cd. de México* (1992), and her edited collections, *Los Medios y los Modos. Partici-*

pación Política y Acción Colectiva de Mujeres (1994) and *Mujeres y ciudades* (1992). She is coeditor, with Dalia Barrera Bassols, of the forthcoming *Mujeres gobernando municipios*.

Carmen Ramos Escandón is researcher at the Center for Sociology and Social Anthropology Research (CIESAS) in Guadalajara, Mexico. She is a historian with an interest in women's history and gender formation processes. Her authored and edited books include *Presencia y Transparencia* (1987), *Género en perspectiva* (1991), *Género e historia* (1992), and *Mujeres y Revolución* (1993). She has also contributed chapters to several books on women's movements, feminism, and Mexican politics. Her most recent publication is the chapter "Gendering Mexican History" in *Gender Politics in Latin America* (edited by Liz Dore, 1997).

Victoria E. Rodríguez has a B.A. from the Instituto Tecnológico y de Estudios Superiores de Monterrey and a Ph.D. in political science from the University of California, Berkeley. Currently she is associate professor at the Lyndon B. Johnson School of Public Affairs at the University of Texas at Austin. She is author and coeditor, with Peter Ward, of several books, chapters, and articles on state and local government in Mexico. She is author of *Decentralization in Mexico: From Reforma Municipal to Solidaridad to Nuevo Federalismo* (Westview Press, 1997) and of several articles and book chapters dealing with Mexican politics and public administration.

Kathleen Staudt received her Ph.D. from the University of Wisconsin. She is professor of political science at the University of Texas at El Paso (UTEP). She has published over fifty refereed articles and ten books, the latest of which include *Women, International Development and Politics: The Bureaucratic Mire* (1990; expanded and updated, 1997), *Managing Development* (1991), and *Free Trade? Informal Economies at the U.S.-Mexico Border* (1998).

Lynn Stephen is professor of anthropology at Northeastern University. She is the author of *Women and Social Movements in Latin America: Power from Below* (1997), *Hear My Testimony: María Teresa Tula, Human Rights Activist of El Salvador* (1994), and *Zapotec Women* (1991). She is the coeditor of *Class, Politics and Popular Religion in Mexico and Central America* (1990). She is currently researching the movement for indigenous autonomy in Mexico and the impact of economic restructuring and changes in land reform policy in rural Chiapas and Oaxaca. This material will appear in a forthcoming book, *Between NAFTA and Zapata: History, Nationalism and Indigenous Identity in Southern Mexico*.

María Luisa Tarrés received her doctorate in sociology from the University of Paris. She is researcher at the Centro de Estudios Sociológicos, El Colegio de México, where she also teaches. Her principal research interests include social and political participation of various sectors (especially women), social movements, and collective action. She is the editor of *La voluntad de ser: Mujeres en los noventa* (1993) and (with Marta Lamas, Alicia Martínez, and Esperanza Tuñón) of *Encuentros y desencuentros: El movimiento amplio de mujeres en México* (1995). She is author of numerous chapters and articles in major academic journals. Her latest edited collection is *Género y cultura en América Latina* (1998).

Lilia Venegas has a master's degree in social anthropology and is a doctoral candidate in sociology at the Universidad Nacional Autónoma de México. She is researcher at the Instituto Nacional de Antrolopología e Historia and also teaches at the Instituto Tecnológico y de Estudios Superiores de Monterrey in Mexico City. She is author of several chapters and articles dealing with women's involvement in local politics and is coauthor, with Dalia Barrera Bassols, of *Testimonios de participación popular femenina en defensa del voto. Ciudad Juárez, Chihuahua, 1982–1986* (1992).

Index

A/Z. *See* De la A a la Z
Abortion, 7, 30, 51, 59, 66, 82, 107, 111, 146
Adultery, 89
Affidamento, 17, 104, 106, 108
Affirmative action, 10, 49, 50–51, 53–55,
   185–186, 188, 190–191
Alcaldeas, 198–200
Alemán, Miguel, 99–101
Alianza de Mujeres de México, 100
Alianza Nacional Femenina, 98
Almazán, Juan, 98, 99
Alvarez, Griselda, 4, 5
Alvarez, María, 8
Alvarez, Sonia, 16n, 50, 81
Amorós, Celia, 105
Anti-feminism, 81
Argentina, 10, 16, 44, 45, 51, 60, 63, 67
Argentinian Women's Council, 52
ARIC. *See* Asociación Rural de Interés
   Colectivo
Arizpe, Lourdes, 3
Asociación Cívica Revolucionaria, 143
Asociación Rural de Interés Colectivo
   (ARIC), 152
Aspe, Pedro, 175
Avila Camacho, Manuel, 98–99, 111, 108,
   168
Ayala, Susana, 210, 217
Ayuntamientos, 197–199, 200–202

Barone de Castellanos, Cecilia, 210, 213, 214
Barrig, Maruja, 223
Barrio, Francisco, 184, 205, 206, 209
Belize, 47
Bennett, Vivienne, 6
Bhutto, Benazir, 28n
Blachman, Morris, 222
Boccia, Maria Luisa, 111–112
Bolivia, 10, 50, 52, 63
Botello, Consuelo, 9
Brazil, 10, 33, 44, 65, 67, 73, 75,
   196

Brazilian Commissions on the Status of
   Women, 33
Brazil's National Council on Women's
   Rights, 74
Budgeting. *See* Public expenditures
Bunster, Ximena, 223

Cabildo, 200
Cabinet positions. *See* Women and formal
   politics, in cabinet positions
Cacicas, 203
Caciques, 151
Caldeira, Teresa, 223
Callistas, 95
Camino Verde, 210
Camp, Roderic Ai, 2, 18, 45, 55
Campaign finances, 180
Cano, Gabriela, 104, 108–109
Capitalism, 225
Cárdenas, Cuauhtémoc, 204, 217
Cárdenas, Lázaro, 94, 95, 96–98, 111, 205
Cardenismo, 94
Cardenistas, 95, 97
Carranza, Venustiano, 5, 91
Carrera, Laura, 108, 111
Carrillo Puerto, Elvia, 91–92
Casa de Cultura Reyes Heroles, 109
Castellanos, Héctor, 213
Castillo Ledón, Amalia Caballero de, 98,
   100–101
Catholicism, 32, 44, 45, 55, 59, 65, 95–96,
   133, 141, 152
CCRI. *See* Consejo Clandestino
   Revolucionario Indígena
CEDAW. *See* Convention on the
   Elimination of All Forms of
   Discrimination Against Women
CEN. *See* Comité Ejecutivo Nacional
Central America, 221, 226
Central Independiente de Obreros
   Agrícolas y Campesinos (CIOAC),
   152

Cetina Gutiérrez, Rita, 91
CFM. *See* Consejo Feminista
    Mexicano
Chamber of Deputies, 170, 175, 181
Chamorro, Violeta, 75
Chaney, Elsa, 15, 31, 45, 67, 222
Chapa, María Elena, 11, 14
Chapa, Ester, 101
Chiapas, 3, 18, 71, 111, 133, 147–149, 151,
    220
Chiapas Women's Convention, 147,
    159–162
Child care. *See* Day care
Chile, 16, 45, 47, 52, 56, 57, 60, 63, 64, 67, 73,
    75, 78, 196, 222
Chumacera, Gaby, 213, 214
Ciller, Tansu, 28n
CIOAC. *See* Central Independiente de
    Obreros Agrícolas y Campesinos
Ciudad Juárez, 19, 205, 206, 214
Civic culture, 117, 118, 121
Class issues, 94, 105, 117, 123, 124–125, 149,
    211, 224
CNC. *See* Confederación Nacional
    Campesina
CND. *See* Convención Nacional
    Democrática
CNI. *See* Convención Nacional Indígena
CNM. *See* Convención Nacional de Mujeres
CNOP. *See* Confederación Nacional de
    Organizaciones Populares
CNPA. *See* Coordinadora Nacional Plan de
    Ayala
CNTE. *See* Coordinadora Nacional
    de Trabajadores de la
    Educación
Coalición de Mujeres Feministas,
    106
Coalitions, 4, 25, 34, 35, 87, 106, 124, 181
Código Federal de Instituciones y
    Procedimientos Electorales (COFIPE),
    10
COFIPE. *See* Código Federal de
    Instituciones y Procedimientos
    Electorales
Cohen, Jean, 189
Collective action, 44, 56, 60, 65, 118, 131,
    133
Colombia, 45, 196
Colonias, 207, 208
Colosio, Luis Donaldo, 108, 111
Comisión Nacional de Derechos Humanos,
    159
Comité de Defensa Popular, 120

Comité Ejecutivo Nacional (CEN),
    175
Comité Nacional Femenil, 98
Comités de Vecinos, 209
Communism, 95
Comunidades Eclesiásticas de Base, 143
CONAMUP. *See* Coordinadora Nacional
    del Movimiento Urbano Popular
CONAPO. *See* Consejo Nacional de
    Población
Confederación Femenil Mexicana, 93
Confederación Nacional Campesina (CNC),
    14
Confederación Nacional de Organizaciones
    Populares (CNOP), 14, 72
Congreso de Mujeres por el Cambio, 183
CONPAZ. *See* Coordinación de Organismos
    No-gubernamentales por la Paz de
    Chiapas
Consejo Clandestino Revolucionario
    Indígena (CCRI), 157
Consejo Feminista Mexicano (CFM), 92
Consejo Nacional de la Mujer (CNM), 52,
    53
Consejo Nacional de Población (CONAPO),
    33, 198
Consejo para la Integración de la Mujer, 183
Consejo Político Nacional, 185
Conservatism, political, 80, 99
Consolidated land invasion neighborhoods,
    120–122, 127
Convención Nacional de Mujeres (CNM),
    147, 160–161
Convención Nacional Democrática (CND),
    159, 160–161
Convención Nacional Indígena (CNI), 161
Convention on the Elimination of All
    Forms of Discrimination Against
    Women (CEDAW), 49, 50–51, 74
Coordinación de Organismos No-
    gubernamentales por la Paz de
    Chiapas (CONPAZ), 159
Coordinadora Feminista of Mexico City,
    106
Coordinadora Nacional del Movimiento
    Urbano Popular (CONAMUP), 74,
    122–123,
    148
Coordinadora Nacional de Trabajadores de
    la Educación (CNTE), 74
Coordinadora Nacional Plan de Ayala
    (CNPA), 152–153
Costa Rica, 47
Coyunturas, 181–191

Craske, Nikki, 9, 16
Critical Mass, 9, 10, 15, 19, 25–26, 34, 38–39,
    60, 80. *See also* Representation
Cuba, 44, 47, 50, 147
Culture and Politics. *See* Women and
    formal politics, cultural context and

Day care, 82, 117, 153
Declaration from the Lacandon Jungle, 160
De la A a la Z (A/Z), 17, 103, 107–109,
    112–113
de la Cruz, Sor Juana Inés, 104
de la Madrid, Miguel, 176
Democracia Proletaria, 143
Democracy, 133, 205
Democracy, rule of law, 222
Democratic openings, 197
Democratic transition, 3, 5, 18, 75, 83,
    109–111, 144, 147–149, 158, 159, 180,
    195, 197, 203, 206, 219, 221, 225–227
Democratization, 146, 147, 148, 159–162
Desarrollo Integral de la Familia (DIF), 212
Día Internacional contra la Violencia hacia
    las Mujeres, 161
Diario Oficial de la Federación, 98, 101
Díaz, Porfirio, 88
Díaz Ordaz, Gustavo, 208
DIF. *See* Desarrollo Integral de la Familia
Divorce, 74, 94
Doble jornada, 69
Domestic violence, 123, 136, 139, 146, 149,
    159–160, 179–180, 191. *See also*
    Violence against women

Early Money Is Like Yeast (EMILY). *See*
    Emily's List
Earthquake in Mexico City (1985), 6,
    122–123, 133
Eber, Christine, 154
Economic crises, 60, 71, 76, 118, 144, 195
Economic factors in politics, 56–57, 64, 65,
    70, 220
Ecuador, 10, 44, 74, 196
Education
    higher, 171–172, 176
    private, 171
    women and, 4, 30, 38–39, 76, 78, 81, 108,
        118, 136–137, 149, 170–173, 177,
        179–180
Ejército Zapatista de Liberación Nacional
    (EZLN), 149–159
El Closet de Sor Juana, 7
Elections, 10, 25–26, 42, 53, 60, 111. *See also*
    Voting

Electoral politics, 124, 180, 184, 205
    and fraud, 210
Electoral reforms, 64
El Financiero, 149
Elías Calles, Plutarco, 95
Elites, political, 64, 88, 168, 182, 186
El Machete, 96
El Salvador, 10, 63, 147
EMILY's List, 31
Employment, women and, 4, 5, 8, 60, 81, 93,
    94, 117, 136–137, 225
Engendered policy outcomes. *See* Gender
    and policy
Enlightenment, the, 66, 73
Environment, 136–137
Equal Rights Amendment, United States
    (ERA), 73
ERA. *See* Equal Rights Amendment, United
    States
Erazo, Viviana, 105
Erundina, Luiza, 196
Espinosa, Patricia, 14
Ethnicity, 70, 105, 123, 153, 224. *See also*
    Race
Executive branch. *See* Women and formal
    politics, as heads of state
EZLN. *See* Ejército Zapatista de Liberación
    Nacional

Family, 193, 211. *See also* Kinship and
    recruitment into formal politics
Family planning. *See* Reproductive rights
FDN. *See* Frente Democrático Nacional
Federación de Mujeres Cubanas, 51
Federación Mexicana de Asociaciones
    Privadas de Salud y Desarrollo
    Comunitario (FEMAP), 33n
Federal district, 1, 100
Feijoó, María del Carmen, 223
Female voter turnout, 227
FEMAP. *See* Federación Mexicana de
    Asociaciones Privadas de Salud y
    Desarrollo Comunitario
Feminism, 89, 112, 133–135, 146, 162,
    179–180, 187, 215, 223
Feminist Congress of the Yucatan (1916), 91
Feminist League of the Yucatan, 93
Feminist movements, 131, 133–135, 146,
    163, 186, 179–180, 187. *See also*
    Women's movements
Feminist organizations, 19, 24–26, 30, 32–34,
    39, 44, 50, 59, 64–65, 66, 76, 87, 92, 97,
    103, 107. *See also* Women, and social
    activism

Feminist research, 222–225
Fernández, Aurora, 99
Fernández Meijide, Graciela, 49
Figueroa, Andrés, 96
First Indigenous Congress, 151
First National Plan for Equal Opportunity
  for Women (1988), 195
FMLN. *See* Frente Farabundo Martí de
  Liberación Nacional
FNALIDM. *See* Frente Nacional por la
  Liberación y los Derechos de las
  Mujeres
Ford Foundation, 203
Fourth Latin American Congress (1987),
  104
Foweraker, Joe, 6, 16, 58, 221
FPTyL. *See* Frente Popular Tierra y Libertad
Frente Democrático Nacional (FDN), 204
Frente Farabundo Martí de Liberación
  Nacional (FMLN), 147
Frente Nacional por la Liberación y los
  Derechos de las Mujeres (FNALIDM),
  106
Frente Popular Tierra y Libertad (FPTyL),
  120, 127–128
Frente Sandinista de Liberación Nacional
  (FSLN), 147
Frente Unico Pro Derechos de la Mujer
  (FUPDM), 17, 87, 92–94, 95–97, 101
Frente Zapatista de Liberación Nacional
  (FZLN), 161
Friedman, Elizabeth, 221
FSLN. *See* Frente Sandinista de Liberación
  Nacional
FUPDM. *See* Frente Unico Pro Derechos de
  la Mujer
FZLN. *See* Frente Zapatista de Liberación
  Nacional

Galeana, Benita, 109
Galindo, Hermila, 91
Ganando Espacios, 180
Garavito, Rosalbina, 8
García, Amalia, 108
García, Refugio (Cuca), 92, 96
García Flores, Margarita, 100
Gay and lesbian issues in politics, 7
GEM. *See* Grupo de Educación Popular con
  Mujeres
Gender
  equality, 4, 66, 67, 149, 162, 195, 197
  identity in politics, 118, 187, 189–190
  and policy, 4, 7, 24, 34–37, 38–39, 42, 55,
    57–59, 64, 65–67, 70, 79, 81, 112, 117,

  125, 133, 134, 139, 144, 150, 179–180,
    186, 190–191, 195, 197, 203, 219, 221,
    226
  and political power, 124, 126–129,
    134–135, 139, 146, 181, 187–188,
    193–195, 199–200, 215
  solidarity in politics, 6–9, 60–61, 70, 95,
    103, 105, 112–113, 190–191, 221
Gender-fair policy outcomes, 24–26, 34–37,
  38–39
Gendered political agenda, 190–191, 203,
  219
Gómez de León, José, 33
Gordillo, Elba Esther, 8, 14
Grassroots organizations, 49, 65, 66, 68, 76,
  116, 123–126, 146, 151, 154, 169–170,
  179, 189, 219, 220, 226. *See also* Social
  movements
Green, Rosario, 220
Grupo de Educación Popular con Mujeres
  (GEM), 108
Grupo Espartaco, 143
Guatemala, 63

HDI. *See* United Nations Human
  Development Index
Heads of state, women. *See* Women and
  formal politics, as heads of state
Health care, 117, 136, 146, 149
Hernández, Blanca, 215
Hernández, Ruth, 213
Hernández, Silvia, 174, 176–177
Hernández Castillo, Rosalva Aída, 153–154
Herrera, Alejandro, 210–211
Hidalgo, María de Sánchez, 208–209
Hirschman, Albert O., 103, 105
Honduras, 45
Housing, 117, 119–122, 127, 136–137, 146
Human development in Mexico, 29–30, 38
Human rights, 71, 73, 88, 116, 118, 133,
  136–137, 146, 159, 160, 170

IADB. *See* Inter-American Development
  Bank
Ibarra de Piedra, Rosario, 33, 47
Illiteracy, 4
Incháustegui, Teresa, 9, 17, 19, 111, 108, 221
Income disparities, 125. *See also* Class issues
Indigenous groups in Mexico, 3, 15, 131,
  133, 135, 189
Indigenous women, 52, 95, 99, 135, 139,
  149, 160, 174
INEGI. *See* Instituto Nacional de
  Estadística, Geografía e Informática

Inequality, 4, 30, 38–39, 109, 117, 160–161, 198, 225. *See also* Class issues
Institutional politics, 34–37, 38, 41, 49, 59, 72, 131, 179, 181, 221
Instituto Nacional de Estadística, Geografía e Informática (INEGI), 4n
Instituto Tecnológico Autónomo de México (ITAM), 171–172, 175
Instituto Tecnológico y de Estudios Superiores de Monterrey (ITESM), 171
Insurgencia Nacional de Mujeres, 174
Integration of policy demands and formal politics, 189
Integration of women into formal politics, 182, 191–192
Inter-American Development Bank (IADB), 4n
International Women's Day, 110
Inter-parliamentary Union (IPU), 2, 26
Inter-parliamentary Union Symposium (1989), 23
IPU. *See* Inter-parliamentary Union
Italian feminists, 104
ITAM. *See* Instituto Tecnológico Autónomo de México
ITESM. *See* Instituto Tecnológico y de Estudios Superiores de Monterrey

Jaquette, Jane, 9, 16n, 19, 81, 219
Jiménez, Patria, 7
Jiménez Palacios, Aurora, 4
Judicial branch. *See* Women and formal politics, in the judiciary
Jusidman, Clara, 8

Kaplan, Temma, 224
Kinship and recruitment into formal politics, 173, 177, 213
Kirkwood, Julieta, 23
Kollontai, Alejandra, 92

Labor unions, 64, 67–68, 146, 152, 169–170
Lacandon Jungle. *See* Declaration from the Lacandon Jungle
La Jornada, 111
Lamas, Marta, 9, 17, 19, 108, 224
Land invasions, 119–122, 127
La Realidad, 158
Latin America, 226
Leadership
women and the church, 153–154
women in local government, 49, 65, 68, 76, 100, 194, 196

women and the military, 155–157
women and NGOs, 170, 179, 186–187, 219–220, 226
women and political parties, 168–170, 174, 180–181, 184, 185, 188, 205, 216, 220
women and social activism, 42, 66, 69–70, 75–76, 87, 96, 105, 116, 117–118, 126, 129, 134, 142–143, 146, 148, 189
Legislative branch. *See* Women and formal politics, legislatures
Ley de Cupos, 10–15, 16, 35, 57
Liberal League of Reformist Women, 93
Liberation Theology Catholicism, 150, 154
Lideresas, 68
Línea de las Masas, 143
Literacy, 75
Local government, 49, 65, 68, 76, 100
Loría, Cecilia, 108

Madres de la Plaza de Mayo, 69, 74, 223–224
Major Ana María, 155
Maoism, 151–152, 155
Maquiladoras, 30, 217
Marriage, 89
Martínez, Alicia, 9, 17, 19, 30n, 189, 221
Martínez, Lorena, 57
Martínez Cantú, Rafaela, 208, 213
Marxism, 132–133, 189, 224
Marxist feminism, 96
Massolo, Alejandra, 19, 27
Maximato, 93, 94
Media, 31–32, 205
Menem, Carlos, 53
Mercado, Patricia, 108, 111
Mesa de Otay, 215
Mexican Anticlerical League, 93
Mexican Communist Party, 92–94
Mexican National Commission for Women (1983–1992), 52
Mexican Secretary of Foreign Relations, 14
Mexican Women's University, 98
Mexico, 44, 57, 60
Mexico City Legislative Assembly, 11
Miguel de la Madrid, 198
Milicianos, 157
Military, impact on politics, 42–43, 56, 65, 71
Minimum wage, 30–31
Mobilization, political, 3, 18, 63–66, 67–76, 74, 95, 132, 182, 221, 223, 226
Molyneux, Maxine, 33, 117
Monsiváis, Carlos, 109

Moreno, María de los Angeles, 7, 175, 176, 220
Motherhood, 44, 50, 57–58, 64, 65, 78, 81
    politicization of, 56–57, 168, 223
Movimiento para la Emancipación de las Mujeres, 66
Mujeres en Solidaridad, 221
Mújica, Francisco J., 96
Municipo Libre, 99, 198

National Preparatory School, 172
National Revolutionary Youth Movement of the PRI, 174
National School of Economics, 175
National Solidarity Program, 221
National University, 175
National Women's Committee of the PNR, 98
Neighborhood activism, 179, 193–194
Neighborhood organizations. *See* Grassroots organizations
Neocardenista, 205
NGOs. *See* Nongovernmental organizations
Nicaragua, 10, 45, 63, 73, 75, 147, 226
1917 Mexican Constitution, 44
19th of September Garment Workers' Union, 68
Nongovernmental organizations (NGOs), 2, 6, 17, 18, 56, 68, 159, 131–132, 170, 179, 186–187, 219–220, 226
    and activities, 136–137
    background, 134–135
    and clientele, 132–134, 139, 140
    clientele of, 179
    and formal politics, 140
    in Mexico, 133
    organization of, 141–142
    and services, 140–141
    and women's leadership, 140–142
Northern border issues, 206–207, 216, 217

Offe, Claus, 189
Opposition parties, 15, 42, 148, 182
Organización Independiente de Mujeres Indígenas, 159

PAN. *See* Partido Acción Nacional
Pan American League for the Advancement of Women, 92
Panismo, 211
Panistas, 19, 184, 204–205, 207–211, 216–217
Paraguay, 44, 45, 63, 74, 75
Paredes, Beatriz, 5, 8, 14, 174–175, 177
Paredes Ramos, Higinio, 174–175

Parliamentary systems, 34–35
Participatory democracy. *See* Democratic transition
Partido Acción Nacional (PAN), 1, 3, 8, 11, 45, 55, 133, 168–170, 183–186, 198–200
Partido de la Revolución Democrática (PRD), 1, 3, 8, 11, 35, 45, 53, 68, 76, 107, 109, 110, 111, 112, 168–170, 183–186, 198–200, 202–203, 204
Partido del Trabajo (PT), 45, 211
Partido Mexicano de los Trabajadores (PMT), 143
Partido Nacional Revolucionario (PNR), 92–94, 95
Partido Revolucionario de los Trabajadores (PRT), 47, 106, 143
Partido Revolucionario Institucional (PRI), 1, 3, 7, 8, 11, 44, 45, 53, 54, 57, 73, 100, 107, 110, 111, 112, 151, 168, 174, 177, 182–191, 198–200, 216–217
Partido Revolucionario Mexicano (PRM), 100
Partido Socialista Unificado de México (PSUM), 143
Party militancy, 207–211
P'as Joloviletik, 159
Payán, Ana Rosa, 8
Peasant organizations, 149–159, 160, 174, 179, 189
Perelli, Carina, 223
Perón, Eva, 45, 79
Peru, 10, 45, 57, 63, 67, 75, 78, 80, 222, 226
PIEM. *See* Programa Interdisciplinario de Estudios de la Mujer
PMT. *See* Partido Mexicano de los Trabajadores
PNR. *See* Partido Nacional Revolucionario
Political activism, 42, 217
Political efficacy, 188–190, 190–191, 194
Political legitimization, 189
Political machines. *See* Women, political "machinery" of
Porfiriato, 17, 87, 90
Postmodernism, 224
Poverty. *See* Women, and poverty
PR. *See* Proportional Representation
PRD. *See* Partido de la Revolución Democrática
Prefeitas, 196
Presidencialismo, 185–186
    local, 200
PRI. *See* Partido Revolucionario Institucional
Priístas, 106, 107, 109, 111, 182, 204

PRM. *See* Partido Revolucionario Mexicano
Programa Interdisciplinario de Estudios de
la Mujer (PIEM), 203
Programa Nacional de Solidaridad
(National Solidarity Program,
PRONASOL), 72–73
Promoción Política de la Mujer, 212
PRONASOL. *See* Programa Nacional de
Solidaridad (National Solidarity
Program)
Property rights, 153. *See also* Land
invasions
Proportional Representation (PR), 14–15,
34–36, 38–39, 80, 200
Protestantism, 153–154
PRT. *See* Partido Revolucionario de los
Trabajadores
PSUM. *See* Partido Socialista Unificado de
México
PT. *See* Partido del Trabajo
Public expenditures, 17, 30, 129
Public services, 117, 118, 121,123–126, 194
Public utilities. *See* Public services
Putnam, Robert, 219

Quotas in formal politics, 9–15, 34–37,
38–39, 42, 47, 49, 53–55, 183–186, 188,
190–191, 216, 219, 225

Race, 70, 105, 123, 153, 159, 159, 224
Radcliffe, Sarah, 224
Rallies. *See* Social protests
Ramos Escandón, Carmen, 4, 17
Rape, 139, 146, 149, 156, 159, 160, 191
Recruitment, of women into formal politics,
168–170, 170–173, 176–177, 182
and kinship, 173, 193, 206–210, 211
Reform, political, 80, 95, 97, 144, 181, 183,
189–190, 195, 203, 206
Regidores, 200–201, 213
Representation, 9–15, 26–30, 34–37, 38, 49,
50–51, 74–76, 110, 136, 168–170, 180,
194, 199
Reproductive rights, 7, 8, 30, 58, 66,
136–137, 146, 149, 160, 195
Revolutionary Feminist Party, 93
Revolutionary Law of Women, 149–151
Revolutionary movements, 63, 67, 116
Ríos Cárdenas, María, 94
Rivas Mercado, Antonieta, 92
Robles, Rosario, 8, 108, 111
Robles de Mendoza, Margarita, 92, 96
Rodríguez, Victoria E., 220
Rodríguez Cabo, Matilde, 96

Rosaldo, Michelle, 162
Rosas Magallón, Salvador, 208
Rovira, Guiomar, 155
Ruffo, Ernesto, 204, 209, 212, 213
Ruiz, Bishop Samuel, 155
Ruiz Cortines, Adolfo, 100–101
Rural social movements, 146, 199

Salinas de Gortari, Carlos, 53, 72, 168, 172,
175, 176–177, 221
Salinismo, 184
Samaniego, Norma, 175, 176
Sandinista Front, 10
Sauri, Dulce María, 14
Second National Congress of Women
Workers and Peasants, 94
Second National Plan for Equal
Opportunity for Women (1993), 195
SERNAM. *See* Servicio Nacional de la
Mujer
Servicio Nacional de la Mujer (SERNAM),
16, 45, 52, 56
Sexenios, 186
Sexual harrassment, 191
Sinarquista, 209
Sindicato Nacional de Trabajadores de la
Educación (SNTE), 14, 69,
Single-Member systems (SM), 14–15, 35–37
SM. *See* Single-Member systems
SNTE. *See* Sindicato Nacional de
Trabajadores de la Educación
Social activism, 42, 66, 69–70, 75–76, 87, 96,
105, 116, 117–118, 126, 129, 134,
142–143, 146, 148, 189. *See also*
Women, and social activism
Social movements, 3, 5–6, 17, 32–34, 39, 226
Social protests, 116, 121, 124–126, 127, 214
Social reproduction. *See* Civic culture
Soldaderas, 91
Sor Filotea, 104
Soto, Cecilia, 34, 47
Soto, Roxana, 210
Southern Cone, 71, 75, 221, 226
Staudt, Kathleen, 9, 15, 53
Stephen, Lynn, 6, 18
Student activism, 119–123, 146, 208
Student uprising in Mexico City (1968), 6,
68, 119
Suffrage. *See* Woman suffrage
Supermadre, 15, 16, 31, 71, 75, 222

Tarrés, María Luisa, 6, 18
Terán, Héctor, 204, 212
Territorially based protests, 123–126, 129

and urban popular movements, 125, 126–129
Thatcher, Margaret, 28
Third National Congress of Women Workers and Peasants, 94
Tijuana, 19, 204, 206, 213, 214
Torres, Elena, 92
Transportation, 117, 118, 121
Treviño, Jacinto B., 96

UN. *See* United Nations
UNAM. *See* Universidad Nacional Autónoma de México
UNDP. *See* United Nations Development Programme
UNICEF. *See* United Nations International Culture and Education Fund
Unidad Femenina pro Miguel Alemán, 99
Unión del Pueblo (UP), 151
Unión de Uniones (UU), 152
Unión de Usuarios y Servicios Públicos, 212
United Nations (UN), 24, 42
United Nations Conference in Beijing (1995), 9, 24, 33, 51–52
United Nations Conference in Mexico City (1975), 32
United Nations Development Programme (UNDP), 15, 24, 29
United Nations Division for the Advancement of Women, 26
United Nations Fourth World Congress on Women (1995). *See* United Nations Conference in Beijing
United Nations Human Development Index (HDI), 29–30
United Nations Human Development Report, 24
United Nations International Culture and Education Fund (UNICEF), 196
United Nations International Year of the Woman, 182, 226
Universidad Nacional Autónoma de México (UNAM), 119
UP. *See* Unión del Pueblo
Urban popular movements, 17, 33, 64, 65, 68, 72, 76, 116, 118–123, 126–129, 135, 146, 196, 200–202, 217
Uruguay, 74, 75, 224
UU. *See* Unión de Uniones

Varela, Estela, 214, 215–216
Vasconcelos, Jose, 92
Venegas, Lilia, 19
Venezuela, 10, 196, 221

Villa, Pancho, 90
Violence against women, 12, 32–33, 52, 66, 71, 94, 136–137, 139, 146, 149, 159–160, 179–180, 191. *See also* Domestic violence
Voting, 25–26, 33–34, 78, 184, 205–206, 222

Wage inequality, 30–33, 65, 74, 82, 117
Westwood, Sallie, 224
White Guards (Guardias Blancas), 148, 157, 160
Woman suffrage, 4, 32, 44, 74, 79, 91, 95, 97–100, 108–109, 131, 182, 197
Women
  and the electoral process, 2, 24–26, 33–34, 39
  health of, 117, 136–139, 146, 179–180, 195
  and the informal economy, 4, 15, 30, 56–57, 64, 65, 70, 72, 94, 118, 123–124, 128, 139, 162, 220
  and labor unions, 25, 64, 67–68, 146, 152, 169–170
  ministries of, 51–53
  movements of, 7, 24–26, 38–39, 44, 59, 66–67, 87, 97, 103–105, 112, 131, 133–135, 146, 163, 179–180, 186, 187, 219, 224, 226. *See also* Feminist movements
  and political activism, 3–6, 18, 42, 217
  and political coalitions, 4, 8, 31–34, 38–39
  political interests of, 6–9, 28, 41, 43, 55, 57, 64, 65, 79, 81–83, 93, 117, 126, 136, 150, 156, 186, 195
  political "machinery" of, 24–26, 39
  and political mobilization, 3, 16, 18, 63–66, 67–76, 74, 95, 132, 182, 221, 223, 226
  and political parties, 4, 5, 18, 27–28, 34, 35, 43, 55–57, 67, 73, 80, 168–170, 174, 180–181, 184, 205, 216, 220
  and poverty, 139, 159, 194, 196
  and proportional representation, 14–15, 34–36, 38–39, 80, 200
  Regional Council of CONAMUP, 122–123, 148
  representation in cabinet positions, 42, 45, 50–51, 51–53, 169: in Latin America, 45; in Mexico, 45, 54
  Revolutionary Law of, 155, 158, 161
  rights of, 73–74, 87, 88–90, 93–94, 97, 118, 149, 160
  and social activism, 5–6, 17–18, 19, 24–26, 42, 66, 69–70, 75–76, 87, 96, 105,

116, 117–118, 126, 129, 134, 142–143, 146, 148, 189
and the state, 50, 58, 66, 71, 72–73, 90, 219, 226
and voting, 25–26, 33–34, 39
Women and formal politics
  in cabinet positions, 26–30, 42, 45, 50–51, 51–53, 70, 169
  coalitions, 4, 8, 31–34, 38–39, 124, 181
  cultural context and, 30–34, 38, 44, 53, 60, 64, 109–110, 194, 195, 197–198, 206, 215, 220–222
  and family, 214
  as heads of state, 5, 8, 27, 28, 49, 168–170, 182–186, 196, 198
  in the judiciary, 168–170, 174–177
  in Latin America, 4, 6–9, 24, 28, 42–44, 49, 56, 59, 63–64, 69–70, 72, 75, 78, 82, 91, 104–106, 175, 196–197, 220, 222, 223
  in legislatures, 168–170, 174–177, 182–186, 212–216, 220
  in local government, 4, 38–39, 121, 124, 126, 168–170, 184, 193–195, 199, 200, 216, 220
  in Mexico, 2, 6–9, 18, 24, 27–30, 31–33, 34–37, 38–39, 45, 49, 50, 76, 87, 88,

122–123, 131, 167–168, 174–177, 179–180, 186, 190–191, 202–203, 204, 209, 219, 220–222
  in nongovernmental organizations, 134–139, 144
  in revolutionary movements, 3, 17, 63, 67, 87, 90–94, 116, 126, 147–149, 150, 157
  in the United States, 1, 2, 167–168, 170, 220, 223
  worldwide, 9, 15, 26–30, 32, 34–37, 38, 52, 54, 167–168, 220, 223
World Bank, 29, 32
World Bank World Development Report, 32
World Values Survey 1990–1993, 167n
World War II, 99

Zamarrón, Hermilia, 92
Zapata, Emiliano, 91
Zapatista Army of National Liberation, 147
Zapatista movement, 148–149
Zapatista women, 18, 133, 147, 149, 157
Zedillo, Ernesto, 53, 172, 176–177, 220
Zendejas, Adelina, 95, 96
Zona del Río, 208